LABOR/MANAGEMENT RELATIONS AMONG GOVERNMENT EMPLOYEES

Public Sector Contemporary Issues Series

Edited by Harry Kershen

Baywood Publishing Company, Inc.

Farmingdale, New York

This is the second volume in the *Public Sector Contemporary Issues Series* prepared under the direction of Harry Kershen and manuscript editor Claire Meirowitz.

Library of Congress Catalog Card Number: 82-22711
ISBN: 0-89503-033-0

© 1983, Baywood Publishing Co., Inc.

Library of Congress Cataloging in Publication Data
Main entry under title:

Labor/management relations among government employees.

(Public sector contemporary issues series ; 2)
"Based on material published in the Journal of collective negotiations in the public sector"—P.
Includes bibliographical references.
1. Collective bargaining—Government employees—United States—Addresses, essays, lectures. 2. Employee-management relations in government—United States—Addresses, essays, lectures. I. Kershen, Harry.
II. Series
HD8005.6.U5L3 1983   331'.04135'0000973 82-22711
ISBN 0-89503-033-0

Preface

These chapters on collective bargaining for municipal, state, and federal employees constitute the second volume in an anthology series based on material published in the *Journal of Collective Negotiations in the Public Sector.* Other books planned for the series will cover such topics as strikes in the public sector and collective bargaining in the armed forces, health field, police and fire fighters, as well as government employees.

The public employees discussed in this volume are commonly considered government workers, that is, persons employed directly by a municipality, county, state, or federal agency. Employees of public school districts and public colleges and universities are often covered under separate legislation; they were, therefore, excluded from this book, as were military personnel.

The collection of material in this book is divided into five parts: 1) an overview and general introduction; 2) municipal employees; 3) state employees; 4) federal employees; and 5) proposed national legislation. The chapters were selected for their long-range relevance and varied perspective, as well as for their analyses of problem areas encountered in governmental employer-employee relations. Practical advice is interspersed among chapters describing theories, studies, laws, case precedents, and administrative rulings.

Each chapter is followed by a group of discussion questions, that are intended to spur classroom discussion and thought. In some cases, the questions are meant to arouse debate and encourage the reader to challenge the viewpoint expressed in the chapter.

We hope readers will find this collection as absorbing, thought-provoking, and useful as we did.

Harry Kershen, Ph.D.
Claire Meirowitz

Table of Contents

PART I
AN OVERVIEW

The importance of employer-employee relationships in governmental settings can hardly be overemphasized. With the growth in public employment at every level, in 1975 nearly one of every five nonagricultural workers in the United States was employed by government, mostly at the state and local level. The total number of persons employed by municipal, state, and federal governments more than doubled in the twenty years from 1955 to 1975, from 7.4 million to 15 million.

Given these numbers, it is clear that the potential for labor-management conflict exists and that such strife has the potential for disrupting the lives of nearly every resident of this country. Governmental services, by their very nature, tend to affect the daily routine of citizens directly or indirectly. Thus, the strikes and crises of the past few years among air traffic controllers, police officers, fire fighters, and sanitation workers, to name a few, have brought the issue of public sector labor relations into the living rooms of America. This intense focus has served to bolster the call for better ways of dealing with public sector crises and bargaining.

In this part of the volume, Overton and Wortman present a brief general introduction to collective bargaining in the public sector, examining the definition and characteristics of negotiations and describing the goals of bargaining from opposing perspectives.

Honadle lists models of public sector wage determination, while Henkel and Wood examine the frustrations of state workers negotiations when the legislatures have the final voice in the appropriation of funds. Sulzner views the major issues of the 1980's for the public workers as productivity and job security.

CHAPTER 1

One More Time: What Is Collective Bargaining in the Public Sector All About?

CRAIG E. OVERTON
MAX S. WORTMAN, JR.

In the United States, we live in an extremely complex environment. Just think about the social structure, the general state of the economy (i.e., the unemployment situation, the rate of inflation caused by demand-pull and/or cost-push, and the controls that the government has imposed to try to halt these rampant trends), the increasing government intervention in labor-management relations, and the hardening of attitudes on the part of management, union leaders, and the public-at-large. If collective bargaining, which in itself is an extremely complex subject, is added to these complex issues, we obtain an even more complicated system. The purpose of this article is to examine collective bargaining as it relates to the public sector.

Seldom does a day go by when the term "collective bargaining" is not discussed by the general public within a community. It may be mentioned in its relationship to school teachers in the community demanding more money, or policemen who want a shorter work week, or garbage collectors who want better trucks. Although we may all talk about collective bargaining, few of us are able to define it. Indeed, each individual may even have a good idea of whether he or she is "for" or "against" it. Some try to define collective bargaining in terms of its end result when a conflict is resolved or a strike occurs; others describe it in terms of the process followed to resolve a conflict while trying to beat a strike deadline; still others might define collective bargaining as a power process whereby each side wields as much power as possible with the more powerful side winning.

Taylor and Witney indicated that the issue of public employee collective bargaining reached unprecedented proportions during the decade of the sixties.

Table 1. Public Employment from 1947 to 1973 in the United States
(In Thousands)

Year	Type of Government		
	Federal	State and Local	Total
1947	1,892	3,582	5,474
1948	1,863	3,787	5,650
1949	1,908	3,948	5,856
1950	1,928	4,098	6,026
1951	2,302	4,087	6,389
1952	2,420	4,180	6,609
1953	2,305	4,340	6,645
1954	2,188	4,563	6,751
1955	2,187	4,727	6,914
1956	2,209	5,069	7,277
1957	2,217	5,399	7,616
1958	2,191	5,648	7,839
1959	2,233	5,850	8,083
1960	2,270	6,083	8,353
1961	2,279	6,315	8,594
1962	2,340	6,550	8,890
1963	2,358	6,868	9,225
1964	2,348	7,248	9,596
1965	2,378	7,696	10,074
1966	2,564	8,227	10,792
1967	2,719	8,679	11,398
1968	2,737	9,109	11,845
1969	2,758	9,444	12,202
1970	2,705	9,830	12,535
1971	2,664	10,191	12,855
1972	2,650	10,640	13,290
1973	2,663	11,079	13,742

Source: *Monthly Labor Review,* Vol. No. 1 (January, 1975), p. 103.

The changing composition of the labor force in the United States has brought with it a rapid rise in government employment. In 1930, about six per cent of the civilian labor force was engaged in public employment [1]. By 1973, government employees constituted nearly nineteen per cent of the total number of employees on nonagricultural payrolls. At the close of that year, federal, state, and local governments employed a total of 13,742,000 workers. Government employment has increased approximately two and one-half times since 1947, when it totaled 5,474,000 (see Table 1).

In addition, Taylor and Witney reported that the greatest gains have been at the state and local levels and not at the federal level, as is often mistakenly believed [1]. The largest segment (approximately one-third) of public employees at the state and local levels are persons associated with education. Although federal employment increased by 143 per cent, state and local employment increased by about 309 per cent from 1947 to 1973. Of the 13,742,000 government employees in 1973, 11,079,000 were employed at the state and local level. If the current trend continues, sixteen million persons could be employed by all levels of government by 1977.

Defining Collective Bargaining in the Public Sector

The right to bargain collectively in the public sector is a realtively new concept in the United States. Although federal policy regarding employee organizations dates back to 1883 when the Pendleton Act was passed, significant expansion of collective bargaining in the public sector did not take place until President John F. Kennedy signed Executive Order 10988 on January 17, 1962. This order provided collective bargaining for federal employees and was the impetus needed for major organizing efforts on state and local levels.

What is collective bargaining in the public sector? The term "collective bargaining" means "the performance of the mutual obligations of the public employer and the exclusive representative to meet at reasonable times, to confer and negotiate in good faith, and to execute a written agreement with respect to wages, hours, and other terms and conditions of employment, except that by any such obligation neither party shall be compelled to agree to a proposal, or be required to make a concession" [2].

The term "public sector" includes all personnel who are employed by the government at the federal, state, and local levels.

MEETINGS AT REASONABLE TIMES

Let us examine the above definition of collective bargaining in detail . . . *to bargain collectively means the performance of the mutual obligations of the public employer and the exclusive representative to meet at reasonable times . . .* After the employees in a governmental unit or agency have been organized into an appropriate bargaining unit and have been recognized as being represented by an appropriate bargaining agent (a union or professional association), the public employer must then meet with the bargaining representatives of the union at reasonable times. The term "reasonable times" has been defined by several National Labor Relations Board (NLRB) decisions involving cases in the private sector. These definitions have been carried directly into the public sector and have been used as guidelines. For example, meetings requested on Sundays or late at night are considered to be unreasonable meeting times. If contract negotiations are held during regular working hours, the negotiators usually are compensated at their regular rate of pay since there are frequently contract clauses providing wages or salaries for these negotiating sessions.

GOOD FAITH

... *to confer and negotiate in good faith* .... The general laws of the individual states require that bargaining be in good faith. Good faith bargaining is not defined in concrete terms. In order to obtain a definition, it is necessary to look at decisions made by the National Labor Relations Board and the courts. Since the area of collective bargaining in the public sector is relatively new, the only decisions that provide guidance in this area are those that have taken place in the private sector. Since the definition of collective bargaining in the public sector is so similar to the definition of collective bargaining in the private sector, one can assume that an understanding of good faith would be similar.

The National Labor Relations Board has held that the element of "good faith" is lacking if an employer:

1. refuses to respond to a union's request for a bargaining conference;
2. refuses to send representatives who have power to negotiate;
3. constantly shifts his position in regard to contract terms;
4. decides not to enter into a collective bargaining agreement;
5. deliberately delays and hampers the progress of negotiations;
6. unilaterally grants concessions to the employees while negotiations with the union are pending;
7. engages in a campaign to undermine the union;
8. insists upon contracting with the employees rather than with the union;
9. rejects union demands without offering counterproposals;
10. refuses to put into a written contract negotiated terms that had been agreed upon.

Although these provisions refer to the employer, it is obvious that these same provisions would bind unions [3]. The duty to bargain in good faith is a duty to approach negotiations with an open mind and with a sincere purpose to reach an agreement.

A WRITTEN AGREEMENT OF TERMS AND CONDITIONS

... *to execute a written agreement with respect to wages, hours, and other terms and conditions of employment* .... All states require that the contract be in written form. In this way, employers are prohibited from attempts to circumvent the union (or vice versa) by confusing verbal agreements. The written contract covers just about any issue, including items such as: pay for time worked; pay for time not worked (such as holidays, vacations, call-in pay, and call-back pay); severance pay plans; pension plans; control of work scheduling; seniority procedures; and grievance procedures. With regard to the different contracts (i.e., police, fire, teachers, etc.) in the public sector, over 200 items in fringe benefits alone can be negotiated.

CONCESSIONS OR AGREEMENT TO PROPOSALS NONCOMPULSORY

... *except that by any such obligation neither party shall be compelled to agree to a proposal, or be required to make a concession* . . . . Neither the employer nor the union is compelled to agree to a proposal or grant concessions. However, each party must continue to bargain in good faith and to offer counter-proposals until an agreement is reached, or an impasse has occurred, or one of the parties ceases to negotiate, due to no fault of the other party. If either party attempts to gain unilateral control over some of the terms and conditions of employment through a counterproposal, that party is not bargaining in good faith. If there is disagreement and an impasse is reached, many states have legislated the steps to be taken. Eight states have implemented "compulsory arbitration" to cover selected groups. For example, the compulsory arbitration statute in Wyoming covers only firefighters. The compulsory arbitration laws in Alaska, Michigan, Oregon, Pennsylvania, Rhode Island, South Dakota, and Wisconsin cover all state and local employees. In addition, the States of Hawaii and Pennsylvania have extended a limited right to strike to employees in the public sector.

Characteristics of Collective Bargaining

Now that collective bargaining has been defined, some of its characteristics may be examined. Some persons view collective bargaining as the relationship between two different groups, some see this relationship solely as a power position, while still others see collective bargaining as a continuous process of communications between employees (and their organization) and employers (and their organization).

THE RELATIONSHIP OF TWO ORGANIZATIONS— MANAGEMENT AND EMPLOYEES [4]

Even though collective bargaining takes place between individuals, these individuals are the representatives of organizations. Nowhere in the field of collective bargaining do individuals bargain for themselves. Negotiations always take place between the representatives of organizations. Therefore, collective bargaining is the relationship of two organizations—management and labor.

In most circumstances, the individual worker is so insignificant as a part of the total work force that he or she has no bargaining power. When an individual alone tries to change an unsatisfactory condition, he has little bargaining power. For example, if a worker is displeased with his working conditions, the only thing he can do is quit and look for another job or continue to work under those dissatisfying conditions. When workers join unions, management must deal with a group that collectively has much more power. In most instances, collective bargaining, rather than individual bargaining, results in occupational improvement rather than job stagnation, economic security rather than economic insecurity, and employee influence rather than employee indifference.

Through the interactions of unions and managements, collective bargaining has become a two-party process in which each side offers proposals and counterproposals for the mutual benefit of all concerned. The survival of both organizations has become dependent on both recognizing and assuming their responsibility in jointly reaching agreements.

PURE POWER RELATIONSHIP BETWEEN MANAGEMENT AND UNION [4, p. 9]

Although a power relationship may exist in the private sector, the same type of power relationship does not exist in the public sector. Both managements and unions attempt through their limited economic power to retain the functions under their jurisdictions during negotiations. However, each side tries to encroach upon the other's functions. With few exceptions, employees in the public sector may not strike and employers may not lock out employess. Thus, the strike and the lockout may not be used, and this power relationship is severely limited (particularly when contrasted to the private sector). Collective bargaining aids the parties in the definition and explanation of the assignment of functions without which constant turmoil would exist.

CONTINUOUS PROCESS OF COMMUNICATION BETWEEN LABOR AND MANAGEMENT [4, p. 10]

It has taken many years for the private sector to learn that collective bargaining is a crisis atmosphere is not as efficient as continuous collective bargaining. (Some still have not learned this.) The words "continuous collective bargaining" are used to mean that managements and unions bargain collectively during negotiations, administration, interpretation, and enforcement of the labor agreement.

Most state and local governments have tried to implement this concept by mandatorily instituting bargaining at least three months prior to the last day on which money can be appropriated for a contract. Thus agreement may be reached before the end of the three-month period or negotiations may go on longer.

Collective bargaining has matured in the private sector; it is just beginning to grow in the public sector. During its life span, collective bargaining has been changing, growing, and developing. It definitely involves more and more employees. Although collective bargaining has changed constantly, it has grown into one of our society's most protected rights. Through this process of determining the price of labor, collective bargaining provides one of the means for the effective use of labor in a complex world.

THE REASONS FOR COLLECTIVE BARGAINING IN THE PUBLIC SECTOR

Why did collective bargaining occur in the public sector? — The main factor that distinguishes the United States from any other form of government is democracy. This basic philosophy has been so ingrained in all American citizens that employment is viewed as a democratic event as well. Although employees understand that managers must direct, control, and supervise their activities, they feel that they should be an integral part of an organization's operations. One of the most effective and efficient ways of becoming such an integral part is through collective bargaining.

The majority of workers in the private sector have had the right to organize and bargain collectively since 1935 when the National Labor Relations Act (sometimes known as the Wagner Act) was passed. Since that date, workers in the public sector have seen their counterparts in the private sector obtain benefits that they did not have. As more and more persons were employed in the public sector and observed the benefits gained in the private sector that were perceived as a direct result of collective bargaining, they too began to form unions or associations in order to bargain with their employers regarding terms and conditions of employment.

The impetus that President John F. Kennedy gave to collective bargaining for federal employees, when he signed Executive Order 10988 on January 17, 1962, had a great effect on other parts of the public sector as well.

Why is collective bargaining necessary in the public sector? — One of the most important aspects of collective bargaining is that it equalizes power between employees and managers. Decisions regarding an employee's terms and conditions of employment are made bilaterally rather than unilaterally. To a great extent, collective bargaining resolves the economic conflict between employer and employee over the terms and conditions of employment. It assures the worker that the rights and privileges he possesses will be protected. Collective bargaining also enhances the satisfaction of the worker's sociological and psychological needs in any organization. Because it tends to be a democratic process, economic political, social, and psychological conflicts are resolved through a meeting of minds, and thus it aids in the attainment of the overall goals of the organizational operations.

Why do persons in the public sector become members of a bargaining unit? — Obviously some workers join unions or associations automatically, because it is required under a union shop contract. These workers who must join the union give relatively little thought to this action because it is one of the conditions of employment.

In agencies that do not require union membership as a condition of employment, a variety of issues may be raised as to why persons elect to become members of a bargaining unit. Initially scholars believed that workers joined unions primarily on economic grounds because they thought that workers were at the mercy of their employer with respect to wages, especially in times of job scarcity. The only way that employers could be forced to pay adequate wages and provide reasonable working conditions was for employees to join forces through a bargaining unit. This remains a significant reason why employees join unions.

In addition to economic considerations, workers also become members of a bargaining unit in order to satisfy a variety of social and psychological needs. The union (or association) can provide a worker with a sense of security, status, a feeling of independence with respect to his employer, and the satisfaction of group membership [5].

Goals of Collective Bargaining in the Public Sector

When it comes to collective bargaining in the public and private sectors, the major difference is that the profit motive is far removed (if it exists at all) in the public sector. As we all know, the public sector obtains its financial resources from the taxpayer, whereas the private sector obtains its resources primarily from the consumer. The unions' objectives are basically the same in both sectors when they develop their collective bargaining policy, but managements' objectives are somewhat different.

In developing managerial collective bargaining policy, Harbison and Coleman state that managements try to accomplish a number of goals [6]. These goals as applied to the public sector follow.

RETENTION OF EFFECTIVE CONTROL
OVER THE ORGANIZATION

Usually management officials in a state, city or town are either elected by the population or appointed by elected government officials. Understandably, these individuals want to unilaterally make decisions, for they may lose their jobs if they do not follow the wishes of the voting public. Managements feel that if they can retain effective control this would help to preserve and strengthen their own organization.

ESTABLISHMENT OF STABLE, PREDICTABLE
RELATIONS WITH THE UNIONS

If management is guaranteed by the union leadership that the union will act in a responsible manner and will cooperate with management in an effort to provide maximum efficiency, this would aid management in day-to-day operations. This is an aim of most managements in their collective bargaining policies.

ADVANCEMENT OF THE PERSONAL
AMBITIONS OF MANAGERS

All managers have their own personal goals and interests. Whether or not individual managers are able to reconcile their gials with those of the organization will have a direct bearing on the success or failure of bargaining.

The objectives that unions have when they develop their collective bargaining policy are as follows [6, pp. 12-17].

PROMOTION OF THE ECONOMIC
WELFARE OF THE MEMBERSHIP

The primary objective of the union leadership is to obtain economic security for the employees. These economic gains may take the form of wages, better fringe benefits, or employment security. In so doing, it is felt that these leaders are preserving and strengthening the union.

PROMOTION OF BROAD SOCIAL OBJECTIVES

The leadership of the union in the public sector believes that human welfare and human rights are paramount to any other rights. They strive constantly to attain these for the membership.

ACQUISITION OF ADDITIONAL CONTROL OVER JOBS

One form of job control is obtained through contract clauses such as seniority, joint union-management discussions on technological change, and subcontracting. This control assures the employees that there will be work for them to do, because it cannot be given to someone else. Another form of job control comes in the form of the increased decision-making ability and responsibility. When workers are given the right to make decisions that affect them directly, they are then able to exercise more control over their day-to-day operations.

ADVANCEMENT OF THE PERSONAL
AMBITIONS OF UNION LEADERS

Just as managers wish to fulfill their goals through the organization, so do union leaders. They are anxious to promote their own personal goals. If they are able to merge these goals with those of the organization, they may be able to gain prestige and self-actualization by their approach to collective bargaining.

Although these attitudes help to form collective bargaining policies for each side, the basic public goal in collective bargaining is to reduce labor-management conflict in our society.

Trends in Public Sector Collective Bargaining

Collective bargaining in the public sector serves to:

1. identify the basic conflicting issues between labor and management;
2. determine the reasons for such conflict;
3. enhance a rapid resolution of these labor-management conflicts;
4. provide a process whereby future conflicts may be aired and a system that will be used to solve these conflicts.

Through collective bargaining, group conflict is resolved by making a compromise between the goals of labor and management. Although both parties may not be completely satisfied with the solution, society as a whole benefits from the rapid resolution of the conflict.

Although this is the way it should be, one need not look far to see the trends that are evolving. Signs of increased militancy in public sector bargaining and the spread of unions and professional associations appeared in the late 1960's. The decade of the 1970's began with a strike by the postal workers. Although it was illegal for these workers to strike, strike they did. Although the postmaster general was forbidden to bargain with strikers, bargain he did. Although postal workers who struck were supposed to be fired, none were. Instead, the strike ended after negotiations took place, the strikers were all reinstated, and their demands were met by Congress.

In addition to the postal workers, thousands of teachers, policemen, firemen, sanitation workers, etc., strike every year in many cities and towns across the United States. One new weapon used by workers has been to call in sick. Using this approach, the air traffic controllers in the early 1970's caused delays, disrupted flight schedules, and some cancelled flights. The same results were achieved through the sick-out as through a so-called strike.

Traditionally, unions have been more militant than associations. However, as each group tries to increase its power over terms and conditions of employment, there seems to be very little difference between them in the 1970's.

As more and more workers in the public sector join unions, courts will be asked to give opinions on the right of workers to join unions. One such case has already been tried. According to Sloane and Witney, an issue was brought to the Eighth Circuit Court of Appeals in 1969 [7]. The issue presented in the *Woodward* case was

> whether public employees discharged because of union membership have a right to seek injunctions and sue those public officials who discharged

them for damages. A solution to the basic issue required a determination of whether public employees have a constitutionally protected right to belong to a union.

The court ruled that workers are protected if they join a union or an association by the First and Fourteenth Amendments to the Constitution and that suit may be brought for damages under Section 1 of the Civil Rights Act of 1871. It is probable that awards and decisions of this kind will someday be tried before the Supreme Court of the United States. Until that day, states will continue to vary widely in interpreting the rights of the public employee involved in the collective bargaining process [7, p. 521].

REFERENCES

1. B. J. Taylor and F. Witney, *Labor Relations Law*, Prentice-Hall, Inc., New Jersey, p. 503, 1971.
2. *General Laws of Hawaii, 1970*, p. 13.
3. *Labor Law Course*, 20th ed., Commerce Clearing House, Inc., Chicago, p. 1653, 1970.
4. C. W. Randle and M. S. Wortman, Jr., *Collective Bargaining: Principles and Practices*, 2nd ed., Houghton Mifflin Company, Boston, p. 9, 1966.
5. J. B. Miner, *Personnel Psychology,* The Macmillan Company, New York, p. 285, 1969.
6. F. H. Harbison and J. R. Coleman, *Goals and Strategy in Collective Bargaining*, Harper and Bros., New York, pp. 6-17, 1957.
7. A. A. Sloane and F. Witney, *Labor Relations,* 2nd ed., Prentice-Hall, Inc., New Jersey, p. 520, 1972.

Discussion Questions

1. Compare and contrast power relationships in the public sector with those in the private sector.
2. The authors define the term "continuous collective bargaining" very specifically. Would you agree that collective bargaining is the process used at the junctures cited? Why or why not?
3. Do you agree that employees feel they should be an integral part of a business organization's operations in a democratic society? Has this concept historically been an accepted part of the work ethos in the United States?

Reprinted from Journal of Collective Negotiations in the Public Sector Vol. 5(1), 1976

CHAPTER 2

A Model of the Public Sector Wage Determination Process – With Special Reference to Institutional Factors

BETH WALTER HONADLE

Existing models of public sector wage determination have tended to view the situation from a level far removed from the actual process of collective bargaining [1].[1] Yet the overall goal of governments to maximize votes [2, 3], for example, does not directly affect wages any more than the profit-making goal of private firms directly affects the wages that they pay. The point is not that such goals are unimportant, because they do constrain the decision-making options open to subordinate organizational actors [4]. Rather, for purposes of explaining compensation outcomes, the motivations and intraorganizational inducements of the individuals who are directly responsible for negotiating a labor agreement are critical. Once the analysis is brought to this level, such overarching factors as the economic pressures of alternative wages and the institutional/legal constraints governing development of the formal bargaining relationship may be introduced as limitations on the parties' latitude in reaching agreements.

[1] One notable exception is that of Thomas A. Kochan and Hoyt N. Wheeler in reference [1].

This article[2] describes the public sector wage determination process to show how certain factors close to the collective bargaining process itself affect the behavior of the participants and the outcomes of negotiations.

Figure 1 depicts a very general "model" of the public sector wage determination process which identifies critical factors affecting compensation outcomes that are often overlooked in wage determination studies.[3] It is intended as a guide to major points in the wage determination process having the potential to influence the employees' compensation package. Identification of these points in the system can be used to aid data collection and to guide the analysis of compensation outcomes.

ELEMENTS AND RELATIONSHIPS IN THE PROCESS

The "model" traces six general paths from the impending expiration of a labor contract (A) to the attainment of a new accord containing the employees' terms and conditions of employment (X). These various routes are not meant to be exhaustive; rather, they are the most common courses in the general process of wage determination. Moreover, the routes are not presented in equal detail. The most detailed of these is the one in which the formal duty to bargain rests with the parties.

One path (A-B-C-D-X) illustrates a situation in which, according to official labor relations policy (B), the public employer has no legally binding duty to bargain (C) with employees. In the absence of such a formal requirement, informal (collective or individual) bargaining (D) between the two sides leads to new compensation provisions (X) [6, 7].[4,5] All of the other routes in this system assume that the employer is required, by law, to bargain over compensation matters with the employees.

Typically the requirement to bargain (E) includes such items as the criteria to be used in bargaining unit determination (F), the scope of negotiable subjects (G), and the rights and obligations of management and labor, including "unfair" practices on the part of either party (H). Cross-sectional analyses have been mistaken in assuming that collective bargaining (in those places where it is

[2] The author gratefully acknowledges the contributions of Roy W. Bahl, Jr. and Larry D. Schroeder of Syracuse University to this article. It is a revised version of parts of two chapters of her doctoral dissertation, which was completed in 1979 at the Metropolitan Studies Program at Syracuse University under a grant from the National Science Foundation.
[3] For a detailed case study employing this approach see reference [5].
[4] Reference [6] tells how public teachers in Indiana bargained individual agreements with their employers prior to the formal requirement for collective bargaining. This allowed considerable variation among employees with respect to compensation outcomes.
[5] Reference [7] observes: "As in other parts of the coutry, much of the collective bargaining activity in the southeast is of the *defacto* type. In the absence of state legislation or city ordinance, management, because it decides it is advisable, agrees to bargain collectively and to sign labor agreements. Although these agreements are not enforceable in court, they almost always are respected by the parties."

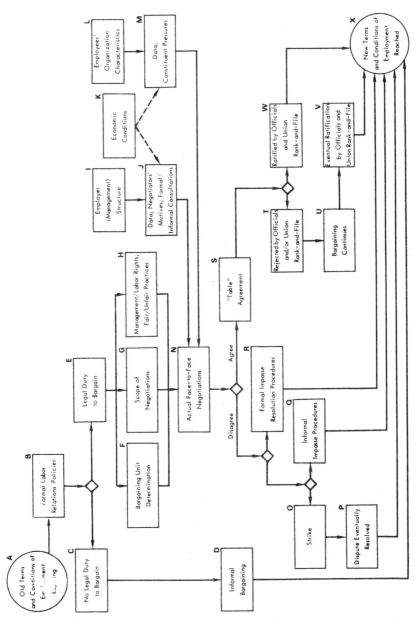

Figure 1.

required) is constant from place to place. Bargaining units may be broad or narrow in terms of the different kinds of employees included in them. Several fragmented bargaining units, for instance, may enable public employees to engage in a pattern of "leapfrogging" wage adjustments over each other. The range of negotiable issues may be quite comprehensive, or it may exclude particular items (e.g., pensions) from consideration at the bargaining table. Finally, states and localities differ over the guaranteed rights of the parties in their formal labor relations (e.g., the right to dues deductions from union members' paychecks). All of these institutional provisions have consequences for the outcomes of negotiations, and their diversity should be recognized [8]. Appendix 1 is a summary of some of these labor relations policies for the fifty states.

Given the formal duty to bargain (E), each subordinate governmental unit must respond to the mandate. Such responses necessarily entail immediate alterations and continuing evolution in the organizational structure of management (I). It has been shown, for example, that in most cases management has become more centralized and specialized (i.e., in the field of labor relations) as the bargaining relationship "matures." This follows the initial reaction of the governmental units to superimpose a capability for dealing with labor relations over the existing (precollective bargaining) management structure, which usually proves inadequate.[6]

The organizational structure of the public employer has important consequences for wage determination. For example, the motives of staff in the organizational subunit responsible for carrying out negotiations will affect their stands at the bargaining table. Thus, if the employer's negotiator(s) report(s) directly to the budget director, s/he (they) may be rewarded for keeping the total cost of a settlement under an imposed budget ceiling. On the other hand, if a negotiator is directly accountable to a personnel department head, who is primarily concerned — by training and experience — with recruitment and internal incentive systems, s/he may be rewarded within the organization for achieving a very different agreement.[7] In addition to the channeling of organizational rewards for individuals' performance, management structure also affects the employer's ability (and propensity) to collect and analyze data (J) on such relevant factors as alternative wages in the area, projections about inflation, and shortages (surpluses) of different types of labor in the area.

Likewise, the employees' organizational characteristics (L) are of considerable importance in shaping the focus of negotiations. Thus, while the opportunity

---

[6] Reference [9] states: "bargaining forces a centralization of authority within management which overcomes the fragmentation of control over various issues typical in a nonunionized unit of local government."

[7] "Major purposes cannot be ascertained by scientific or economic analysis . . . . What is a secondary purpose for one, is a major purpose for another. To quote Miles' law: 'Where one stands depends upon where one sits.' " Miles is Rufus Miles, formerly Assistant Secretary for Administration at HEW [10, p. 20].

wage establishes the range of a settlement, the point within that range at which agreement ultimately occurs is largely dependent on the experience, professionalism, constituent interests, and other organizational characteristics associated with the union. For example, in a union whose constituents are mostly located at the bottom of the position classification system, it would be rational for the elected union leadership to press for wage increases on a uniform cents-per-hour basis. Conversely, a union with members clustered mainly in the upper half of the position classification system is better off pursuing equal percentage increases. That is, union leaders, who are elected by the rank-and-file, attempt to pursue courses of action that are of greater benefit to the majority of their constituents. In short, the union as an organization will affect the types of data that are collected and the nature of constituent pressures on the leadership (L). The data the two sides collect (J and M), which are influenced by market conditions themselves (K), are important in the outcomes of actual negotiations (N).

Once the parties enter actual face-to-face negotiations (N), a number of general possibilities can ensue. The parties might not be able to agree on a new contract and would have to turn to a set of formal impasse resolution procedures (R), such as fact-finding and mediation, to resolve differences to reach an agreement (X). In the absence of specified impasse resolution procedures, either the parties resort to informal dispute settling procedures (Q), leading to a new agreement (X), or a strike (O) occurs, after which the dispute is eventually resolved (P) is one or another fashion and a new agreement is adopted (X). Finally, the parties could reach a "table" agreement (S), which would require the ultimate approval of the union membership and of elected officials (i.e., the mayor and/or the legislature, depending on local legal provisions). Such ratification is usually *pro forma*, however, because intraorganizational management consultations (J) generally ensure executive and legislative support throughout the process. Also, the fact that management and employees both delegated bargaining authority to their respective representatives in the first place implies general endorsement of their judgment. If the "table" agreement were rejected (T), bargaining would continue (U) until approval could be won (V) and a new agreement achieved (X). Usually, though, ratification should occur (W), and the outcomes (X) are those contained in the negotiated "table" agreement (S).

SUMMARY AND RESEARCH IMPLICATIONS OF THE MODEL

The model focuses attention on the complex institutional relationships involved in public sector wage determination processes in general, which, in conjunction with knowledge about competing wages in an area, can help to explain compensation outcomes. Thus, in addition to expecting the opportunity wage to be a major factor in determining the range of wages in the public sector, legal, historical, and organizational factors are also expected to affect directly the terms of negotiated contracts.

This means that any serious attempt to analyze local public sector wage determination should begin with a consideration of the likely effects of legal restrictions on and provisions for local governments' duty to bargain with employees as well as the development of the local jurisdiction's organizational responses to such legal provisions imposed from above. The steps in the wage determination process could also be examined in order to analyze the differing perceptions and roles of the various actors directly involved in negotiations.

Most importantly, this model supports the view expressed by Kochan and Wheeler: "Clearly, if a theory of bargaining outcomes is to be developed which has any explanatory power, the dependent variable should be measured at the level at which the complex and subtle process of bargaining takes place." [1, p. 389] This view, of course, implies analysis of both direct wages and the indirect fringe benefits provisions resulting from negotiations.

REFERENCES

1. T. A. Kochan and H. N. Wheeler, Municipal Collective Bargaining: A Model and Analysis of Bargaining Outcomes, D. Lewin, P. Feuille, and T. A. Kochan (eds.), *Public Sector Labor Relations: Analysis and Readings,* Thomas Horton and Daughters, Glen Ridge, pp. 387-411, 1977.
2. M. W. Reder, The Theory of Employment and Wages in the Public Sector, D. S. Hamermesh (ed.), *Labor in the Public and Nonprofit Sectors,* Princeton University Press, Princeton, pp. 1-48, 1975.
3. J. E. Annable, Jr., A Theory of Wage Determination in Public Employment, *Quarterly Review of Economics and Business, 14,* pp. 43-58, Winter 1974.
4. H. Simon, On the Concept of Organizational Goal (Chapter XII), *Administrative Behavior: A Study of Decision-Making Processes in Administrative Organization,* Third Edition, The Free Press, New York, pp. 257-278, 1976.
5. B. Walter Honadle, Collective Bargaining and Public Employee Compensation: A Case Study of Blue-Collar Wage Determination in Syracuse, New York, Syracuse University doctoral dissertation, 1979.
6. G. A. Moore, The Effect of Collective Bargaining on Internal Salary Structures in Public Schools, *Industrial and Labor Relations Review, 29,* pp. 352-362, April 1976.
7. F. A. Nigro, Public Management and Unions in the Southeast, *Southern Review of Public Administration, 1,* pp. 144-145, September 1977.
8. R. D. Horton, D. Lewin, and J. W. Kuhn, Some Impacts of Collective Bargaining on Local Government: A Diversity Thesis, *Administration and Society, 7,* pp. 497-516, February 1976.
9. J. F. Burton, Jr., Local Government Bargaining and Management Structure, Lewin, et al. (eds.), *Public Sector Labor Relations: Analysis and Readings,* Thomas Horton and Daughters, Glen Ridge, pp. 101-112, 1977.
10. H. Seidman, *Politics, Position, and Power: The Dynamics of Federal Organizations,* The Oxford University Press, New York, 1970.

APPENDIX 1.
State by State Comparison of Selected Public Sector Labor Relations Policies

State	Coverage	Scope of Negotiations	Mediation	Fact Finding	Arbitration	Strike
Alabama	Firefighters	Salaries and other conditions of employment	N/A	N/A	N/A	Prohibited
	Teachers	Consultation regarding educational policy	N/A	N/A	N/A	N/A
Alaska	All except teachers	Wages, hours, and other terms and conditions of employment	Agency may appoint mediator or parties may select one	N/A	Required by law enforcement, fire and hospital disputes; required after strike injunction, otherwise optional	Limited
	Teachers	Matters related to employment and professional duties	At request of either party	N/A	N/A	N/A
Arizona	Does not have a collective bargaining statute for public employees.					
Arkansas	Does not have a collective bargaining statute for public employees.					
California	State employees	Wages, hours, and other terms and conditions of employment	At request of either party	N/A	N/A	Prohibited
	Local government employees	All matters relating to employment conditions and employer-employee relations	Parties may select mediator Costs shared equally by parties	N/A	N/A	Prohibited

California (Cont'd.)	Teachers	Wages, hours, and terms and conditions of employment; consultation on policy matters	Mediator appointed by Educational Employment Relations Board at no cost to parties; or at request of either party	If no settlement after 15 days of mediation either party may ask for fact finding		Prohibited
Colorado						
Connecticut	State employees	Wages, hours, and other conditions of employment; Merit system excluded	May be requested from State Board of Mediation and Arbitration	Either party may request fact finding from SBMA	Permitted	Prohibited
	Municipal employees	Wages, hours, and other conditions of employment	May be requested from State Board of Mediation and Arbitration	Requested by either party; cost shared equally	Used if either side rejects fact finders' report	Prohibited
	Teachers	Salaries and all other conditions of employment	At request of either party	If mediation fails	N/A	Prohibited
Delaware	All public employees, except teachers	Wages, salaries, hours, vacations, sick leave, grievance procedure, and other terms and conditions of employment	N/A	N/A	For any matter except wages and salaries	Prohibited
	Public school employees	Salaries, employee benefits, working conditions	Parties select a mediator; costs shared equally	May be used; costs divided equally	Prohibited	Prohibited

State	Coverage	Scope of Negotiations	Mediation	Fact Finding	Arbitration	Strike
Florida	All public employees	Wages, hours, terms and conditions of employment; excluding pensions	At request of either party; costs shared equally by parties	If mediator not appointed, or at request of either party; if report rejected, legislative hearings held	N/A	Prohibited
Georgia	State employees	Wages, rates of pay, hours, working conditions, and all other terms and conditions of employment	N/A	Mandatory after 30 days	N/A	Prohibited
Hawaii	All public employees	Wages, hours, and other terms and conditions of employment	Appointed by and costs borne by Board	15 days after impasse, costs borne by Public Employment Relations Board; firefighters excluded	Permitted	Limited
Idaho	Municipal employees	Bargaining permitted if municipality desires	N/A	N/A	N/A	N/A
	Firefighters	Wages, rates of pay working conditions	N/A	Begins after 30 days of negotiation; costs shared equally	N/A	Prohibited during term of contract
	Teachers	Matters and conditions subject to negotiations by agreement of parties	Procedures and allocation of costs determined by parties	Appointments by parties or state Superintendent of instruction	N/A	N/A
Illinois	State employees	Wages, hours, and other terms and conditions of employment	At request of either party	At request of either party	Voluntary	Prohibited

Illinois (cont'd.)

Firefighters	Wages, hours, conditions of employment	N/A	Used if impasse exists; advisory only	N/A	N/A
Indiana — All public employees	Wages, hours, other terms and conditions of employment	60 days prior to contract expiration either party or Board may order it; costs borne by Board	If negotiation does not produce agreement in 30 days costs shared equally by parties	Permitted	Prohibited
Teachers	Salaries, wages, hours and salary and wage related fringe benefits	At request of either party; or Board may initiate mediator; costs borne by Board	If mediator cannot get settlement in 5 days Board may initiate 45 days before budget submission	Permitted	Prohibited
Iowa — All public employees	Wages, hours, vacations, insurance holidays, leaves, shift differential, overtime, seniority, transfer procedures, job classification, health and safety, evaluation, staff reduction, in-service training	Begins 120 days prior to budget submission date; mediator appointed by Board	Begins 10 days after mediator is appointed	Permitted	Prohibited
Kansas — All public employees except teachers	Salaries, wages, hours, vacations, sick leave, holiday retirement, insurance, clothing, overtime, jury duty pay, grievance procedures	Either party or PERB may request	Initiated 7 days after appointment of mediator; costs borne by Board	Permitted	Prohibited
Teachers	Salaries, wages, hours, and terms and conditions of professional service	Appointed by Secretary of Human Resources	At request of either party or mediator	Permitted	Prohibited

State	Coverage	Scope of Negotiations	Mediation	Fact Finding	Arbitration	Strike
Kentucky	Police (in counties of over 300,000)	Wages, hours, terms and conditions of employment	N/A	N/A	N/A	Prohibited
	Firefighters (in cities of over 300,000)	Wages, hours, and other conditions of employment	Commissioner of Labor may mediate after 30 days of bargaining	At request of either party	N/A	Prohibited
Louisiana	Does not have a collective bargaining statute for public employees.					
Maine	State employees	Wage and salary schedules, work schedules, vacation and sick leave, general working conditions, overtime practices, values and valuations	At request of either party or Board	At request of either party	If impasse not resolved within 45 days	Prohibited
	Municipal employees	Wages, hours, and working conditions	At request of either party or Board; costs borne by State (first 3 days)	At request of either party; costs shared equally	At request of either party; costs shared equally	Prohibited
	University of Maine employees	Wages, hours, working conditions and grievance arbitration	At request of either party or Board; costs borne by Board and parties	Same as municipal employees	Follows mediation and fact finding advisory with respect to wages, pensions and insurance; binding for other subjects; costs shared equally	Prohibited

State	Coverage	Scope				Strikes
Maryland	Teachers	Salaries, wages, hours, and other working conditions; tenure excluded	Upon consent of both parties	Costs of panel shared equally by parties	Permitted	Prohibited
Massachusetts	All public employees	Wages, hours, standards of productivity and performance, and other terms and conditions of employment	Either party may request	After 20 days of mediation, either party may request	Voluntary, excluding police and firefighters	Prohibited
Michigan	Municipal and local government employees	Rates of pay, wages, hours of employment	If impasse unresolved, 30 days prior to contract expiration	Parties share costs equally; either party may request	N/A	Prohibited
	Police and Firefighters	N/A	Permitted	N/A	Permitted after 30 days of mediation	Prohibited
Minnesota	All public employees	Grievance procedures and terms and conditions of employment	Permitted	N/A	Parties share costs equally	Limited
Mississippi	Does not have a collective bargaining statute for public employees.					
Missouri	All public employees	Salaries and other conditions of employment	N/A	N/A	N/A	Prohibited
Montana	All public employees	Wages, hours, fringe benefits, and other conditions of employment	Either party may request	At request of either party	Voluntary	For firefighters only: prohibited
Nebraska	All public employees	Terms and conditions of employment, including wages and hours	Permitted	Permitted	Court hearing	Prohibited

APPENDIX 1. (Cont'd.)

State	Coverage	Scope of Negotiations	Mediation	Fact Finding	Arbitration	Strike
Nevada	Local government employees	Wide range of terms and conditions of employment	Mandatory	Voluntary	Voluntary	Prohibited
New Hampshire	All public employees	Wages, hours, and other conditions of employment	Voluntarily	Voluntarily or within 45 days of budget submission date; parties share costs equally	May use voluntarily on non-cost items	Prohibited
New Jersey	All public employees	Terms and conditions of employment and grievance procedures	At request of either party; Employment Relations Commission pays costs	Employment Relations Commission recommends or invokes if mediation fails; costs found by Commission	Voluntary	Prohibited
New Mexico	State employees	Terms and conditions of employment	Voluntary	At request of either party; costs shared equally by parties	Prohibited unless Board directs; costs shared equally	Prohibited
New York	All public employees, except NYC	Terms and conditions of employment, grievance procedures	Appointed and paid for by PERB at request of either party or on motion of PERB	Appointed and paid by PERB (nonbinding)	Voluntary	Prohibited
North Carolina	All public employees	No bargaining rights; prohibited; all contracts illegal and void	N/A	N/A	N/A	N/A
North Dakota	All public employees	Salary, hours, and other terms and conditions of employment	At request of both parties	If mediation fails	N/A	Prohibited

32

Does not have a collective bargaining statute for public employees.

State	Employees covered	Scope of bargaining				Strike
Ohio	Does not have a collective bargaining statute for public employees.					
Oklahoma	Police, fire, municipal employees	Wages, salaries, hours, rates of pay, grievances, working conditions and all other terms and conditions of employment	N/A	After 30 days of bargaining	N/A	Prohibited
	Public school employees	Professionals: matters affecting professional services; non-professionals: terms and conditions of employment	Parties set up own impasse procedure	In absence of an agreed impasse procedure	Parties set up own impasse procedure	Prohibited
Oregon	All public employees, except mass transit	Direct or indirect monetary benefits, hours, vacations, leave, grievance procedures, and other conditions of employment	At request of either party after reasonable period of negotiations	After 15 days of mediation, costs shared equally by the parties	Permitted by agreement; costs shared equally; mandatory for police and fire	Permitted (with limitations)
Pennsylvania	All public employees	Wages, hours, terms and conditions of employment	After 21 days or 150 days prior to budget submission date	Named by Labor Relations Board; state pays half the cost, parties each pay one fourth	Voluntary for most employees	Limited
	Police, Firefighters	Compensation, hours, working conditions retirement pensions and other benefits	N/A	N/A	At request of either party upon reaching impasse	N/A

State	Coverage	Scope of Negotiations	Mediation	Fact Finding	Arbitration	Strike
Rhode Island	State employees	Wages, hours, and other conditions of employment	N/A	Required after 30 days of bargaining	Advisory as to wages; binding as to all other issues	Prohibited
	Municipal employees	Hours, salaries, working conditions and all other terms and conditions of employment	Either party may request if no agreement reached within 30 days	N/A	Either party may request if mediation not requested or fails; costs shared equally by parties	Prohibited
	Teachers	Hours, salary, working conditions and all other terms and conditions of employment	Parties may submit to mediation if there is no settlement after 30 days of bargaining	N/A	If mediation fails; costs borne equally by parties	Prohibited
	Firefighters	Wages, rates of pay, hours, working conditions and all other terms and conditions of employment	N/A	N/A	Mandatory if no agreement after 30 days of bargaining; costs shared equally by parties	Prohibited
	Police	Wages, rates of pay, hours, working conditions and all other terms and conditions of employment	N/A	N/A	Mandatory if no agreement after 30 days of bargaining; costs shared equally by parties	Prohibited
South Carolina	Does not have a collective bargaining statute for public employees.					
South Dakota	All public employees	Grievance procedures and conditions of employment, rates of pay, wages, hours of employment	Parties may adopt their own procedure for dispute settlement	Parties may adopt their own procedure for dispute settlement	Parties may adopt their own procedure for dispute settlement	Prohibited

Tennessee	Teachers	Salaries, grievance procedure, fringe benefits, working conditions	At request of either party	If mediation fails; either party may request	N/A	
Texas	All public employees, except police and fire	Bargaining prohibited	N/A	N/A	N/A	Prohibited
	Police, Firefighters	Wages, hours, working conditions and other terms and conditions of employment	After 60 days of bargaining	N/A	Not compulsory; costs shared equally	Prohibited
Utah	Does not have a collective bargaining statute for public employees.					
Vermont	State employees	Terms, tenure and conditions of employment; wage and salary schedule; work schedule; vacation	Either party may request	At request of either party in a deadlock; fact finders may mediate and parties may agree is advance to be bound by recommendations	N/A	Prohibited
	Municipal employees	Wages, hours, conditions of employment, excluding managerial prerogatives	Either party may request; costs shared by parties	After 15 days of mediation	May voluntarily agree to arbitration	Limited
	Teachers	Salary, related economic conditions of employment, and any other agreed upon terms	Parties may agree to mediators; costs shared equally by parties	At request of either party; costs shared equally by parties	N/A	Prohibited
Virginia	Does not have a collective bargaining statute for public employees.					

APPENDIX 1. (Cont'd.)

State	Coverage	Scope of Negotiations	Mediation	Fact Finding	Arbitration	Strike
Washington	Municipal employees	Wages, hours, and working conditions; civil service system excluded	For police in certain size jurisdictions; for firefighters after 45 days of bargaining	After 10 days of mediation	If no agreement within 45 days of commencement of mediation	Prohibited
	Teachers	Curriculum, textbook, in-service training, student teaching programs, personnel, hiring and assignment practices, leaves of absence, salaries, salary schedules	At request of either party	At request of either party	N/A	Prohibited
West Virginia	Does not have a collective bargaining statute for public employees.					
Wisconsin	State employees	Wage rates, hours and conditions of employment	Either party may request	Parties may request; costs shared equally by parties	May voluntarily agree to arbitration	Prohibited
	Municipal employees	Wages, hours, conditions of employment	Voluntary	Either party may request; fact finder may mediate; costs shared equally by parties	For police: either party may request arbitration; costs shared equally by parties	Limited
Wyoming	Firefighters	Wages, rates of pay, working conditions and all other terms and conditions of employment	N/A	N/A	Required if no agreement reached within 30 days	N/A

NOTE: N/A = not available from source.
SOURCE: Compiled by author; based on U.S. Department of Labor, Labor-Management Services Administration, *Summary of Public Sector Labor Relations Policies: Statutes, Attorney Generals' Opinions and Selected Court Decisions*, Washington, D.C.: U.S. Government Printing Office, 1979.

36

Discussion Questions

1. Describe how the motives of the public employer's staff in the organizational sub-unit responsible for the negotiations can affect wage determination.
2. Discuss the constituency of a sample union and how that union's composition affects its bargaining options and stances.
3. In the model shown, where and how would these factors be involved: budgetary constraints, management rights, legislative pressures.

Reprinted from Journal of Collective Negotiations in the Public Sector Vol. 10(2), 1981

CHAPTER 3

Collective Bargaining by State Workers: Legislatures Have the Final Voice in the Appropriation of Funds

JAN W. HENKEL
NORMAN J. WOOD

There has been a trend in public sector bargaining for the executive branch of government to increasingly gain effective authority for labor relations, with a corresponding loss of influence by the legislative branch. For example, in state government the executive branch, through department or agency heads, usually has the primary responsibility for labor relations and the job of negotiating labor contracts with public employee unions. Now, recent court decisions have upset

38

this relationship by ruling that the state legislative branch--rather than the executive--has the ultimate power over the economic content of public employee labor contract negotiations. In effect, the wage and fringe benefits that state officials may concede in public employee bargaining have been ruled to be subject to the approval of state legislatures.

This paper examines three recent court rulings which have held that a collective bargaining agreement negotiated by a state public employee association is subject to subsequent appropriation of funds by the state legislature. A comparison of state statutes authorizing collective bargaining and the right of the legislature not to finance the collective bargaining agreement is presented. The difficulties that the court decisions impose on public employee bargaining will be considered and some possible remedies will be suggested.

THE CASES

In 1977 the Florida legislature refused to appropriate the funds necessary to implement salary increases at the level called for in the collective bargaining agreement negotiated by the union representing 5,000 faculty and professional employees and the state board of regents. Thus the question of whether the legislature or a state agency has the power to establish salary increases at a particular level for organized public employees was decided in *United Faculty of Florida, etc. v. Bd. of Regents* [1].

The agreement negotiated in 1976 by the union contained a "reopener" clause. The provision stipulated that certain monetary terms relating to the 1977-78 portion of the two year agreement were open to further negotiation. When the two sides subsequently failed to reach agreement regarding faculty salaries for 1977-78, the state legislature scheduled hearings on the matter as required by state law. Right before the hearings were to begin, however, the impasse was resolved. The two sides agreed to a salary increase of 8.85 per cent or a total of $6.6 million.

Unfortunately for the union, the Florida legislature in a special session appropriated only $5.1 million of the amount requested. An accompanying letter of intent stipulated that salary increases should not exceed 7.1 per cent. The union informed the board that it should transfer funds from other line items so that the agreed pay increase of 8.85 per cent could be met. When the board refused, the union sued, contending that "sufficient monies were appropriated in (other) items of the Appropriations Act to allow implementation of the collective bargaining agreement between the parties [1, at 1074]."

The Florida Court of Appeals unanimously affirmed the position taken by the board. In support of its decision, the court emphasized that the legislature did not appropriate an indeterminate amount of money that the board could spend as it saw fit. Moreover, the letter of intent imposed a 7.1 per cent ceiling on pay increases and enjoyed the force and effect of law, as it was mandated by state statute. The board, therefore, could increase faculty salaries by the exact amount appropriated for the purpose and no more. In other words, the Florida legislature had the final and dispositive word concerning any union contract involving faculty salaries.

> [The Florida Public Employment Relations Act] operates to make all collective bargaining agreements subject to the approval, though the medium of appropriations, of the legislative body. That the legislative body might not provide full funding for the collective bargaining agreement was a contingency well known to the parties before, during, and after negotiations [1, at 1078].

The significance of *United Faculty of Florida* is not so much that the court upheld the validity of the legislative veto, but that the Florida legislature is the twenty-first state to have affirmatively addressed the issue and the twenty-first state to have confirmed that the power of the state legislature in this area is absolute. An examination of the laws of the fifty states indicates that thirty provide for some form of collective bargaining in the public sector. Many have separate provisions dealing with the rights of narrowly defined groups. Fourteen states separately provide for collective bargaining for teachers, twelve for municipal and/or county employees, and fifteen for police and/or fire fighters. Four states, Mississippi, North Carolina, Texas, and Utah, do not allow collective bargaining of any sort for state employees.

Of the thirty states that permit collective bargaining by state employees, twenty have a statute explicitly stating that the monetary terms of any agreement are subject to the appropriations process of the state legislature. The remaining ten have not denied the validity of the legislative veto. They simply have not addressed the issue, probably because the constitution in each state stipulates that only the legislature has the power to appropriate state funds. For example, the constitution of West Virginia provides that "[A]ll public money shall be paid out and disbursed only pursuant to appropriations first made by the legislature" [Art 10§3]

Table 1 presents a summary of the states that allow collective bargaining for public employees and the state statutes specifying a legislative veto.

There are only two other cases where courts have faced the question of whether the collective bargaining agreement negotiated by a public employee association is subject to subsequent appropriation of funds by the state legislature. In Delaware the public employee union negotiated a collective bargaining agreement with the Division of Adult Corrections of the Department of Health and Social Services, which specified that the Department would assume the full cost of the family coverage of the health insurance plan. When the legislature refused to appropriate the necessary funds, the union brought suit to enforce the collective bargaining agreement. In 1972, the Delaware Court to Chancery in *State v. American Fed. of State, County and Municipal Employees Loc. 1726* [2], held that although a state agency may be authorized to enter into

Table 1. State Laws Granting Bargaining Rights to State Public Employees

State	Collective Bargaining for State Employees	Legislative Veto
Alabama	Firefighters: join union; present proposals Teachers: meet and confer	N/A[a]
Alaska	Public Employees: O/CB[b] Teachers: O/CB Ferry System Employees: O/CB	Yes
Arizona	Public Employees: Meet and discuss	No reference[c]
Arkansas	Public Employees: join union	No reference
California	State Employees: O/CB State Non-Civil Service: O/CB State Civil Service & Non-Academic: meet and confer, file grievances Local Employees: O/CB Firefighters: organize, meet and confer School Employees: O/CB Higher Education Employees: O/CB	Yes
Colorado	Public Employees: O/CB	No reference
Connecticut	State Employees: O/CB Municipal Employees: O/CB Teachers: O/CB	Yes
Delaware	Public Employees: O/CB Teachers: O/CB Transportation Employees: O/CB	Yes
Florida	Public Employees: O/CB	Yes
Georgia	Firefighters: O/CB Public Employees: O/CB Municipal Employees: O/CB	N/A
Hawaii		Yes
Idaho	Firefighters: O/CB Teachers: O/CB	N/A
Illinois	State Employees: O/CB Firefighters: advisory arbitration	Yes
Indiana	State Employees: grievance procedure[d] Teachers: O/CB	N/A
Iowa	Public Employees: O/CB Firefighters: advisory arbitration	Yes
Kansas	Public Employees: O/CB Teachers: O/CB	Yes
Kentucky	Firefighters: O/CB Police: O/CB	N/A
Louisiana	Public Employees: O/CB	No reference
Maine	State Employees: O/CB Municipal Employees: O/CB University Employees: O/CB	Yes
Maryland	State Employees: grievance procedure Certificated School Employees: O/CB Noncertificated School Employees: O/CB	N/A

Table 1. (Cont'd.)

State	Collective Bargaining for State Employees	Legislative Veto	State	Collective Bargaining for State Employees	State
Massachusetts	Public Employees: O/CB; Police and Firefighters: supplemental impasse procedures	Yes	Oklahoma	Police and Firefighters: O/CB; School Employees: O/CB	N/A
Michigan	Public Employees: O/CB; Police and Firefighters: supplemental binding arbitration	No reference	Oregon	State, Municipal, and School Employees: O/CB	Yes
Minnesota	State, Municipal, School Employees: O/CB	Yes	Pennsylvania	State, Municipal, and School Employees: O/CB; Police and Firefighters: supplemental arbitration procedure	Yes
Mississippi	No Provisions	N/A	Rhode Island	State Employees: O/CB; Municipal Employees: O/CB; Police: O/CB; Firefighters: O/CB; Teachers: O/CB	No reference
Missouri	Public Employee: O/CB	N/A			
Montana	Public Employees: O/CB; Nurses: O/CB	Yes			
Nebraska	Public and Utility Employees: O/CB; Teachers: O/CB	Yes	South Carolina	State Employees: grievance procedure; County and Municipal Employees: grievance procedure[g]	N/A
Nevada	Municipal and School Employees: O/CB	N/A			
New Hampshire	Public Employees: O/CB	Yes	South Dakota	Public Employees: O/CB; Teachers: O/CB	Yes
New Jersey	Public Employees: O/CB; Police and firefighters: supplemental binding arbitration	No reference	Tennessee	Transit Employees: O/CB[h]	
New Mexico	State Employees: O/CB	N/A	Texas	Public Employees: collective bargaining is prohibited[i]; Police and Firefighters: O/CB[j]	N/A
New York	Public Employees: O/CB	Yes			
North Carolina	Public Employees: state law prohibits[e] collective bargaining	N/A	Utah	Public Employees: state law prohibits bargaining[k]; State Employees: grievance procedure	N/A
North Dakota	Public Employees: O/CB[f]; Teachers: O/CB	No reference			

State	Category	
Ohio	Public Employees: communicate views, grievance	N/A
Virginia	Public Employees: prohibited from bargaining/	N/A
Washington	Public Employees: organize and collective bargain."	No reference
	State Employees: O/CB	
	Post Employees: O/CB	
	Teachers: O/CB	
	Community College Employees: O/CB	
Vermont	State Employees: O/CB	Yes
	Municipal Employees: O/CB	
	Teachers: O/CB	
West Virginia	Public Employees: discussion and agreements	No
Wisconsin	State Employees: O/CB	Yes
	Municipal and School Employees: O/CB	
	Fire fighters: O/CB	
Wyoming		N/A

[a] In this table, "N/A" or "not applicable" is used under the last three categories when the state in question has no provision for public employee collective bargaining. Of these, the states of Georgia, Ohio, Texas, and Virginia have a separate statute prohibiting strikes by public employees.

[b] In this table, "O/CB" stands for "organize and collective bargain."

[c] In this table, "No Reference" is used under the last three categories when the state in question makes some provision for public employee collective bargaining, but the provision makes no reference to the category in question.

[d] Indiana's comprehensive statute on collective bargaining in the public sector, Ind. Code Ann. §22-6-4-1, was declared unconstitutional in *Indiana Education Employment Relations Board v. Benton Community School District*, 365 N.E. 2d 752 (1977).

[e] However, the case of *Atkins v. City of Charlotte*, 296 F. Supp. 1068 (W.D.N.C. 1969) held that public employees do have the right to join labor unions.

[f] In addition, N.D. codes §34-11 requires the creation by a mediation board to resolve disputes between public employees and employers.

[g] The grievance procedure established for county and municipal employees in South Carolina must be specifically adopted by the locality before it goes into effect.

[h] In addition, Tennessee authorizes payroll deduction from the compensation of state employees to an employee organization.

[i] However, Texas authorizes payroll deductions from compensation by state employees to an employee organization.

[j] The collective bargaining rights of police and firefighters are subject to being adopted by the locality.

[k] However, the attorney general of Utah has ruled that employees at the state and local level may join labor unions.

[l] The Virginia Supreme Court has ruled that, absent specific legislation, collective bargaining agreements in the public sector are invalid. *Commonwealth of Virginia v. Arlington County Board* 217 Va. 558 (1977).

collective bargaining agreements with public employee unions, the agreement does not bind the legislature to appropriate the necessary funds. The court noted, "[O]ur Constitution forbids the expenditure of public funds without appropriation, and the power to appropriate cannot be delegated." [2, at 367]

In *California State Employees Association v. Flournoy* [3], the state court of appeals was faced with a fact situation similar to that in *United Faculty of Florida*. Although the California Board of Regents recommended faculty salary increases of 7 per cent for the 1970-71 fiscal year, the governor's proposed budget set the increase at 5 per cent. The legislature reacted even more strongly and failed to appropriate *any* funds for faculty salary increases. Even though the faculty was not unionized, a class action suit was filed to force the legislature to appropriate funds at the 7 per cent level recommended by the board. In the ensuing litigation the court held that even though the state constitution granted authority to the state board of regents to *establish* faculty salaries, it vested the authority to *appropriate funds* for salaries solely in the state legislature. The court concluded that the power of appropriation was not delegable by the legislature to any other body.

EFFECTS OF THESE DECISIONS

The primary impact of these decisions on collective bargaining in the public sector is to increase the effective authority of the legislative branch with a corresponding loss of influence by the executive branch. However, the general trend in public labor relations has been the opposite: in recent years the executive branch has tended to become the more dominant in the handling of the bargaining relationship.

The reason for this trend is that the executive branch has clear advantages at the bargaining table. First, the executive can coordinate bargaining with the preparation of the budget, which is usually its responsibility, and with its overall legislative program. Also, the executive will be responsible for administering the labor agreement, a job which can best be handled by officials who negotiated the labor contract. Second, the executive is able to develop a unified policy and confront the union with a single management position. The divisions characteristic of legislative negotiating committees, where each legislator has his or her own political power base, are not present when management is able to negotiate within guidelines set by the chief executive's office.

The major disadvantage of having the legislative branch, or one of its standing committees, represent management in collective bargaining is that legislators are unlikely to be effective negotiators. They usually lack experience in labor negotiations. They do not have detailed knowledge of most issues that are subject to negotiations, such as work rules and job security, grievance procedures, union security, and other personnnel issues. Also since state legislators are part-time officials, they usually do not have sufficient time to become knowledgeable in these areas or sufficient time to participate in time consuming labor contract negotiations.

POSSIBLE REMEDIES

Since the state executive branch has assumed the responsibility for both the negotiation and administration of labor contracts, the recent court rulings, which reinforce the authority of the legislative branch, may tend to destabilize existing bargaining relationships. Institutional or informal arrangements need to be developed to insure the effective delegation of authority from the legislative branch to the management negotiators in the executive branch. Two mechanisms could help to solve this problem: prior commitment of legislators through consultation, and restrictions on the role of the legislature on nonwage labor issues.

First, labor negotiators in the executive branch should attempt to secure the commitment of legislators to a proposed contract by consulting with them in advance, even to the extent of accepting guidelines set by the legislators. This procedure would improve communications between the executive and legislative branches and still allow the legislators to participate in setting labor relations policy.

Second, executive authority for labor relations can be further supported by the enactment of state legislation that assigns all responsibilities for labor contract negotiations to the executive office in every unit of state government. Additional features of such legislation could enhance executive authority, such as provisions that: 1) the legislative body can only review those portions of a negotiated agreement that require funds for implementation or conflict with existing law; 2) purely administrative items, such as grievance procedures and work rules should not be subject to a legislative veto; 3) if the legislature does reject a contract provision negotiated by the executive branch, it may only return the rejected agreement to the executive for further negotiations and; 4) the legislative body be prohibited from participating directly in any negotiation.

Such a statute, voted by a state legislature, would be completely consistent with the recent court rulings we have cited, since the legislature would retain complete control of the purse strings. However, it would clearly support and define the bargaining authority of the executive. Together with an effort to improve communications between the executive and the legislature, such legislation would represent one important step toward coordinating the roles of the executive and legislative branches in state labor relations.

REFERENCES

1. *United Faculty of Florida, etc. v. Board of Regents*, 365 So. 2d 1073 (Fla. A pp. 1979).
2. *State v. American Federation of State, County, and Municipal Employees, Local 1726*, 298 A 2d 362 (Del. Ch. 1972).
3. *California State Employees Association v. Flournoy*, 32 Cal. App. 3d 219 (1973).

Discussion Questions

1. What is the point of negotiating with a local government sub-unit if the state legislature has the final say? Discuss.
2. What are the advantages held by the executive branch of the state government at the bargaining table? How "real" are these advantages?
3. What might be the effect of executive branch negotiators consulting in advance with legislators to get a commitment for the proposed contract?

Reprinted from Journal of Collective Negotiations in the Public Sector Vol. 11(4), 1982

CHAPTER 4

Productivity and Job Security: The Issues of the 1980's in U.S. Public Sector Labor Relations

GEORGE T. SULZNER

The period of rapid expansion of government employment that occurred during the 1960's and into the late 1970's has ended. Vincent Barabba, Director of the U.S. Bureau of the Census, stated: "Government employment is projected to increase less rapidly than total civilian employment during the 1980's, a reversal of historical trends." [1, p. 38] While the number of state and local government employees per 1,000 persons nearly doubled from 1960 to 1978 and the ratio at the federal level remained constant, the projection for the current decade is for a virtual standstill in the growth of government employment relative to the growth of the population [1, p. 38].

The consequences for government managers and employees are rather clear and aptly summed up in the statement that in the near future, governments in the United States will have to "do more with less." It is not simply a question of limiting growth. The public is concerned also about improving the efficiency and quality of government services while reducing the cost of government. Proposition 13 in California and Proposition 2 1/2 in Massachusetts are two of the most dramatic examples of this development. Operating within this context and, in the early 1980's, in a setting where public confidence in the ability of government to solve problems is very low, it is hardly surprising that worker productivity and job security are issues high on the agenda of public sector unions. Whether they can be dealt with effectively may determine significantly the viability and continued existence of government employee unions in the United States. From the present vantage point, the prospects do not appear favorable.

PRODUCTIVITY IN THE PUBLIC SERVICE

Measuring government productivity is a relatively recent concern and has only been systematically examined within the federal government since 1967. Using a measurement system developed by the Bureau of Labor Statistics involving an efficiency measure (the ratio of outputs to inputs) and applied to fifty federal agencies, the U.S. Office of Personnel Management reported that productivity growth (output per employee year) averaged 1.4 per cent per annum from 1967 through 1978 [2]. There is no comparable data available for state and local governments. Recognizing the limits of looking at productivity simply from an efficiency perspective which necessarily ignores other important dimensions of governmental service, it remains, however, a useful task to examine factors that contribute to or detract from government employee productivity.

Productivity seems to be affected by the dynamic interaction of three kinds of factors:

1. *People Factors*, consisting of elements associated with the motivation and skills of employees;
2. *Process Factors,* composed of elements connected to work systems and technology, and;
3. *Product Factors,* comprised of elements that affect the quantity and quality of service delivery.

This paper focuses on the process and people factors and it must be sufficient to note simply that as the nature of the problems engaging governments and the framework within which governments function become more complex, product factors seem to have a net negative impact on employee productivity.

Let us examine some key people and process factors more closely, assess their relative support in the contemporary public sector environment in the Northeast and North Central areas of the United States (the places where government unions are most active), and look at how public collective bargaining might relate to employee productivity issues.

When the most important people factors that aid or hinder productivity are identified, expectations about significant productivity gains for government enterprises must be restrained. Motivational and skill related incentives for increased productivity, such as enhanced employee participation, monetary rewards, job enrichment schemes, increased training and employee development programs—all part of the modern litany of personnel management theory—do not carry a lot of weight when public administrators and elected officials are confronting a constricting economic environment. Those agencies most likely to advocate these policies for employees, personnel and human resource units, are the usual targets for substantial budgetary recisions. Elements linked to productivity decline, like level funding of budgets, hiring and promotion freezes, reductions-in-force and in-grade, and high rates of employee turn-overs, seem in the ascendency at the present time.

A similar relationship appears to exist for the positive and negative components of the process factors that affect productivity. In this instance, however, the net impact is greater because process factors have been found to be the main ingredients of productivity change [3]. Again, positive contributors such as rationalizing work functions through planning techniques and operations analysis, the implementation of effective performance evaluation methods, regular capital investment in materials, equipment and facilities, and sustained commitment to research and development activities, have never been promoted consistently in the highly charged political atmosphere and severely constrained budgetary milieu of public management. Not surprisingly, as Roger Lubin noted in a recent article, little systematic thinking about investment in technology occurs outside the Department of Defense or the protective services [4]. The excessive clearance procedures for launching innovative projects, which are tied to rigid control and monitoring mechanisms, the instability of periodic departmental reorganizations, and the relatively short time frame facing government officials for fulfilling mission objectives, are additional obstacles to productivity growth in the public sector. Productivity increases in government during the 1980's will be modest at best.

COLLECTIVE BARGAINING AND PUBLIC SERVICE PRODUCTIVITY

How does collective bargaining bear on this issue? Roberts and Bittle reported in a recent issue of *Federationist* about five contemporary studies that show union workers are more productive than nonunion workers in the private sector. The common explanation relates to the higher motivation and skill of union workers and the greater stability of the work environment. Because of favorable wages and benefits, worker morale is higher, turnover is lower, security is greater, and management is more effective [5]. Thus, it appears that where collective bargaining can operate within fairly wide parameters, both the people and process factors related to productivity can be addressed affirmatively. This is evidenced in the growing number of agreements that establish labor-management committees to discuss matters of mutual concern, especially items dealing with the quality of work life and the field of health and safety [6]. While few deal with productivity directly, the general improvement in the attitudes of the parties as a result of these structured communications can spill over into the formal negotiations and possibly facilitate the handling of sensitive productivity concerns [7].

Whether private sector experiences can be transferred to the public realm is yet to be determined. There is evidence, certainly, that management operations, communication with employees, and employee participation all improve with the advent of collective bargaining within government agencies [8]. Public management initiatives are restrained beyond the limiting political and budgetary perspectives already mentioned, however, by being subject also to civil service regulations that inhibit administrative flexibility to protect the service from patronage abuse. The relevant illustration here is the difficulty of introducing job enrichment programs in the midst of traditional position classification systems.

Unions also have difficulties dealing with productivity issues when the short-term effect of technological innovation is loss of jobs. If care is not taken to cushion the possible adverse consequences of the introduction of productivity raising technology, unions undoubtedly will not cooperate in productivity improvement schemes. Public managers, perhaps because of particularly forceful management rights provisions in statute and contract, have seemed too often to lack sensitivity to the union viewpoint on work life after operational change. Because government unions are prohibited from striking and excluded normally from bargaining about position classifications, contracting-out of government work, reorganization of government services, and reduction-in-force decisions, their concerns are sometimes ignored. Surely this is a problem that joint committees or worker councils can attend with potentially beneficial results.

What seems abundantly clear is that a "bandaid" approach to increasing public sector productivity simply will not work. Major resource commitments in human and economic terms must be made if progress is to occur. Additionally, the restructions on collective bargaining in government must be removed if unions are to be agents of rather than roadblocks to change [9].[1] Realistically, it does not look like any of these things will happen in the 1980's, and we can expect a further shrinking of the jurisdiction of government, justified at least in part by references to the sluggish productivity of public employees and enterprises.

---

[1] Rudolph A. Oswald strongly supports this perspective in Bargaining and Productivity in the Public Sector: A Union View [9].

JOB SECURITY IN THE PUBLIC SERVICE

Public sector employment, as we have discussed earlier, will expand modestly throughout this decade. Projections by the U.S. Bureau of the Census and the U.S. Bureau of Labor Statistics call for a gain of about two million state and local employees during this period and nearly 150,000 federal employees. This forecast is based on the assumption that while "real" GNP may grow at an annual average rate of 3.6 per cent for the 1980's, government purchases of goods and services are seen to increase by only 1.5 per cent per annum, compared to personal consumption expenditures and gross private domestic investment rises of 4.0 and 4.1 per cent, respectively [1, pp. 37, 39].

Furthermore, government employment gains will be distributed unevenly throughout the country and among occupations. Growth will occur in the sun belt states and decline in the Northeast and North Central states, sections of the county where public employees are most heavily organized. Growth is anticipated for the health care and public safety fields; retrenchment for education, environmental and public works employees. The demand for professional, technical, and protective service workers will increase, while the need for clericals, blue collar workers, and managers/administrators will be less [1, pp. 38, 39].

Even if public sector unions had experience with handling reductions in employment of their constituents, which they do not, the uneven effects of very slow growth would create internal organizational problems for them because of a trend in recent years to organize agencies wall-to-wall, regardless of employee function, and to consolidate representation across departmental boundaries.

COLLECTIVE BARGAINING AND JOB SECURITY IN THE PUBLIC SERVICE

Public employee organizations have not had much success bargaining about issues that touch the job security of government workers. This ineffectiveness, to some extent is related to the circumstance that public sector bargaining organizations matured during a period of time when public employment was growing rapidly. Job security simply was not viewed as an important issue for most of the bargaining history of government unions. As a result, they have had very little experience in dealing with this topic in negotiations. A dramatic case in point is a recently negotiated agreement with the Trial Court of Massachusetts and the nonprofessional staff and clerical employees, which ignores layoff matters completely. Layoffs were just never thought to be a possibility, even though three months after the contract was signed, layoffs for bargaining unit members seem probable.

Moreover, within government, administrators have an especially pressing obligation to respond to public wants whether they be demands for increases or cutbacks in service and programs. The corresponding management right to direct the workforce and take whatever actions are necessary to promote efficient and accountable operations is deeply ingrained in the lexicon of public managers and is always spelled out in contract articles. For example, an agreement governing a bargaining unit at a United States Veterans Administration Medical Center states that:

> Management officials of the agency retain the right. . . :
>
> A. To direct employees of the Veterans Administration;
> B. To hire, promote, transfer, assign and retain employees. . . . to suspend, demote, discharge, or take other disciplinary action against employees;
> C. To relieve employees from duties because of lack of work or for other legitimate reasons; . . . . [10].

Another striking instance is the language of the contract for the Trial Court of Massachusetts, which besides supplying an exhaustive list of management prerogatives, pointedly calls attention to the fact that, "The listing of specific rights of management in this agreement is not intended to be, nor shall be, restrictive of, or a waiver of, the rights of management not listed and specifically surrendered herein, whether or not such rights have been exercised by the employer in the past." [11]

Is it any wonder, given the above representative citations, that public sector negotiations have not been a widely used vehicle for dealing head on with subjects involving work assignments, transfers, contracting-out-of-work, relocations of facilities, and layoffs of employees? All, as policies, generally have been held by appropriate adjudicatory bodies to be outside the scope of bargaining for public employee unions. Bargaining organizations' impact has been limited to handling the implementation of management decisions in this realm and attempting to soften the blow when it falls on bargaining unit members members.

At a state university the retrenchment clause states that "while it is recognized that the employer may retrench one or more members of the bargaining unit whenever the employer determines that such retrenchment is required for financial or programatic reasons, the parties agree that the advice of faculty and librarians will be sought. . ." [12] The rest of a very detailed provision provides for advance notice and access to relevant information to the affected bargaining organization; an opportunity to comment on the preliminary retrenchment plan; criteria that must be addressed specifically in the actual retrenchment plan; an order of retrenchment that must be followed when bargaining unit members are being retrenched; and relocation assistance plus recall rights for individuals who are actually retrenched.

A similar contractual layoff relationship exists between the Lawrence and Memorial Hospitals of New London, Connecticut, and its unionized nurses. The agreement relates, "In any reduction-in-force for a period of more than four (4) weeks, the hospital shall make such reductions in the number in each position classification as it determines the needs of the hospital require and within each position classification the hospital shall be governed by the following considerations in selecting employees for layoffs: . . . " [13] The remaining relevant sections of the article proceed to specify factors that must be taken into consideration and that qualify management's discretion to choose who will be laid off; establish bumping rights and recall rights for employees actually retrenched; and set forth two weeks as the minimum advance notice targeted employees must receive before their jobs end.

Both these references illustrate the underlying strategy of public sector unions' handling of job security through collective bargaining agreements. They cannot guarantee jobs, and they ordinarily are excluded from participating in the actual layoff decision. Through the contract, unions attempt to make the procedures for implementing the decision as complex and drawn out as possible in order to buy time to deal with the issue through the political process. This game plan, however, may not be terribly rewarding currently when labor's political capital is quite diminished. Graham Wilson observed, recently, "American unions enjoy a mixed reputation and little popularity. Union leaders, even on economic matters, are less trusted than any other socially prominent leaders." [14]

The dilemma facing governments in the United States as we move through the 1980's is the dual demand for smaller workforces and increased productivity. Insecure workers typically have low productivity rates, while productive employees theoretically could work themselves out of a job by demonstrating that fewer workers are needed to maintain a satisfactory level of government services. In this decade, the viability of public sector labor relations will be severely tested, and the outcome will have a telling effect on whether governments can do more with less.

REFERENCES

1. V. P. Barabba, Demographic Change and the Public Work Force, *Proceedings of the Second Public Management Research Conference, The Brookings Institute, November 17-18, 1980,* United States Office of Personnel Management, Washington, D.C., November, 1980.
2. *Measuring Federal Productivity,* United States Office of Personnel Management, Office of Productivity Programs, Washington, D.C., p. 22, February, 1980.
3. J. Bodoff, *The Effect of Innovation on Productivity in the Serivce Industries,* National Science Foundation, Office of R and D Assessment, Washington, D.C., August, 1975.
4. R. Lubin, Productivity and Capital Investment: How State and Local Officials Can Increase Productivity, *Intergovernmental Personnel Notes,* pp. 18-24, March/April, 1981.

5. M. Roberts and W. E. Bittle, The Union Contract: A Solid Investment, *Federationist, 88*:5, pp. 8-10, May, 1981.
6. *Labor Management Committees in the Public Sector: A Practitioner Guide,* Midwest Center for Public Sector Relations, Bloomington, Indiana, 1979.
7. G. T. Sulzner, The Impact of Labor Management Committees on Personnel Policies and Practices at Twenty Federal Bargaining Units, *Journal of Collective Negotiations in the Public Sector, 11*:1, pp. 37-45, 1982.
8. G. T. Sulzner, *The Impact of Labor-Management Relations Upon Selected Federal Personnel Policies and Practices,* United States Office of Personnel Management, Washington, D.C., January, 1979.
9. R. A. Oswald, Bargaining and Productivity in the Public Sector: A Union View, in *Collective Bargaining and Productivity,* G. Summers, et al., (eds.), pp. 85-87, Industrial Relations Research, Madison, Wisconsin, 1975.
10. *Agreement Between the Veterans Administration Hospital, Boston, Massachusetts and Local No. 2143, American Federation of Government Employees,* duration expiration November 20, 1981, p. 3.
11. *Agreement Between Chief Administrative Justice of the Trial Court of Massachusetts and the Office and Professional Employees International Union, Local 6, AFL-CIO,* duration expiration June 30, 1983, p. 44.
12. *Agreement Between MSP/FSU/MTA, NEA and the Board of Trustees of the University of Massachusetts,* duration expiration June 30, 1983, Article 22, Section 1, p. 43.
13. *Agreement Between the Lawrence and Memorial Hospitals, New London, Connecticut and Lawrence Memorial Hospital Registered Professional Nurses, Unit No. 22, Connecticut Health Care Associates,* duration expiration June 30, 1981, p. 30.
14. G. K. Wilson, *Unions in American National Politics,* St. Martin's Press, New York, pp. 1 and 148, 1979.

Discussion Questions

1. Discuss the studies that show union workers to be more productive than non-union workers in the private sector. How does the public sector differ?
2. Describe union problems in dealing with productivity issues that might lead to a reduction of the work-force and consequent loss of jobs.
3. Why are public sector unions inexperienced in handling job security issues? Discuss trends.

PART II
MUNICIPAL EMPLOYEES

The four chapters in this section deal with municipal employees in a bargaining or strike framework. The authors share an underlying assumption that is overtly stated in Chapter 5: that public employee unions are political, at least in the sense of using the public opinion to bolster their positions.

Of necessity, the taxpayers are silent partners at the bargaining table in all public employee negotiations. At the municipal level, however, the public tends to be in close proximity—they are often friends, neighbors, and relatives of municipal board members and negotiators. In addition, the services jeopardized by a breakdown in negotiations are tangible: the garbage would pile up, the houses might burn down, the snow would remain to clog the streets, and so on. Thus, the pressures are greater at the municipal level than at state and federal levels.

In Chapter 5, Michael Marmo examines the effectiveness of political activities and connections for municipal unions in a large city. Mary W. Henderson, in Chapter 6 speaks from the rueful experience of dealing with a strike among general city workers. Her advice to municipal officials on the proper posture to assume before and during a strike is based on that experience. Taken as a totality, the four chapters reflect part of the range of problems faced by municipal officials—elected or appointed—in dealing with organized local government employees. In Chapter 7 Joseph W. Wilson questions the survival of pension plans within the governmental structure. In Chapter 8 Donald E. Pursell and William D. Torrence describe the impact of compulsory arbitration on a municipal budget.

The chapters also present a spectrum of philosophical issues that are seldom analyzed: ranging from "Who is the public?" to "Do municipal officials represent only taxpayers?" to "What are the ethical and moral problems in dealing with unions that represent your neighbors?"

CHAPTER 5

*Public Employee Unions –
The Political Imperative*

MICHAEL MARMO

In the United States most private sector unions exhibit a basically economic orientation. For them, forays into the political thicket are sporadic and tend to involve peripheral issues. To use a cliche, private sector unions are essentially "bread and butter" organizations. As such, they tend to eschew politics. It would be erroneous to deny that political factors are important to some private sector unions. However, for most, political considerations remain subordinate to their overriding economic concerns.

In marked contrast to private sector unions, their public employee counterparts appear to be vitally concerned with political action. According to Chester A. Newland, "The outstanding characteristic of public employee unions which is basic to an understanding of governmental labor-management relations is their heavy dependence upon political power and their methods to accomplish their goals" [1]. Although both private and public sector unions engage in political activities, Newland maintains that the basic distinction between them is that ". . . public employee unions are primarily political organizations" [1].

This article examines the political nature of municipal public employee unions by looking at the activities during the 1960's of three unions representing workers of the City of New York. They are: The Uniformed Sanitationmen's Association (USA); Transport Workers Union, Local 100 (TWU); and the Social Service Employees Union (SSEU). In examining these unions, three generalizations emerge about their political activity. First, each was convinced that since it operated in a political context it must have an effective political organization. Second, because of this belief, each union had or tried to develop an organization that would maximize its political effectiveness. Third, the extent to which each was successful in developing political "clout" greatly affected its collective bargaining goals.

Why Politics?

Let us consider the attitude of these unions toward the importance of political power. The Uniformed Sanitationmen's Association's commitment to political activity goes back to their president John DeLury's early experience. In the 1940's, the USA was locked in a representational struggle with two other union groups to determine which organization would get bargaining rights for sanitationmen. The USA won the election, helped in large part by the intervention of Mayor Fiorello LaGuardia. LaGuardia was convinced that John DeLury was the man with whom he wanted to deal. It was from this experience that DeLury saw the need to develop a strong political base. He felt that politicians understood and responded to club style political help, and he was determined to develop a well-disciplined political machine. The USA saw political activity not as an alternative to "bread and butter" issues but as vital to the achievement of collective bargaining objectives.

Like the USA, the Transport Workers Union, Local 100, believed that collective bargaining power is closely related to political power. As the Union's international president, Matthew Guinan, stated, "We're interested in politics because a lot of the things that

we bargain for involve legislation and the political situation" [2].
Daniel Gilmartin, the president of Local 100, elaborated on this
point:

> In Local 100, the difference between good and bad legislation can
> mean job security, or better working conditions, or improved retirement
> benefits, or other additional benefits. The whole transit job is subject to
> the political process. It is governed by laws and regulations produced by
> the legislature, or by some agency of government . . . It should be clear
> then that political action is bread and butter in this local. It is a power-
> ful ally at the collective bargaining table [3].

The youngest of the three unions, the Social Service Employees
Union, was not established until 1964. While lacking the history of
political involvement of the sanitationmen and transit workers, the
SSEU shared their belief in political activity. Martin Morganstern,
president of the SSEU, believed that all things a public employee
union were concerned with, including "bread and butter" items,
were more easily attainable if the union had a strong political organization to back its demands. He envied the USA's political
strength. "At this point we are not the sanitationmen," stated
Morganstern, "but we hope to move that way [4]." Unlike the
USA and the TWU, the welfare workers gave an additional reason
for being concerned with politics. According to Morganstern, the
SSEU had to be politically active because it should be interested in
social issues as well as the welfare of its members. "Major public
policy issues are at stake in welfare matters and we feel it is inappropriate to limit our actions to the collective bargaining front,"
he elaborated [4].

The Modus Operandi

Because of their belief that the ability to achieve their "bread
and butter" demands was closely related to their political power,
each union had tried to develop an effective political organization.
The sanitationmen and the transit workers used their own organizations to perform the traditional political chores that deliver votes
to a candidate. The welfare workers, on the other hand, tried to
enlist the aid of other community groups in order to exert political
influence. The kind of political organization each union had in the
1960's was to some extent a reflection of the nature of its members' work, the size of the union, and their previous political
influence.

The kind of work sanitationmen perform made it fairly easy for
them to engage in "politicking." They were in constant touch with

people and used this opportunity to spread their political ideas. "They're like Yogi Berra," explained union official Al Katz, "they may not have the best grammar, but they love to talk to people, and people like to listen to what they have to say." During the 1961 Democratic mayoral primary, one of the candidates charged that more than 3,000 sanitation employees were campaigning for his opponent while they were working. A top union leader answered the charge, "We damn well politicked while we were working. What's wrong with that?" He continued:

> Sure we campaign while we work. So what? People would have a right to complain if we weren't picking up the garbage while we're campaigning, but we do. Politicians don't resign their jobs when they are running for office—so why shouldn't our people be allowed to campaign while they're working [5]?

In addition to "politicking" on the job, the USA was unusually effective in mobilizing off-duty workers. Because their days off were rotated, there were potentially 1,600 men available for canvassing six days a week. The ability to put men in the field, one of the main reasons for the USA's political strength, was facilitated by an extensive filing system, which listed every sanitationman and retiree with breakdowns by borough, assembly district, congressional district, and all other election districts. The listing of retired workers was especially important since these older people usually have more time in which to campaign.

Basically, the USA had three categories of political workers. The first, composed of the union's 100-member wage negotiating committee, had the most political experience and were usually asked to perform higher level jobs. The bulk of the political work, however, was carried out by the union's 600-man steward body, which was converted to a political action committee at election time. This committee did most of the political legwork for the union, such as canvassing and handing out campaign literature. Finally, if an election was deemed important enough, union leaders solicited the help of the rank-and-file members. "We are able to go at a moment's notice," said the union's Director of Political Activity, Al Katz. "If a politician needs people, I look in my files and can send them right out [5]."

Since the sanitationmen had such a fine reputation as a political power, their usual mode of operation was to hold back and wait for a candidate to ask for the union's endorsement. In deciding who to support, the USA followed the Gompersian dictum to "support your friends and defeat your enemies." "We're not tied to nobody's kite," John DeLury stated. "We've backed Republicans and Democrats who've been favorable to labor. We're not an adjunct to either party [6]." The USA was recognized as the most active and politically effective among civil service groups in New York City. The extent to which politicians coveted their support was evidenced in a statement by Edward N. Costikyan, the former head of Tammany Hall. He was reported to have said, "I would rather have John DeLury's sanitationmen with me in an election than half the party headquarters in town [5]."

Like the USA, the Transport Workers Union in New York City ran a formidable political organization. John O'Connell, union vice-president, attributed the success of the rank-and-file to the nature of their work. In the performance of their job activities most TWU members came in contact with numerous voters daily. The union staff members ought to be good at political activities, reasoned O'Connell, since they had to be skilled politicians in order to maintain their positions of leadership in the union.

When the TWU supported a candidate it did not work through the political clubs of the candidate's party. Instead, the union set up its own storefronts, manned and supported exclusively by TWU personnel. The Transport Workers' leaders believed that people came into their storefronts who wouldn't go to political clubs. Also, they felt that the political clubs were lazy. "Our people get out and do the job," maintained John O'Connell, "they tell the people in the clubs to get off their backsides and get out and ring doorbells [7]."

In addition to manning storefronts, the TWU performed a variety of other political duties. The union found out whether its own members were registered to vote. Unregistered members received a phone call. Union staff people then set up meetings, sent out leaflets, and telephoned members urging them to vote for the preferred candidates. The union maintained eight sound trucks of its own to blare forth statements on behalf of its candidates. Union staff members organized street corner rallies, talked to voters, and distributed campaign literature door-to-door and at shopping centers. The union claimed it could mobilize 75-100 men on a week night and more than 200 on weekends. In addition to manpower, the TWU contributed money to the campaigns of favored candidates.

Since the TWU was known to be an effective political organization its backing was greatly desired by most local politicians. Decisions as to which candidates were to be backed were made by the local's executive board. In major elections such as those for mayor, the board delved deeply into a candidate's past. When lesser offices, such as the city council or state legislature were involved, candidates themselves normally took the initiative by asking for a TWU endorsement. If a man had been a friend of the union in the past, he would be given the endorsement. The backgrounds of new candidates were checked out rather carefully to determine whether they were pro-labor. "They all tell you that their father or grand-father was a member of a union and they worked their way through school at night," related TWU Local 100 president, Daniel Gilmartin. "However," he added, "checks of their background often reveal conservative leanings and sometimes even the backing of the Conservative Party [8]." Although most of the candidates supported were Democrats, the union sometimes supported liberal Republicans.

In comparison to the Sanitationmen's Association and the Trans-port Workers Union, the Social Service Employees Union was only beginning to lay the foundation for a political organization. In fact, in its formative years the welfare workers' union was not interested in establishing an ongoing political apparatus. Instead, it attempted to interest other groups in joining it on an *ad hoc* basis to mount political pressure. The folly of this strategy was all too apparent. The SSEU was repeatedly unable to mobilize other groups. As a small union without the membership or organization to exert polit-ical influence, the welfare workers were often frustrated at the bargaining table.

After an abortive strike in 1965, the SSEU began actively re-cruiting the support of other groups in the hope that together they could exert influence on the city as the union itself could not. The SSEU established a five-person speakers' bureau to attend any meeting to which they were able to get invitations. In this way, the SSEU hoped to get support from various community or-ganizations. When a second strike ensued in 1967, the SSEU leaders cultivated working relationships with spokesmen for wel-fare recipients. They also spent considerable effort trying to enlist the support of influential members of the Black and Puerto Rican communities. In 1969 they made additional attempts to mobilize public support through advertisements and contacts with scores of liberal leaders.

The welfare workers' attempts to join with other groups for political purposes were doomed to failure. It was not possible to convince these other groups that their interests were best served by an alliance with the SSEU. The N.Y.C. Welfare Department divided welfare recipients from welfare workers during the 1965 strike by adopting a policy of generosity toward its clients. The union alleged that the Welfare Department gave out money readily in order to avoid incidents with welfare recipients. The union's efforts to enlist the support of minority leaders was probably hampered by the City, which attempted to characterize the 1967 strike a "strike against the poor [4]." The SSEU asserted in 1969 that "the City administration is calculating that it can blatantly ignore union demands and a possible disruption of services because the general public is not involved [9]." The union was undoubtedly right in its assessment of the City's strategy. Unfortunately for the SSEU, the City was probably correct in assuming the general public was not much interested in the fate of welfare workers.

In 1969, the SSEU changed strategy. After several years of failure to mobilize other groups, the union leaders made a move they felt would establish the groundwork for an ongoing political organization. The SSEU merged with Local 371 of the American Federation of State, County, and Municipal Employees. The merger was not dictated solely by political considerations, but it substantially increased the political "clout" of the welfare workers. By merging with the AFSCME local, the SSEU became a part of and reaped the advantages of affiliation with AFSCME District Council 37. The Council, which represented over 100,000 public employees in New York City, had long been aware of the need for a strong political organization. It endorsed candidates, contributed money to political campaigns, and lobbied for favorable legislation. In addition, Victor Gotbaum, the Executive Director of the Council, was a political intimate of Mayor John Lindsay. Through merger, the Social Service Employees Union had achieved that which it could not realize on its own. It had become part of an effective political organization capable of exerting pressure to achieve "bread and butter" goals.

Another political advantage of the SSEU's merger with Local 371 was that it ceased to be an independent union and became an integral part of the organized labor movement. Explaining the SSEU's unsuccessful strike in 1965, A. H. Raskin correctly observed, "The union was not affiliated with the labor movement so Mayor Wagner could treat them cavalierly without fearing repercussions [10]." Association with organized labor would prevent a recurrence of such treatment.

The Collective Bargaining Payoff

Political activity by public employee unions was only a means to achieve their collective bargaining goals. The Uniformed Sanitationmen's Association was rather successful in wielding political power. For example, in the 1961 negotiations with the City government, USA president John DeLury attempted to support his demands with the argument that he was only seeking benefits that were already prevailing practice in private industry. When the logic of this argument failed to sway the position of City negotiators, DeLury was not averse to using a different form of persuasion. He intimated that the political support of his union, legendary for its effectiveness, would be given to Mayor Wagner only if a good collective bargaining agreement was reached.

The agreement was reached in July, 1961. However, certain contract provisions needed State legislative approval before they could be enacted. Generally, such bills had no chance of passing in the N.Y. State Legislature unless they were accompanied by home-rule messages from the City Council. Thus the usual procedure for enacting a contract provision that requires State legislation was as follows: a collective bargaining agreement was reached; a home-rule message was passed by the City Council; then a bill was introduced in the State Legislature, where it was subject to usual legislative procedure.

In March, 1962, the City Council considered a home-rule request on a provision of the 1961 agreement. Under consideration was a measure giving sanitationmen the option of retiring after 25 years of service. The minority leader of the Council, Stanley M. Isaacs, accused the Wagner administration of having made a primary election campaign deal the previous summer to provide these benefits in return for election support. Of course, the Democratic majority leader denied the charge, defending the previous summer's agreement as being the result of normal collective bargaining. In a sense he was right, for political pressure was normal for public employee unions.

The sanitationmen enjoyed the political advantage of friendship with Governor Nelson Rockefeller. In 1963, Rockefeller, who had vetoed a similar bill the year before, signed a bill providing for the 25-year pension option for sanitationmen. He gave no explanation for his change of heart, but from that point on Mr. Rockefeller received strong political support from the USA. The Governor, in turn, became a forceful proponent of the interests of sanitationmen.

At no time was the value of Rockefeller's friendship with the USA more evident than in their 1968 strike. Mayor Lindsay, with whom the USA had not yet established a *quid pro quo* political relationship, wanted to mount a show of force by using the National Guard and the employees from other City departments to break the strike. Governor Rockefeller refused to call out the National Guard. He told Lindsay he thought there were "other possible solutions [11]." Assuming complete control of the situation, Rockefeller got Lindsay to arrange for John DeLury's temporary release from jail so that the three of them could meet. After talking with DeLury and the Mayor for several minutes, Rockefeller dismissed Lindsay and his aides. The Governor and his labor advisors continued to meet with Mr. DeLury and his staff leaving Mayor Lindsay completely out of the discussions.

Throughout the subsequent maneuvering involved in this dispute, Governor Rockefeller sought to impose a settlement that was acceptable to his old political ally, John DeLury. The Governor's stance led Mr. Lindsay to complain privately about the "unholy alliance" between Rockefeller and the USA president [12]. For his part, DeLury had every right to expect the Governor's staunch support. How could he have expected anything less from the man who responded to DeLury's endorsement of his gubernatorial candidacy several years earlier by lifting the diminutive union leader in his arms before a throng of appreciative unionists and giving him a warm embrace?

The Transport Workers Union, Local 100, and the Social Service Employees Union also had dealings with Governor Rockefeller. In 1966, both groups sought exemption from the Condon-Wadlin Act, which provided that striking public employees in New York State could not receive wage increases for a period of three years after their strike was terminated. However, the politically strong TWU and the relatively weak SSEU were treated quite differently.

In mid-February, 1966, a new flare-up of the 12-day transit strike that had paralyzed New York City beginning on January 1 of that year, seemed imminent. More than a month after the strike had been concluded, a State Supreme Court Justice ruled that the returning strikers could not receive wage increases before January, 1969, in accordance with the penalty provisions of the Condon-Wadlin Act. Faced with the prospect of a new transit walkout to protest this action, Governor Nelson Rockefeller hastily introduced legislation to permit the Transit Authority to pay its employees the raises they won in the recently ended strike.

As the Legislature was considering the Governor's measure, a delegation from the SSEU urged Mr. Rockefeller to include them in the exemption bill. The question of penalties for the welfare workers was being argued in the courts at that very moment since they too had recently ended a strike. The SSEU group was told by a Rockefeller aide that the bill had already been printed and could not be amended. Two days later, the Governor's bill exempting only transit workers was passed.

In denouncing Governor Rockefeller for not including the

welfare workers in his exemption, the Democratic minority leader of the State Senate, Joseph Zaretzki, stated, "The two cases are absolutely the same. There isn't an ounce of logic in his position—He's just being blindly stubborn [13]." But the two cases were not absolutely the same. The transit union had 35,000 members and maintained an extremely powerful lobby at the state level. This compared with less than 5,000 members in the politically insignificant SSEU. After Governor Rockefeller's bill was made law, the *New York Times* reported, "Both parties seemed to agree that the Governor's bill was, in essence, a reflection of the influence of a large union in an election year . . . [13]."

There was a considerable amount of public speculation at the time to the effect that a deal was made between the Transport Workers Union and Governor Rockefeller. It was alleged that the union was to give Mr. Rockefeller its tacit approval in his upcoming bid for reelection in return for his sponsorship and support of the bill to exempt the transit workers from the penalties of the Condon-Wadlin Act. There was support for the belief that a deal had been made. After leaving a meeting at which the TWU thanked the Governor for his support, the union's international president Matthew Guinan said:

> We have 100,000 members (statewide) and we can only make a recommendation to our members. They don't have to follow the recommendation. But this action by the Governor sits well with the members [14].

The Social Service Employees Union, a politically weak group at that time, was in no position to reach a similar accommodation with the Governor.

There was an additional reason why only the TWU was exempted from the penalty provision of the Condon-Wadlin Act in Rockefeller's bill. Two extremely powerful political groups in the state, the New York City Central Labor Council and the State Chapter of the AFL-CIO, both supported the bill. The SSEU was not affiliated with the organized labor movement at that time and, consequently, did not enjoy their support.

Conclusion

The foregoing examination of three public employee unions in New York City shows that each union was convinced that since it operated within a political context it must have an effective political organization. Each union had or tried to develop such an organization. Its political "clout," or lack of it, greatly affected its ability to achieve its collective bargaining goals. Rather than being an abandonment of the "bread and butter" orientation characteristic of American unions, the political involvement of these public employee groups was directly supportive of those economic issues.

REFERENCES

1. Chester A. Newland, "Trends in Public Employee Unionization," *The Journal of Politics* (August, 1964), p. 586.
2. Personal interview with Matthew Guinan, held in Mr. Guinan's office at 1980 Broadway, New York, New York, on March 4, 1970.
3. Daniel Gilmartin, "Around Local 100," *TWU Express*, November, 1966, p. 6.
4. Personal interview with Martin Morganstern, held in Mr. Morganstern's office at 817 Broadway, New York, New York, on March 10, 1970.
5. Personal interview with Alfred Katz, held in Mr. Katz's office at 23-25 Cliff Street, New York, New York, on February 16, 1970.
6. "Sanitation Union Backing DeSapio," *New York Times*, October 1, 1963, p. 25.
7. Personal interview with John O'Connell, held in Mr. O'Connell's office at 1980 Broadway, New York, New York, on March 3, 1970.
8. Personal interview with Daniel Gilmartin, held in Mr. Gilmartin's office at 1980 Broadway, New York, New York, on February 27, 1970.
9. Letter by Edward Perlmutter, Legislative Representative of SSEU, to union members, November 13, 1968. I saw a copy in the files of the SSEU.
10. Personal interview with A. H. Raskin, held in Mr. Raskin's office at 229 W. 43d Street, New York, New York, on March 13, and March 16, 1970.
11. "Mediator's Garbage Strike Offer Promptly Rejected by the Mayor," *New York Times*, February 9, 1968, p. 1.
12. "Garbage Strike Is Ended," *New York Times*, February 11, 1968, p. 1.
13. "Transit Pay Bill Passed . . .," *New York Times*, February 17, 1966, p. 1.
14. "Labor In 2 Moods Greets Governor," *New York Times*, February 18, 1966, p. 18.

Discussion Questions

1. Would you agree that public employee unions are primarily political organizations? Why or why not?
2. Discuss the underlying assumptions, economic ramifications, and ethics of politicized public employee unions.
3. Name and discuss the factors that helped account for the Uniformed Sanitation Men's Association's political strength.

Reprinted from Journal of Collective Negotiations in the Public Sector Vol. 4(4), 1975

CHAPTER 6

How to Deal with a Strike as an Elected Official

MARY W. HENDERSON

If the goal of good employer–employee relations is to avoid a strike, then perhaps I'm not too well qualified to give you advice, since we recently had a strike. However, if you want to hear from the voice of experience, then I guess I'm qualified, at least to tell you how we dealt with the strike in Redwood City. There may be some lessons for you in our experience.

Let me give you some background. Redwood City, population 58,000, has about 400 employees and three bargaining units: the Police Officers Association; the International Association of Fire Fighters, AFL–CIO; and the Service Employees International Union, AFL–CIO (SEIU).

Salary adjustments are made effective January 1 in Redwood City. About 70% of our general budget goes for salaries and other employee costs. Our police and fire groups and the city came to terms by mid-December. Agreements were within the then-existing guidelines of 5.5%.

However, the City and the SEIU, representing general employees, were unable to agree. SEIU's original demands added up to a 46%

salary and fringe benefit package and involved numerous items, including agency shop and compulsory binding arbitration of grievances.

Although a marathon last-ditch session was held from 4 p.m. January 3 until 6 a.m. January 4, the sewage treatment plant people walked off the job at midnight January 4. By 8 a.m. there were picket lines around city facilities. The strike was on.

About 125 of 225 general employees went out. The only service critically affected was the library, both branches were closed for the duration. Redwood City has a franchise for garbage pickup and has a contractual arrangement for the municipal transit operation, thus allowing for full service in two important areas of concern.

The strike lasted 32 days, ending on February 4. The settlement was a two-year agreement averaging 5.25%, no binding arbitration, no agency shop.

I believe there are some important considerations for me to share with you regarding the role of city council members in a strike. First is the question of confidence in your city manager. This is a must if a council is to deal properly and effectively with a strike. A strike is no time to try outguessing your management. Second, remember NO ONE wins in a strike, but councilmen can have long-term effects on employer–employee relations by the manner in which they deal with a strike. Third, no one in his right mind wants a strike, and no council wants to provoke a strike.

In Redwood City, two years ago our manager had recommended that we contract with a private professional labor relations firm to conduct negotiations on our behalf. The Council approved his recommendation. It was probably one of the most important decisions we ever made.

I cannot emphasize too strongly the importance of having negotiators be persons other than the city manager or the council, not just during a strike, but in easing the difficulty of picking up the pieces after the strike ends. Last year, without a strike, we were equally pleased to have professional negotiators, not members of our own staff, representing us. It is a lot better to have employees mad at someone other than the manager and the council, if possible.

Our negotiating team had three members, two from our labor relations firm and our city personnel director. The union made a number of efforts to discredit our team, which didn't work, and they tried hard to involve council members and the manager directly in the negotiations. That, too, failed. Our council's faith in our negotiating team did not waver. If ever we had allowed ourselves to become personally involved, the effectiveness of our team would have been destroyed both in the strike situation and in future negotiations with all our employee groups.

The Redwood City Council is not addicted to blind faith in management advice. Hopefully, the same is true of your councils. The city council must make the decisions and it is vital that a council not simply accept someone else's word, that they understand fully the situation they face. Our labor relations firm and management kept us completely advised on all issues, and they explored with us all possible alternatives and the ramifications thereof. A distinct plus for hiring a labor relations firm was their ability to inform us of labor conditions and council positions and resulting situations in other jurisdictions.

We were not told these things quickly or casually, but thoroughly and in depth. At times these meetings were mentally exhausting sessions. The issues were raised and examined from all sides quite carefully. Often we'd find ourselves arguing with our labor relations people as they practiced "role playing" on us. Literally, they put us through our paces and tested us to be sure we knew not only what we stood for but why, and they measured the strength of our convictions in the process.

The result was that when our council took a position, a THIS-IS-AS-FAR-AS-WE-CAN-GO posture, it was backed by conviction based in knowledge of the issues and a very thorough understanding of both the position and what might be expected to result from our taking it. I must warn you to be very cautious about settling in on a given position. We all know what happens to people who set their feet in concrete. If you are going to change your minds, do it before a strike starts, not later.

If you do take a position that has the possibility of causing a strike, be sure you are prepared to maintain your position when the strike happens. You'll do your city great damage if you fall into a strike and then have second thoughts about your so-called "absolute final position."

After all this if you still have a council position beyond which you are not prepared to go, you may feel comforted in that you have been briefed, measured, tested, and tried by your labor relations team and your management. So you come to the point where you feel strongly and you are prepared to accept a strike rather than to give in to certain employee demands. If you are lucky, the employee representatives will recognize the strength of your position and respond accordingly; then again, you might get a strike.

Thus, you are struck. A strike is not a game, a joke or a contest, believe me. And it is not fun. It might seem like a holiday to the pickets for the first day or so, but that's about all. Things look different when they are still pickets and have missed two pay checks.

When a strike is underway the council's understanding of its role becomes even more important. You may expect to be scowled at and called names by pickets. Shoving can occur, but not if you stay away. You may get slashed tires, rocks through windows, pickets at your business or home or even worse. You may get "hang up" phone calls all night long, or abusive calls to you or your wife, husband, or children. You may expect subtle and not so subtle threats involving your own career, business, or personal life. You may find close personal friends who are also employees of your city are very bitter toward you, and they may demand that you "do something."

You must expect and be prepared to cope calmly with these kinds of things. It is critically important that you, as a council member, maintain a calm, cool and collected posture throughout a strike. If you get angry and yell into a telephone which awakened you every hour from 1 to 5 a.m., you'll just increase the pressure to do more of the same to you, nonstriking employees, management, and other councilmen. Cool it! Your yelling does not help.

Whatever the harassment, don't make an issue of it publicly. If you work at it, you can learn not to answer the phone after midnight and eventually the calls might even stop. Don't allow yourself to be drawn into discussions with pickets or individual employees. Remind them that by agreement, and under the MMB law,[1] negotiating is being done by designated representatives for each side and you will not, CANNOT, discuss the matter with them directly.

There will be continuing efforts and pressures to get each council member mixed into the process. You'll be told you don't understand, that you are stupid or indifferent. Your negotiators will be called names in hopes of discrediting your own team with you.

Meanwhile, you continue to try to appear cheerful, unconcerned and confident. Do NOT discuss the strike with anyone or anywhere other than in your executive sessions. Spare your family and friends

[1] Meyers-Milias-Brown Act is the legislation that governs the conduct of labor relations of all cities in California.

any details. It may prove awkward to them and, worse, damaging to your city.

Then there are the newspapers, television and radio. Everyone who otherwise ignores you becomes interested when there is a strike. Incorrect information may appear in the newspapers. Restrain yourself from setting the record straight. Don't get caught negotiating via the media. A strike is a time for "no comment" from councilmen.

Our council refused to comment during negotiations, saying any statement on the strike would come from our manager or negotiating representative. Our mayor candidly admitted to the council during our strike that he had hurt our position at one point because he answered a reporter's questions. A big story resulted that did not aid our position. The mayor did not make the same mistake again, nor did the rest of us. We issued only one public statement on behalf of the council. It was a prepared statement read by the mayor at a council meeting. We made no other comments and did not permit strikers or the public to speak to us at council meetings on the subject of the strike. They tried hard. Of course not allowing them to speak on the subject resulted in our being accused of gestapo-like tactics, among other things, but we did keep ourselves out of public discussion and, therefore, possible negotiating.

Many on the outside will criticize you and some will offer to help. You must resist the impulse to share with them information that is privileged. This may further the criticism, but you must stick with your agreed procedures if they are to be effective.

Before you get into it, recognize that a strike will make great demands on your time, other than and in addition to the usual demands of being a councilman, which of course must be met. Business-as-usual should be your posture.

Our council spent about 23 hours in 10 special executive sessions during our strike. Before it started we had three special sessions for a total of 6½ hours. Ten special executive sessions in 32 days on top of 4 regular council meetings and business-as-usual is rather demanding. Expect it. Be prepared. All of our executive sessions were held separately from council meetings. The end of a long day and after a tough council meeting is no time to start a discussion of something so important as negotiations. Our longest session was four hours. We sometimes met at noon, often at 4 p.m., and once or twice in the morning. We tried to meet at the convenience of the private business requirements of our members, but our council members were available "on call" during the strike. Our sessions on negotiations were, of course, closed meetings, attended only by the council members, City Manager, his assistant, personnel director, our city attorney, his assistant, and the labor relations firm representatives, usually two or three of them. They were hard working, tiring, but extremely important meetings. We always felt fully informed about the negotiations. You must expect to do this during a strike.

Finally, in summary, I'd like to urge that you, as an elected official, can best deal with a strike if you do these things:

1. Use labor relations experts other than yourselves and your manager to represent you in a strike.
2. Measure your convictions before a strike and the degree of commitment your whole group has. Don't, repeat, DO NOT take a position you think you might not stick with. A firm, consistent, straightforward, and fair position is vital.
3. Remember you are a management representative. The old paternalistic system is gone. You can't represent both employer and employee. More than once our negotiators reminded me, forcefully, that my job is not to be concerned about what is best for employees, but to listen to the demands of their representatives and to remember that I represent management.
4. Plan ahead. Prepare in advance for strike effects. If there is a strike, anticipate possibilities and don't weaken your position by being caught by surprise.
5. Expect threats and harassment to yourself, family, business, and to nonstriking city employees. Be prepared to support your position in spite of ugly, nasty situations that might develop.
6. Be prepared to take the guff, to let appearances belie the facts. Resist the urge to defend yourself. *Do not answer back*, no matter what the provocation. Let the negotiating team guide you in tactics and let them do the talking.
7. Be cheerful, positive, unconcerned appearing. Don't act or look nervous, worried or desperate. It is important you appear to have utmost confidence in the propriety of your position and that position had better be fair and straightforward.
8. Don't disrupt or interfere with those employees still on the job trying to do the work of many. They appreciate your support but don't have time for more than keeping up with the heavy pressures of doing the work of several.
9. Do not make statements on your own to the press or public. It is no time for personal heroics or brinksmanship.

10. Keep in mind that no two strikes are ever the same. What applied in our situation could be just the opposite for yours. Be sure you all understand your tactics and that you all stick to them. It is no time for you to improvise.

11. Remember, although your negotiating team is doing the work, they work for you. You make the policy and determine the tactics which they carry out. Although it may look like they are doing it all, take comfort in your own knowledge of the importance of your role, even though it may be an invisible one.

A strike is a time for quiet thinking, a time for council members to be seen and not heard. Undramatic as it is, this may be your greatest contribution to your community.

Discussion Questions

1. Discuss the concept of having professional negotiators on whom employees can vent their anger after a strike.
2. Why is the advice given to refrain from setting the record straight if incorrect information appears in the newspapers during a strike?
3. Discuss the position of a management representative and the reminder issued to the author that the job of a city council member is not to be concerned about "what is best for the employees but to listen to the demands of their representatives."

Reprinted from Journal of Collective Negotiations in the Public Sector Vol. 4(1), 1975

CHAPTER 7

Can Public Pension Plans Survive under PERISA?

JOSEPH W. WILSON

To help alleviate a myriad of problems involving private pension and profit-sharing plans, Congress passed, in 1974, the "Employee Retirement Income Security Act" (ERISA). This law has effected some very important changes in the private pension movement, particularly by affecting both pension and profit sharing plans from a legal, tax, and acturial viewpoint.

Many in Congress, who think ERISA has strongly benefited private pension plans, now seek to pass a similar law for public pension plans. This proposed law is entitled the "Public Employee Retirement Income Security Act" (PERISA). It would cover all public employee benefit plans except those covered by ERISA. Additionally, the law proposes to establish a single independent agency to administer both PERISA and ERISA.

Although the basic philosophy of the public pension law is commendable, the problems created by such a law could cause a great deal more turmoil in the public sector than ERISA has caused in the private sector. A basic difference in the two sectors, from the standpoint of benefit plans, lies in the methods of funding. Private plans are funded from the profits or earnings of corporations that choose to institute pension plans. These organizations have the means to increase their contributions to their pension trust when their profits or earnings grow. On the other hand, public plans are funded through the general revenue funds of state and local governments. Any increase in fund contributions normally are gained via taxes on the local citizenry. Presently there is a trend in our society to *decrease* taxes, rather than the opposite. Therefore, if PERISA is enacted—with all its stringency—it could bankrupt many local communities that have very low tax revenues and tight municipal budgets.

This paper explores the feasibility of a public pension law and identifies the types of problems such a law might create.

PROVISIONS OF PERISA

If enacted by Congress, PERISA would cover all public plans except those that are unfunded and maintained by employers for the express purpose of providing deferred compensation to management or highly paid employees. This legislation would also require reporting and disclosures to participants, beneficiaries, employees, employee organizations, and the general public.

Benefit plans under both ERISA and PERISA would be governed by the Employee Benefit Administration. The agency would be headed by a five-member board, consisting of officers from the Departments of Labor and the Treasury, two members appointed by the President, and an executive director, who would be chairman of the board of the Employee Benefit Administration. Under PERISA the proposed standards of conduct, fiduciary responsibilities, and prohibited transactions are very similar to the provisions required by ERISA. Although details are still being formulated, plans under PERISA would be treated similarly to private plans. Initially, this fact would make administration of public pensions extremely difficult because at the present time public plans are organized under state laws and each state has slightly different rules. As now proposed, PERISA would preempt most state pension laws, with the exception of state insurance, banking, and security laws, as well as generally applicable criminal laws [1].

CHARACTERISTICS OF PUBLIC PLANS

Membership in state and local government plans has grown more rapidly in the last ten years than employment. In 1972, 98 per cent of all full-time state and local government employees belonged to public pension plans. Thus, most of the 12 million state and local government employees expect to draw pension benefits in the future. During 1975, state and local government maintained

6,630 plans covering 10.4 million active workers and 2.3 million retired people or their beneficiaries. In 1975, the assets of these funds totaled 108 billion dollars, with present growth being at an annual rate of 13 per cent. Benefit payments issued by these funds totaled over 7.5 billion dollars in 1975. Although membership totals have remained fairly constant, benefit payments made by state and local retirement programs exceeded 12 billion dollars during the fiscal year 1978-1979 [2, pp. 2-3]. The number of state and local plans by size of active membership for 1975 is shown in Table 1.

A similarity between public and private pension systems is that a large percentage of all retirement plans have fewer than 100 active members (see Table 2). Also, both public and private pension plans have a small percentage of large plans that cover the majority of employees. Looking at the distribution, by size of public plans, we find 1,206 plans (18% of total) with memberships at 100 members of greater, which cover the majority of public employees. This situation bears a marked resemblance to coverage by private plans, i.e., 17 per cent of the large plans cover the majority of employees. This comparison becomes an extremely important factor for estimation of future public plans that may fail or terminate. During the first two years following the passage of ERISA, the Government Accounting Office (GOA) estimated that 41 per cent of all plan terminations were a direct result of the requirements for compliance

Table 1. Number of State and Local Public Employee
Retirement Systems by Size, 1975

Size of Active Membership	Number of Plans	% of Total
0-4	793	13.7
5-2	1,545	26.7
25-99	1,110	19.2
100-199	332	5.7
200-499	297	5.1
500-999	187	3.2
1,000-4,999	206	3.6
5,000-9,999	60	1.0
10,000 and over	124	2.1
Unknown	1,134[a]	19.6
Total	5,788[b]	

[a] Unknown plans, primarily local plans or police and firefighters having fewer than 100 members.

[b] Total number of plans excludes 842 plans for which data is unavailable.

SOURCE: *Committee on Education and Labor, Pension Task Force Report on Public Employee Retirement Systems,* Washington, D.C., 1978 [3].

Table 2. Number of Private Retirement Plans by Size, 1977

Size of Active Membership	Number of Plans	% of Total[a]
1-10	293,056	63
11-25	57,943	12
26-99	37,814	08
Over 100	77,762	17
Total	466,575[b]	

[a] Figures not exact due to rounding.
[b] Includes plans that come under ERISA for revision.
SOURCE: U.S. Government Accounting Office, *An Actuarial and Economic Analysis of State and Local Government Pension Plans* (Washington, D.C., February, 1980), Report No. PAD-80-1 [4].
U.S. Pension Benefit Guaranty Corporation, *Analysis of Single Employer Defined Benefit Termination,* 1977 [5].

with ERISA's provisions. To be more specific, terminations among small plans (100 members or less) were 20 times greater than among large plans (100 or more members). Approximately 18 per cent of all small private pension plans (roughly 82,000) terminated between December 1974 and July 1977. The remaining 82 per cent of small private plans (about 38,000) have continued, however many report they are having extreme difficulties [6]. Since the provisions of PERISA are quite similar to those of ERISA, it is quite possible that PERISA will be responsible for an 18 per cent failure or termination rate of public plans (about 1120). It also seems probable because public plans are currently experiencing conditions similar to those of private plans just prior to passage of ERISA.

FUNDING AND GROWTH OF PUBLIC PLANS

To give a more in-depth look at public plans we should explore the circumstances surrounding the expansion of governmental services. State and local government employment has expanded more rapidly than either that of the federal government or the private sector. This situation, coupled with the increasing cost of pension plan funding, has placed an expensive burden on state and local governments.

Although seldom publicized, public plans have, for the most part, always been inadequately funded. For example, as early as 1916, the City of New York's public plans were found to be inadequately financed. This situation has also prevailed in many other public plans. Indeed, it seems rare to find an adequately funded public plan. A 1973 report by the Advisory Commission on Intergovernmental Relations concluded that "underfunded, locally administered retirement systems pose an emerging threat to the financial health of local governments." [3]

The term "underfunding" can be interpreted in a number of ways and, therefore, must be explored to gain a clearer understanding for our purpose. First, the term can refer to the inability of the employer to meet continually increasing contributions to the pension plan. This problem, in most instances, stems from the lack of a sound acturial procedure, which should make the proper assumptions about probable future frequencies of death rates, retirement rates, and rates of salary increases. Contributions to the plan, which fall into this category, are generally made on a "pay-as-you-go" basis. Public plans funded in this manner obtain their contributions from general revenues and from taxes earmarked specifically for pensions. Such a haphazard funding method frequently causes underfunding during periods of rising inflation and when the populace is determined to hold down taxes, regardless of their intended use.

The term *underfunded* can also refer to unfunded accrued liabilities. An accrued liability, in pension terminology, is the excess of the pension fund liability over the value of the pension plan assets. Almost all pension plans have some unfunded accrued liability. These liabilities may arise when a retirement plan is established and invested benefits are given to employers for years of service that occurred prior to the establishment of the pension plan. Accrued liabilities may also occur after a plan is established if the plan is amended to increase benefits.

A Presidential Pension Task Force estimated that the unfunded accrued liabilities of all state and local governments was "in excess of $175 billion during the year 1975." [3, pp. 150-155] These liabilities appear to have greatly increased over the last five years to an estimated level of about $225 billion.

At this point, questions arise regarding whether public pension plans have a commitment to accumulate assets to eliminate these liabilities and whether there is a moral or legal commitment concerning the speed at which these liabilities should be eliminated under the provisions of ERISA's minimum funding standards. It is mandatory that private pensions accumulate the necessary assets, so that all accrued liabilities be eliminated over a period of forty years, beginning January, 1975. At present very few private pension plans have fully eliminated these accrued liabilities, and many corporations question how they will accomplish this within the time limit. To illustrate the problem, there are some corporations whose accrued liabilities for their pension plans exceed the total asset value of the corporation. If PERISA is enacted, a similar burden will be placed on public plans.

POSSIBLE IMPACT ON STATE AND LOCAL
TAXES UNDER PERISA STANDARDS

In a study by the Governmental Accounting Office (1980) it was estimated that if the current benefit and financing procedures were continued by state and local governments to the year 2012, benefit payments will exceed estimated contributions [5]. This study, although limited to seventy-two pension plans in eight states, presented an excellent cross-section of all categories of public pension plans. In all instances, the minimum funding standards required by ERISA were used. That is, annual contributions had to include not only amounts to cover the annual costs, but also contain amortization of existing accrued unfunded liabilities over a period of forty years.

This study concluded that if state and local governments adopted funding methods similar to ERISA, they would have to raise the contributions to their pension plans between 100 per cent and 400 per cent. These costs could use up to 50 per cent of the total revenues of state and local governments. Several of the cities gave exact figures. For example, Pittsburg, Pennsylvania stated that for it to meet the ERISA funding standard, 33 per cent of tax revenues would have to be designated for pension costs. This would be a 20 per cent increase in funding—currently Pittsburg allocates 13 per cent of its funds for support of the city's pension plan. Reading, Pennsylvania's pension administration believes that ERISA's standard would take up to 40 per cent of tax revenue, in comparison to the 15 per cent currently being allocated. In both cities officials strongly believe such an alternative would lead to bankruptcy. But they also expressed the opinion that the general citizenry would not accept such dramatic increases in taxation. Or, if the voters did allow such an increase, they would object to such funds being paid into a pension fund [7].

Although the above comments are limited, it is believed that this situation is not unique and in fact prevails throughout the public pension industry. Increased costs that will result from the passage of PERISA with its stringent standards will cause an increasing, severe drain on the tax revenues of local communities.

Some state and local governments are fully aware of the deficiencies in their present funding methods and these communities have initiated steps aimed at correcting them. Such attempts, however, have had limited success, primarily due to the costs involved. A key setback to preventing success in public pension reforms has been voter opposition to any sort of tax increase, regardless of its purpose.

Several California citizens have been leaders in opposing pension reform, especially if it involves increased costs. Proposition 13, which was passed by California voters in 1978, drastically cut back and limited property taxes throughout the state, although these same taxes are a major source of revenue for funding of public pensions by local governments.

Officials in other communities have commented that state or federal governments should make available to cities and local communities the necessary financial support for public pension reform. This stems from the fact that since state and federal governments are pushing for public pension reform, they, therefore, should provide the necessary financial support for such reform.

The idea of major governmental support for public pensions is not new. At present the federal government is heavily involved in state and local government pension plans financing through its grants-in-aid programs. It is estimated that about $1 billion in pension plan contributions are being reimbursed annually to state and local governments. It is a logical assumption for officials to expect increases in such reimbursements if ERISA funding standards are made applicable to public pension plans. Another aspect to the funding of public pension is through revenue sharing. However, this approach is being frowned on by federal government officials. At present, there is a movement in the federal government to greatly reduce or even eliminate revenue sharing.

SUMMARY AND RECOMMENDATIONS

At present, state and local governments are faced with quite a dilemma. On the one hand, they are struggling with current high pension costs, with the voting citizenry resisting higher taxes regardless of the reason. On the other hand, the federal government is attempting to raise current pension costs through the passage of PERISA—a law that will place public plans on a funding schedule similar to those of private pension plans without regard to how these increased costs will be met.

It is recognized that public pension reform is needed in many states, cities, and local communities, but a question arises concerning the amount and type of reform that is needed. The philosophy that all public pensions should adhere to the same standards is as unwise as the philosophy that everyone in the nation should have the same standard of living. A much more realistic approach would be for the government to monitor actions taken by state and local governments to improve the funding of their pension programs and provide them with grants-in-aids to assist in this endeavor.

Passage of PERISA will not guarantee the success of public pensions any more than ERISA has guaranteed success of private pensions. What the government should consider is that pensions, both public and private, were established on a voluntary basis by corporation employees and state and local communities. The federal government has the power to set funding standards but does not have the power to prevent termination of these voluntary programs. Massive termination of private and public pension plans will place an unbearable strain on the already overburdened social programs of our nation.

REFERENCES

1. Bureau of National Affairs, Public Plans, *BNA Report 278,* Washington, D.C., February, 1980.
2. U.S. Department of Commerce, Finance of Employee "Retirement Systems of State and Local Government in 1978-1979," Washington, D.C., 1980.
3. Committee on Education and Labor, *Pension Task Force on Public Employee Retirement Systems,* Washington, D.C., 1978.
4. *Analysis of Single Employer Defined Benefit Termination,* U.S. Pension Benefit Guaranty Corporation, 1977.
5. *An Actuarial and Economic Analysis of State and Local Government Pension Plans,* U.S. Government Accounting Office, Report No. PAD-80-1, Washington, D.C., February, 1980.
6. U.S. Government Accounting Office, Defined Benefit Pension Plans, *Effects on the Termination of Single Employer,* Washington, D.C., April, 1978.
7. Comptroller General of II the United States Funding of State and Local Government Pension Plans, A National Problem, Report HRD 79-66, Washington, D.C., 1980.

Discussion Questions

1. Discuss the concept of public employer sovereignty as it relates to a federal law about pensions and pension rights.
2. Could pension plans bankrupt a governmental unit? Discuss, using among others, New York City as an example.
3. What would be the effect of federal grants-in-aids to state and local governments as a means to improve funding of pension programs? Discuss.

Reprinted from the Journal of Collective Negotiations in the Public Sector Vol. 11(3), 1982

CHAPTER 8

The Impact of Compulsory Arbitration on Municipal Budgets – The Case of Omaha, Nebraska

DONALD E. PURSELL
WILLIAM D. TORRENCE

In an article discussing binding arbitration in government, Chauhan called for the systematic study of the impact of such laws on a variety of activities—one of which is the impact of arbitration awards on state and local budgetary priorities and the level of services [1]. In order to respond to Chauhan's call for analysis, this chapter examines the budgetary priorities and levels of services in the city of Omaha, Nebraska, over a ten-year time period, as a result of arbitration decisions of the Nebraska Commission of Industrial Relations.

Decisions by the Nebraska Commission of Industrial Relations were examined from the perspective of their impact on municipal budgets. Commission awards have the potential of disrupting or even controlling city budget priorities and allocations. By disruption, we mean that budgets must be reshuffled, reallocated, or reorganized during a fiscal year in response to some crisis such as a commission award. Disruption is inconvenient to budget planners for it increases the workload in the budget department. By control, we mean the ability of city officials to guide, manage, direct, and prioritize the city's budget. An outstanding issue relating to compulsory arbitration is the concern that elected officials would find their authority and control over municipal finances usurped by an appointed body.

The Nebraska Commission of Industrial Relations represents a unique entity engaged in compulsory arbitration to resolve labor-management disputes in the public sector of the state. First, the creation and continued existence of the commission is embedded in the constitution of Nebraska as well as subsequent statutory law. Second, the commission's functions follow a judicial approach, with five judges appointed by the governor and individual cases coming before the commission being heard by three-judge panels.[1] When evidence is taken, the rules of evidence prevailing in the trial of civil cases in Nebraska are observed by the commission [3]. Third, orders and findings of the commission may alter or establish wages, conditions of employment, or hours of labor. More specifically:

> In making such findings and order or orders, the Commission of Industrial Relations shall establish rates of pay and conditions of employment which are comparable to the prevalent wage rates paid and conditions of employment maintained for the same or similar work of workers exhibiting like or similar skills under the same or similar working conditions. In establishing wage rates the commission shall take into consideration the overall compensation presently received by the employees, having regard not only to wages for time not worked, including vacations, holidays, and other excused time, and all benefits received, including insurance and pensions, and the continuity and stability of employment enjoyed by the employees. Any order or orders entered may be modified on the commission's own motion or on application by any of the parties affected, but only upon a showing of a change in the conditions from those prevailing at the time the original order was entered [3, p. 51:3615].

Fourth, the commission may order mediation or factfinding or take the disputed issue(s) directly into arbitration. Finally, the decisions of the commission are appealable directly to the state supreme court, thus avoiding a series of intermediate steps.

---

[1] The title of "judge" is still used and is a carry-over from the earlier designation of the commission as the "Nebraska Court of Industrial Relations." The name change was made in 1979.

OMAHA BUDGETS AND AWARDS

Analysis of Omaha city budgets over the interval 1968-1980 provided no support for the hypothesis that compulsory arbitration in the public safety sector shifted resources toward areas where awards were made. Commission awards during the 1970's were centered in the fire and police units of the public safety division.[2] From 1968-1980, Omaha budget resources were allocated away from the public safety sector, implying that wage gains as a result of compulsory arbitration (commission awards) had not shifted resources toward the public safety division.

Consider the data in Table 1. Over the interval 1968-70, Omaha municipal budgets allocated 33.24 per cent of all resources to public safety. At the end of the decade public safety was allocated 26.12 per cent of city budgets 1977-1979.[3] The same pattern persists on actual expenditures. Note, however, that the public safety division spent less than budgeted levels in the first half of the 1970's—before commission awards were made—but overran budgeted amounts during the last half of the 1970's. Despite the tendency of the public safety sector to spend more than budgeted amounts during the latter years of the decade, the trend was definitely down for the public safety division in terms of the total city budget.

Sectors of Omaha city government unaffected by compulsory arbitration and awards were expanding more rapidly than the unionized public safety[4] sector during the period 1968-1980. Departments recording substantial relative increases in Omaha city budgets include public works and the residual category that includes employee benefits. Much of the increase in the residual category is a result of higher social security taxes the city was forced to pay, expenditures more or less beyond its control, unless the city is willing to substantially reduce the number of employees. The residual category was applied to items not elsewhere noted in Table 1.[5] It includes expenses for the city council, mayor's municipal court, employee benefits, and several smaller city functions. Departments that were large relative losers of city budget resources during the interval 1968-1980 include public safety and debt service. Debt service is a function of debt outstanding and interest rates and at least the outstanding debt

[2] Wage awards for fire and police were made under commission awards No. 117, 1975; No. 121, 1975; No. 233, 1977; and No. 240, 1978. Note: No. 233 covered 1978, the others covered the same year as the date of decision.

[3] Comparisons are made over three-year intervals, since any single year may reflect an unusual situation. A rise in interest rates or additional bond financing could distort single year budget proportions.

[4] The police union was incorporated in 1972 and the fire union was organized in 1934, but both unions began collective bargaining with the city in 1971.

[5] Public safety was a smaller portion of expenditures at the end of the study period than at the beginning *if* the residual category is excluded.

Table 1. Omaha City Budgets and Expenditures (as a percentage of total) 1968-1979

Budgeted	Year											
	1968	1969	1970	1971	1972	1973	1974	1975	1976	1977	1978	1979
Law	0.79	0.95	0.87	0.80	0.71	0.71	0.82	0.86	0.83	0.93	0.89	0.88
Personnel	0.32	0.32	0.35	0.33	0.33	0.37	0.44	0.46	0.42	0.43	0.42	0.44
Planning	0.47	0.45	0.42	0.40	0.38	0.39	0.41	0.44	0.42	0.40	0.41	0.42
Human Relations	0.17	0.15	0.23	0.20	0.15	0.19	0.24	0.24	0.25	0.26	0.24	0.27
Finance	.2.02	1.96	1.78	1.65	1.60	1.77	1.50	1.68	1.58	1.77	1.78	1.60
Parks, Recreation and Public Property	7.63	7.49	7.45	7.20	7.00	7.11	7.57	7.84	8.25	8.79	8.59	7.45
Public Safety	35.28	32.83	31.60	29.76	28.21	25.93	26.83	27.36	26.01	26.33	25.29	26.74
Public Works	21.57	21.35	21.28	22.15	19.78	18.67	21.02	25.65	25.27	25.29	26.87	25.71
Library	2.59	2.38	2.21	2.06	1.78	1.69	1.63	1.88	1.91	2.24	2.27	2.26
Debt Service	19.01	20.97	16.94	19.28	27.51	28.04	24.98	17.16	16.22	14.82	14.04	13.10
Residual	10.15	11.15	16.87	16.17	12.55	15.13	14.56	16.43	18.34	18.74	19.20	21.13
Expended												
Law	0.89	0.99	0.94	0.82	0.73	0.80	0.75	0.85	0.87	0.92	0.90	0.87
Personnel	0.34	0.35	0.35	0.34	0.32	0.46	0.45	0.47	0.48	0.49	0.43	0.44
Planning	0.47	0.42	0.43	0.38	0.37	0.44	0.40	0.45	0.44	0.46	0.47	0.43
Human Relations	0.20	0.11	0.21	0.18	0.14	0.21	0.22	0.25	0.26	0.26	0.29	0.33
Finance	2.06	1.99	1.95	2.03	1.91	1.62	1.50	1.64	1.84	1.81	1.83	1.84
Parks, Recreation and Public Property	7.87	8.27	8.52	7.86	7.67	8.32	7.73	8.40	8.45	9.02	8.65	7.85
Public Safety	34.98	34.41	34.85	34.31	29.00	30.93	27.22	27.52	26.74	26.76	26.92	26.40
Public Works	22.06	22.33	22.72	23.84	20.57	24.65	22.94	25.42	25.58	26.32	27.45	29.45
Library	2.60	2.48	2.34	2.19	1.88	2.14	1.75	1.89	1.95	2.29	2.23	2.21
Debt Service	20.65	18.99	18.26	18.79	28.73	20.45	25.79	17.49	16.45	15.17	13.95	12.93
Residual	7.88	9.66	9.43	9.26	8.68	9.98	11.25	15.62	16.94	16.50	16.83	17.16

SOURCE: Compiled from the *Omaha City Annual Budgets* for 1968-1981, using the "Summary of Budgets Appropriations—All Funds."

component is under the direct control of the city.[6] There was some decrease in the proportion of budget resources allocated toward libraries, with little change in the proportion of budget resources allocated parks, recreations, and public properties. Other segments of the budget such as planning, human relations, and personnel department changed little and are relatively small components of Omaha's total budget.

The data do not permit the investigators to determine the reason for the shift in municipal resources. It may be the result of better management in the public safety division or it may reflect policy decisions to place funds in other programs. It may reflect a changing public "taste" for a different mix of public sector goods and services. At the risk of being redundant, it should be emphasized again that resource shifts in the city's budget cannot be linked to compulsory arbitration or commission awards. Note, however, that the authors were unable to analyze the impact of unions in the important area of changes in work rules, conditions, etc.

While compulsory arbitration appears to have had no long range impact on budget resource allocation commission awards did impact allocation during the course of a year. A review of the information in Table 2 indicates that the public safety division experienced a substantially larger budget overrun in one of the two periods when awards were granted by the commission. Commission awards were granted in December 1977 and January 1978 and the absolute budget overrun in 1978 (1.63) was four times that recorded in 1977 (0.43) or 1979 (0.34). Note, however, that no such problem developed after the 1975 awards.[7] This implies support for the hypothesis that cities have lost some control over the resources at their disposal in years in which commission awards are made. Control of budgets and flexibility are seemingly reduced in the short run as a result of arbitration awards.

What happens to the city's budget when an award upsets the budget in a major department such as public safety? Apparently all other departments have to be restricted more aggressively than in nonaward years. Note, for instance, that public works overexpended their budget by 4 per cent (relative) in 1977 and 14.9 per cent (relative) in 1979—nonaward years— but were restrained to a 2.2 per cent (relative) budget override in 1978 (Table 2).[8]

Compulsory arbitration awards would seem to upset budgets most dramatically within the short run or budget year in force at the time the award is granted. In some cases the adjustment process may continue into the next budget year. Pressure to reduce expenditures is evident in the fact that the

---

[6] Lack of debt financing represents a deliberate political policy reflecting control over city finances.

[7] Compare the budgeted and expended data for 1975 in Table 1.

[8] The 1977 decision was handed down on December 21, 1977 and came too late in the year to affect the 1977 budget (less than 10 working days remained in 1977). Case No. 233 had more impact on the 1978 budget than on the 1977 budget.

Table 2. Omaha Budget Differences, Budgeted and Expended[a]

Department	1977 Differences Absolute	1977 Differences Relative	1978 Differences Absolute	1978 Differences Relative	1979 Differences Absolute	1979 Differences Relative	1977-79 Differences Average Relative
Law	−.01	1.0%	+.01	1.1%	+.01	1.1%	1.1%
Personnel	+.06	14.0%	+.01	2.4%	.00	- - - -	5.5%
Planning	+.06	15.0%	+.06	14.6%	+.01	2.4%	10.7%
Human Relations	.00	- - - -	+.05	20.8%	+.06	22.2%	14.3%
Finance	+0.04	2.2%	+.05	2.8%	+.24	15.0%	6.7%
Parks	+.23	2.6%	+.06	0.7%	+.40	5.4%	2.9%
Public Safety	+.43	1.6%	+1.63	6.4%	+.34	1.3%	3.1%
Public Works	1.03	4.0%	+.58	2.2%	3.74	14.5%	7.4%
Library	+.05	2.2%	−.04	1.8%	−.05	2.2%	2.1%
Debt	+.35	2.4%	−.09	0.6%	−.17	1.3%	1.4%
Residual	−2.24	12.0%	−2.37	12.3%	−3.97	18.8%	14.4%

[a] These calculations represent the difference between budgeted amounts and expenditures. The absolute differences are the arithmetic differences (e.g., Public Safety, 1977, 26.33 budgeted, −26.76 expended = 0.43). The relative difference is the percentage difference between the two items. All calculations in Table 2 are derived from Table 1. Overexpended budgets represented by (+); underexpended budgets by (−).

residual component of the budget was underexpended by 18.8 per cent in 1979. The impact of these awards is likely to be more dramatic in the city divisions not directly affected, since commission awards are mandatory. Divisions outside public safety may have their budgets monitored more thoroughly in award years than in a nonaward year. Flexibility is absolutely essential when an uncertain element such as an award to a major component of the budget is likely to be released.

One important issue remains unanswered. If the commission were to announce an award late in the fiscal year, say the last quarter of the fiscal year, the city's budget might be so committed as to make it nearly impossible to change priorities and shifts in allocations in the brief time remaining. The timing of commission awards could have a major impact on a city's ability to meet the award.

The evidence is sketchy and it is not as complete as the authors would like but it seems reasonable to conclude that compulsory arbitration has not interfered with municipal budgeting to the extent that the City of Omaha lost control of its budget. Elected officials retained the authority to control the city's budget in the 1970's despite the granting of awards. Elected officials could have increased the proportion of resources going to public safety had they desired, and there is no support for the contention that awards usurp elected official control. Sectors covered by compulsory arbitration awards during the 1970's had less of a budget share in total city expenditure in 1979 than they had at the beginning of the period under review, 1968.

While there appears to have been no substantial erosion of city control over budgets, the budgets were likely made more complex and uncomfortable to manage. City budget managers undoubtedly had to make unanticipated shifts and reallocations during the course of a year and certainly this caused much anguish to city administrators. Reducing expenditures on equipment and other items that can be postponed did occur after commission awards [4], and the fact that budget overruns were larger and more common following a compulsory arbitration award lends some support to the contention that awards disrupted the budgeting process. Disruption and control, however, are two different elements, and while there was undoubtedly disruption there is no evidence of the city having lost control as a result of the awards.

REFERENCES

1. D. C. Chauhan, The Political and Legal Issues of Binding Arbitration in Government, *Monthly Labor Review, 102*:9, pp. 35-41, 1979.
2. C. A. Olson, The Impact of Arbitration on the Wages of Fire Fighters, *Industrial Relations, 19,* pp. 325-339, Fall, 1980.
3. *Government Employee Relations Report,* Bureau of National Affairs, Inc., pp. 51-3613, Washington, D.C., October 29, 1979.
4. Interview with City Finance Director, March 31, 1980.

Discussion Questions

1. Do you perceive a causal relationship in the rapid expansion of Omaha city government areas unaffected by compulsory arbitration?
2. Speculate on the reasons why Omaha's municipal budget resources were shifted toward certain areas.
3. How does an erosion of a city's administrative control over budget allocations affect the city and its public services? Discuss short and long-term effects.

PART III
STATE EMPLOYEES

In Chapter 9 Haskell reviews the options of centralization or decentralization of bargaining among state government employees. Jack E. Klauser in Chapter 10 describes and illustrates how Hawaii's statewide bargaining units function.

Singer et al. deal with the problems in a right-to-work state in Chapter 11. Swimmer, in Chapter 12, describes the impact of legislative action in California with Proposition 13. Proposition 2½ in Massachusetts id discussed in Chapter 13.

The objective of Part III, then is to highlight a variety of problems and possible solutions inherent in state employer-employee relations.

CHAPTER 9

Centralization or Decentralization of Bargaining among State Government Employees: An Examination of the Options*

MARK A. HASKELL

The question of appropriate bargaining units for state government employees is one that has not received a great deal of attention in recent years, but as the result of greater experience with collective bargaining, state government officials have become aware of the importance of the issue. It has become very clear to many of them that unit definition has a direct impact on how public management organizes itself for bargaining which in turn affects the levels at which important decisions are made and the prospects for uniformity and fairness in the treatment of employees. Experience has also shown that unit proliferation and uncoordinated decentralized bargaining often lead to unintended and unfortunate consequences. For example, in one state where

*This article is based on material developed in a study of collective bargaining in Delaware state government funded by a grant under the Intergovernmental Personnel Act of 1970, P. L. 91-648. Collaborators in the study were Linda Hsu, Project Director and Marcilee Bierlein [1].

fewer than 4500 state government employees are divided into twenty-eight units, a recent study found several cases of contracts altering ostensibly nonnegotiable merit system rules with the result of an unnecessary and undesirable lack of contract uniformity between similar groups of employees [1, Ch. IV].

Following the pattern of centralization of local government bargaining and management structure observed by Burton [2], there has been a clear trend toward centralization at the state government level. This has been the case in the midwest where Derber, Pashler and Ryan observed an emergent decentralization in 1974 [3, p. 72], a conclusion confirmed four years later by Derber, Maxey, and Wetzel [4, p. 1] and also among large states elsewhere, notably New York, Pennsylvania, and New Jersey. In New York, ten units cover approximately 160,000 state employees; in Pennsylvania 90,000 state workers are organized into twenty bargaining units and in New Jersey eleven units, including one for first line supervisors, encompass more than 50,000 employees [5–7].

Obviously with such a small number of units covering such a large number of workers, occupations are very broadly defined. In New Jersey, for example, a professional unit includes physicians, accountants, engineers, and almost 800 other job titles. In that state, the policy of creating statewide units was a direct result of the determination of state government to avoid unit proliferation. Buttressing that determination was a decision of the New Jersey Public Employment Relations Commission (PERC), which established priority for statewide units. While the collective bargaining law specifies "community of interest" as the major criterion for unit determination, PERC focused on the definition of "employer." Thus the Commission commented that "we begin with the elementary observation that the employer is not Trenton State Hospital, Greystone Park State Hospital . . . or any other like facility of administrative unit . . . ; rather it is the State in the person of the Chief Executive." [8, p. 7] Such a definition is not explicit in the New Jersey collective bargaining act, which states that public employer means "the State of New Jersey, or the several counties and municipalities thereof, or any other political subdivision of the State, or a school district, or any special district, or any authority, commission, or board, *or any branch or agency of the public service.*" [9, italics added]. In this decision, PERC also gave weight to the way the state government was structured to handle collective bargaining, i.e., on a centralized basis. The case resulted in PERC's dismissal of ten union petitions to establish various units and the creation instead of three statewide units for:

1. health care and rehabilitation services;
2. operations, maintenance, and services; and
3. all craft employees [8].

Nonetheless, in New Jersey, there remain three units completely within departments; state college faculties, state troopers, and state trooper sergeants. In addition, several other units fall largely within single departments. The most extreme case is the Health Care and Rehabilitations Services unit, where 97 per cent of employees represented are in the Department of Institutes and Agencies [7].

There are similar exceptions to the rule of statewide units in Pennsylvania, where about 80 per cent of all represented employees are found in six units. Clerks in state-owned liquor stores are one example. Other singular units are those encompassing state police and those covering professionals whose units tend to be more narrowly defined than those of nonprofessionals. However, in general, Pennsylvania adheres to the rule of statewide units unless it sees sufficient reason for doing otherwise.

Even New York, which has adhered most closely to the principle of statewide units, has three "vertical" units. These are the faculty and professional staff of the State University system, state police troopers, and state police officers [10].

MANAGEMENT ORGANIZATION FOR BARGAINING

Unit determination and government organization for collective bargaining are closely related and affect one another. Three major approaches to management organization can be discerned. In the first, state government accepts units as historically determined and allows its bargaining and contract administration structure to correspond. In a second, enabling legislation establishing bargaining rights specifies criteria for unit determination. Such criteria are often intended to support centralized authority for bargaining at a particular level, usually the Office of the Governor. In a third approach the law is permissive, but public management moves aggressively to influence a particular bargaining configuration. Generally, the configuration is one involving a high degree of centralization.

Another Middle Atlantic state, Delaware, provides an example of the first approach. Historically, AFSCME and other unions organized groups of employees in the agencies or facilities within departments where they had sufficient support to win representation elections. Since the Governor's Council on Labor, the agency that makes unit determination recommendations, has given heavy weight to the preferences of the employees, the result has been a proliferation of units containing relatively small numbers of employees. In 1978, 4,473 state employees were divided into twenty-eight bargaining units, the largest of them containing 465 employees. Twelve of the units had fewer than 100 employees [1, pp. 9-11].

Burton's analysis of the initial impact of bargaining on management structure accurately described the current situation in Delaware. His study of a number of local jurisdictions revealed that a system of collective bargaining is imposed " . . . on the existing structure of authority with little or no modification. Primary responsibility for negotiations can be assigned to either the executive or legislative branch, but no preexisting center of authority is subordinated or greatly diminished in influence." The result is that "the authority of line managers to negotiate on issues within their discretion will be undefined; multiple centers of power will continue to exist, forcing the labor organization to negotiate with numerous . . . officials on various issues." [2, pp. 128-129] The disadvantage is not solely that of the unions; the situation encourages "whipsawing" — the attempt by unions to apply the most favorable terms negotiated with one department to all of the others. It also provides fertile ground for the political "end-run" with multilateral negotiations and lobbying that might involve the civil service commission, the governor, the legislature, or any combination of the three.

The second organizational approach, where statutory criteria dictate the formation of units that support centralized bargaining, is illustrated by the cases of Pennsylvania and New York. In Pennsylvania, the law provides that the Pennsylvania Labor Relations Board shall "take into consideration that when the Commonwealth is the employer, it will be bargaining on a statewide basis unless issues involve working conditions peculiar to a given governmental employment locale." [11, Art. VI, Sec 604(4)] And since the law specifically states that "the effects of overfragmentization shall be taken into consideration," the statutory provisions seem purposefully weighted toward statewide units.[1]

New York's Taylor Law is not so explicit as Pennsylvania's Act 195 with regard to bargaining unit determination. However, in its applications of the law, the New York Public Employment Relations Board (PERB) has consistently interpreted the standards as requiring "the designation of as few units as possible." [12]

Several other states — Illinois, Alaska, Kansas, Maine, Connecticut, and Vermont — have laws that also express concern about unit fragmentation. For example, Alaska's law states that the "bargaining units shall be as large as is reasonable and unnecessary fragmentation shall be avoided." In Kansas, the law requires that "the effect of overfragmentation and the splintering of a work organization" should be considered in unit determination [13, p. 5].

Of all states, Hawaii and Wisconsin go farthest in specifying the nature of bargaining units. State employees in Wisconsin must be part of one of sixteen units specified in the labor relations law. The main occupational groups are:

1. clerical;
2. blue collar and nonconstruction trades;
3. construction crafts;
4. security and public safety;
5. technical; and
6. professional.

Within the professional category, there can be separate units of employees in areas such as fiscal services, legal services, social services, education, engineering,

[1] Other criteria deal only with the question of exclusion of certain categories of employees such as supervisors, management, confidential employees and prison guards.

and science. The Wisconsin Employee Relations Commission (WERC) has the power to assign employees to the appropriate bargaining units [14, pp. 1390-1391]. In Hawaii, eight mandatory and five optional occupational groups are specified by statute. Employees eligible for optional units may vote to be included in a mandatory unit or remain separate [13, p. 4].

The Minnesota law is specific in designating appropriate units as all or most employees under a single appointing authority, rather than interdepartmental by occupation as in Pennsylvania, New York, and Wisconsin. However, exceptions are permitted if there are professional, geographical, or other considerations affecting employment relations [14, p. 3284]. The result is that Minnesota has ninety-five units, some occupational, some agency-wide, and some drawn geographically. Originally, bargaining was sharply "two-tiered" — i.e., wages and fringe benefits were negotiated on a statewide basis with all or most unions involved and nonmoney items were negotiated with representatives of each bargaining unit [3, pp. 72-73]. The two-tiered system was modified in 1974 to allow a single, centralized negotiation covering wage and nonwage items for all units represented by AFSCME. The management team includes personnel officers from the five largest state departments [4, p. 11]. The Minnesota case is particularly instructive as an example of a situation where, despite a large number of bargaining units, centralized bargaining takes place over issues where uniformity for all employees is desirable. At the same time, negotiations over issues singular to departments, units within departments, or to certain professional groups take place at those levels.

New Jersey provides an example of the third approach to management organization for collective bargaining. Despite the fact that the New Jersey Public Employment Relations Commission's very first decision ordered separate faculty bargaining units for each of the six state colleges [15], the State Office of Collective Bargaining successfully resisted separate negotiations. It achieved this end by convincing the Superior Court to allow it to replace the State Board of Higher Education as "employer" for collective bargaining purposes [16]. The result is one master agreement covering all state colleges (now eight in number) with some bargaining taking place on local issues. And as mentioned earlier, the state's challenge to union petitions for separate units within other departments was upheld by the Public Employment Relations Commission in a decision that established priority for statewide units.

LEGISLATIVE, BUDGET AND
INTERNAL MANAGEMENT COORDINATION

The second and third approaches to unit designation and management organization, characterized as they are by some degree of centralization, lend themselves to internal management coordination, to coordination with the budget process and to some degree of continuing liaison with the legislature. In

Pennsylvania, bargaining timetables are keyed to February 1 of each year, the date on which the governor is required to submit a proposed budget to the legislature for the following fiscal year. Impasse procedures go into effect 150 days before this date, approximately September 1. Bargaining itself must begin at least three weeks earlier to allow time to reach agreement by February 1 [11, Art. VIII]. In practice, however, negotiations are rarely concluded by the budget submission deadline. Since contracts do not expire until June 30, the end of the fiscal year, there is little incentive for unions to attempt to settle by February 1. The period between February and July can be used effectively to build pressure on the governor and legislature.

In a similar way, contracts in New Jersey and Wisconsin are coordinated with the budget processes and fiscal years of those states, with contracts of one year or more typically becoming effective on July 1 and expiring on June 30. In Wisconsin, the labor relations act requires agreements to coincide with the fiscal year or biennium. No specific provision appears in the New Jersey law, but the Office of Collective Bargaining has made it a practice to key contract dates to budget deadlines. In addition, mandatory impasse procedures are also keyed to those deadlines. In New York State, the Taylor Law provides a "statutory impasse" date, 120 days before the end of the fiscal year on March 31, i.e., December 1. The state has, however, continued negotiations well beyond this date in its efforts to secure agreements.

Wisconsin's labor relations system includes formal mechanisms both for liaison with the legislature and for communications between the state Bureau of Collective Bargaining and line agencies. The Joint Legislative Committee on Employment Relations, comprised of the senior leadership of both parties, is kept informed at all stages of negotiation. Agency representatives are convened in a thirty-six member Employment Relations Council, which helps develop management positions, reviews union proposals and, in general, acts as liaison between the bargaining team and the state departments and agencies [4, pp. 7-9].

Two other midwestern states, Minnesota and Kansas, have also established procedures for legislative coordination. In Minnesota no consultation occurs prior to bargaining, but increases in wages and fringe benefits must be approved by the legislature, which may also modify or reject them. In Kansas, the state Finance Council, consisting of eight legislative leaders and the Governor and Lieutenant Governor, must endorse negotiated agreements [4, p. 11]. In general, the success of these arrangements is highly dependent on the degree to which the chief negotiator is genuinely open to advice from sources other than the executive.

In Pennsylvania, all bargaining units negotiate simultaneously. As preparation, management committees that include agency representatives attempt to anticipate union demands and develop and draft bargaining positions. Agency representatives also sit as members of the bargaining teams. Final positions are determined by the state Bureau of Labor Relations (BLR) on the basis of advice from these committees and from the Bureau of Personnel which acts as staff arm to BLR. Critical issues are referred to the Governor or to his/her designee for determination.

Informal liaison with the legislature is undertaken by the director of the BLR, but Pennsylvania is in the position of being able to implement an agreement whether or not the legislature specifically appropriates funds for it. Unconstrained by a line-item budget, the Governor can move agency funds from one category to another. Lacking other options, negotiated salary increases may have to be funded by reductions in force.

In New York, the state Office of Employee Relations (OER), as the Governor's principal representative in matters of public employee relations, has full authority for negotiations. Department personnel are consulted during pre-negotiation planning activities and also sit on bargaining teams. The OER maintains liaison with the Division of Budget in negotiations; an informal liaison with the legislative leadership is maintained through the Governor's office. In the past, funds for negotiated salary increases have not been refused by the legislature, although such items as negotiated health benefits have been rejected. As a result, contracts now include reopeners on items not approved by the legislature.

It has been observed that centralization of the labor relations function occurs because tensions within the management structure require new forms of organization. Three specific tendencies exist:

1. the executive branch gains authority with commensurate losses ensuing for the legislature and civil service commission;
2. authority for labor relations becomes centralized within the executive branch; and
3. labor relations specialists replace budget directors or personnel chiefs in assuming responsibility for contract negotiation and administration [2, pp. 128-130].

The advantages of centralized organization are greater integration of bargaining, budgeting and the overall legislative program, and better coordination of the employer's position on issues affecting line agencies [2, pp. 128-130]. The centralized bargaining system is complete when mechanisms are developed for coordination of bargaining with the legislature, which has the sole authority to appropriate funds, and for coordination with the line agencies, which have responsibility for administering the agreement on a day-to-day basis.

CENTRALIZATION VS DECENTRALIZATION

Many, if not most, observers of public sector labor relations favor centralization of authority for bargaining; established management structures in the larger states reflect this view. Nonetheless, there is a case for decentralization, and it may well be that some combination of the two models leading to a form of two-tier bargaining may be most efficacious for states where decentralization has already gained a foothold.

It is worth observing at this point that while centralization of the labor relations function has objective advantages for state governments, its preeminence has occurred, in part, because it also has political advantages for any administration. In particular, a governor will ordinarily want to exercise firm control over the state's budget; greater control over salary and fringe benefit costs will occur if bargaining is centralized under the authority of the governor than if it is decentralized. Nonetheless, an objective case can be made for centralization and that case will be reviewed below.

First, if it is accepted that uniformity in salaries, fringe benefits, and working conditions is desirable, such uniformity is most easily achieved by way of negotiations with large, preferably statewide, bargaining units. The contract administration process is likewise simplified, and the entire collective bargaining function can be accomplished with a more efficient deployment of staff resources. As a practical matter, agency heads typically have no authority to commit the executive on money items. If the scope of negotiations extends to these matters, the governor or his representative must necessarily be heavily involved.

Viewed from another perspective, it can be said that the scope of bargaining is in part determined by the way bargaining units are defined. On this point, Rock referred to a criterion for unit determination in the Taylor Law, which requires that: "the officials . . . at the level of the unit shall have the power to agree, or to make effective recommendations to other administrative authority or the legislative body with respect to the terms and conditions of employment over which the employees desire to negotiate . . . . " Rock noted that "the . . . clause clearly reflects awareness of the fact that the employer-negotiator in the public service frequently has only limited authority, and that this condition will affect the scope of bargaining." [17]

Second, the prospect of "whipsawing" is raised in the argument for centralization. It occurs when any gain made in an early negotiation leads to union pressure for similar, or possibly better, treatment in subsequent negotiations with other units. The first settlement becomes the floor; no subsequent agreement costs less. The process is aggravated by a tendency for agency heads to identify with subordinates and become advocates for their cause. Subject to little direct pressure from taxpayers, such officials may be willing to commit more resources than would politically vulnerable holders of elective office [18]. Even if only nonmoney demands are at issue, the effect of conceding them may be to raise costs indirectly.

In short, both in terms of management time devoted to the process and in terms of the results, centralization is believed to be the most cost-effective management structure for collective bargaining [19].

The argument for decentralization, or at least for a degree of it, is more subtle. At the most general level, the case for decentralization is identical to the case for a more effective democracy. In large-scale-interdepartmental negotiations, the needs of employees in the smaller units will get less attention than the needs of those in larger units. Rock, who otherwise makes a strong case against unit proliferation, thus granted that a "small minority" if included in a larger unit can argue with some justification that its specialized interests and needs may be subordinated to the wishes of the majority [17]. Kornbluh summarized the issues as follows:

> Collective bargaining structures are often a trade-off between increased power, efficiency, and equitable effects of uniformity on the one hand, and the benefits of more localized decision making on the other . . . [20].

The subordination of minority interests is not only a problem for management, it also poses difficulties for union leaders who may find dissident factions developing within their organizations. This may result in a form of multilateral bargaining where such factions approach employer representatives directly or attempt to form coalitions with management in their own agencies in an effort to bypass the bargaining process [21]. A third possibility is that an agency head may engage in informal negotiations over issues that are not adequately handled in collective bargaining. This may "create rule changes which deviate from statewide agreements." [21]

It is also possible that if a union is unable to resolve the tensions created by diverse employee interests within a single bargaining unit, it may multiply its demands at the bargaining table so as "to placate every group in the union." [18, p. 1190] As a result, bargaining may become protracted and indecisive. Thus, Summers observes that " . . . while multiple bargaining units add to the employer's negotiating burden, that cost may be less than negotiating with a conglomerate union which is trying to represent greater diversity than its internal processes can reconcile." [18, p. 1190]

Another criticism of centralization focuses on situations where it is desirable or necessary for conditions such as work rules and vacation scheduling to differ [21, p. 37, 22]. On a political level, it has been suggested that centralization "may also mean that public sector bargaining becomes more politicized than it needs to be." [21]

There has been very little empirical research on how the degree of centralization of bargaining influences organizational effectiveness and productivity. What data do exist indicate that departmental units are superior to statewide units in those two respects. Martin approached the question by testing whether there were important attitudinal and demographic differences in the separate departments and locations of a statewide bargaining unit in Illinois. Such differences were found, leading the author to conclude that "community of interest might be greater in a departmental or facility unit structure where issues reflecting the different local and departmental working conditions could be better and more easily dealt with than in an occupational unit structure." [19, p. 16]

A similar conclusion was reached by Moore, who studied the influence of alternative bargaining structures on the productivity of state employees in Michigan and on the effectiveness of their agencies. He found departmental units encourage a stronger orientation toward increased productivity than other types by providing flexibility to focus on issues specific to the department's mission. In contrast, occupational units often require uniform performance standards across departments irrespective of distinctive needs and conditions. Further, negotiations tend to focus on occupational interests at the expense of organizational effectiveness and the public welfare [23].

Both of these studies confirmed earlier research of Alutto and Belasco, who concluded that for nurses and teachers, work attitudes and views about bargaining were most significantly related to characteristics of the agency or facility [24].

THE MULTIPLE-TIER OPTION

It is clear that there are advantages to both centralized and decentralized bargaining. To achieve the benefits of both, it is suggested here that two- or three-tier bargaining is the most desirable arrangement. Under two-tier bargaining, economic items and other matters for which statewide uniformity is desirable would be negotiated centrally for all employees. Issues particular to departments would be the subject of a second level or tier of negotiations at the department level and, if necessary, issues of importance to agencies or facilities would be dealt with at a third tier.

Whether multiple-tier bargaining is a formal structure or not, it seems to emerge in any case. For example, in Pennsylvania, negotiations with AFSCME often establish economic patterns for subsequent negotiations with other bargaining units. However, these subsequent negotiations also deal with issues of concern particular to the unit involved. More generally, Begin has noted that various factions engage in forms of multilateral — i.e., decentralized bargaining when their interests are not well represented at the central bargaining table. As one example, even though the New Jersey Office of Collective Bargaining (OCB) had resisted local bargaining in the state colleges it ultimately gave formal sanction to such bargaining which had emerged despite OCB opposition. In Begin's words, "local negotiations . . . should be viewed as natural adaptations to the needs of local employers and employees to respond to local problems." [21]

Although formal two-tier bargaining is not common, states such as Minnesota, Oregon, Hawaii, Washington, Wisconsin, and New York have used it [21]. Typically, as in Oregon and Minnesota, agency staff members are given guidance in the second tier negotiations. In Oregon, agency staff are assisted in negotiations by the central employee relations staff. In Minnesota, the bargaining teams are headed by negotiators from outside the departments, but they include department personnel. In the case of the Minnesota Highway

Department, for example, the team includes the state negotiator, the department's chief personnel officer, five district department officials, an assistant commissioner, and a personnel officer [4, pp. 10-11].

As would be expected, multiple-tier systems permit and justify the existence of large numbers of bargaining units. Oregon has seventy-two and Minnesota has ninety-five units. These systems do not dictate a fixed configuration of bargaining units; rather they accommodate all types depending on what is considered as providing the maximum community of interest.

To achieve this, state laws need not mandate particular types of bargaining units. Rather, they should be appropriate to employees' needs and can be statewide occupational units, departmentwide units, and units within departments. While existing units do not necessarily need to be dismantled, the parties should be urged to move voluntarily to a more rational bargaining structure and incentives should be provided for them to do so. To guard against excessive unit fragmentation, there should be careful specification of the criteria used for the determination of appropriate bargaining units. These criteria can include direct strictures against excessive fragmentation, references to "principles of efficient administration" or other similar wordings.

Clearly multi-tier bargaining cannot succeed unless management organization is adapted to it. A state office must have complete responsibility for centralized negotiations on salaries and fringe benefits. At the minimum, it should provide advice to all department negotiations; preferably, a representative of the central office should be a member of bargaining teams in lower level negotiations. In addition, the central office should prepare information necessary to collective bargaining and should develop and implement labor relations seminars and training programs.

SUMMARY

As public sector bargaining has matured, there has been a tendency for state governments to move toward statewide bargaining units defined by occupation and thus toward centralization of the labor relations function. The advantages of centralization including managerial efficiency and uniformity of contract terms are, however, offset by the subordination of the interests of employees in small units or having specialized occupations. In addition, there is some evidence that attending more directly to the needs of such employees through decentralized collective bargaining can enhance employee morale and the productivity of work units.

Consequently, it is suggested that a trade-off between the benefits of centralized bargaining and those of a decentralized model can be avoided by opting for a multiple-tier structure, thus maintaining the efficiency and uniform treatment provided by the former along with the real possibility of democratic decision making and appropriate treatment of minorities provided by the latter.

On these grounds, public officials and union leaders who are now in a position to influence unit determination and bargaining structures should give serious consideration to a multiple-tier arrangement as an optimal compromise between complete centralization and unit fragmentation.

REFERENCES

1. L. Hsu, M. A. Haskell, and M. Bierlein, *Collective Bargaining in Delaware State Government: Analysis and Recommendations,* Delaware Public Administration Institute, University of Delaware, Newark, Delaware, November 1978.
2. J. F. Burton, Jr., Local Government Bargaining and Management Structure, *Industrial Relations, 11:2,* May 1972.
3. M. Derber, P. Pashler, and M. B. Ryan, *Collective Bargaining by State Governments in the Twelve Midwestern States,* Institute of Labor and Industrial Relations, University of Illinois, Champaign-Urbana, December 1974.
4. M. Derber, C. Maxey, and K. Wetzel, *Public Management's Internal Response to the Demands of Collective Bargaining in the Twelve Midwestern States,* U.S. Department of Labor, Labor Management Services Administration, Washington, 1977.
5. Governor's Office of Employee Relations, State of New York.
6. Bureau of Labor Relations, Commonwealth of Pennsylvania.
7. H. F. Stark, Organizing for Bargaining in New Jersey State Government: 1976, *New Jersey Public Employer-Employee Relations,* Institute of Management and Labor Relations, Rutgers University, 29 July 1977.
8. State of New Jersey, Public Employment Relations Commission, *PERC No. 50,* January 15, 1971.
9. *New Jersey Employer-Employee Relations Act,* Title 34, Sections 34:13A-1 to 34-13A-13.
10. D. H. Wollett, State Government Strategies for Negotiations in an Austere Environment: A Management Perspective, *Labor Law Journal, 27:8,* pp. 506-507, August 1976.
11. Commonwealth of Pennsylvania, *Act No. 195.*
12. H. Milowe, Relationship Between Unit Size and Scope of Bargaining, *PERB News,* New York State Public Employment Relations Board, 8, p. 6, September 1977.
13. U.S. Civil Service Commission, *Labor-Management Relations Issues in State and Local Government, 1,* Washington, D.C. (no date).
14. Commerce Clearing House, *Public Employee Bargaining,* New York, Chicago, Washington, 1977.
15. State of New Jersey, Public Employment Relations Commission, *PERC No. 1,* February 19, 1969.
16. *Association of New Jersey State College Faculties v. The Board of Higher Education* et al., Superior Court of New Jersey, Docket No. L-33784-69 P.O., October 7, 1970.

17. E. Rock, Bargaining Units in the Public Sector: The Problem of Proliferation, J. J. Loewenberg and M. H. Moskow (eds.), *Collective Bargaining in Government: Readings and Cases,* Prentice-Hall, Englewood Cliffs, New Jersey, p. 120, 1972.
18. C. W. Summers, Public Employee Bargaining: A Political Perspective, *Yale Law Journal, 83:*6, pp. 1173-1175, May 1974.
19. J. E. Martin, Appropriate Bargaining Units for State Employees, Unpublished paper, Wayne State University, no date.
20. H. Kornbluh, Public Schools — Multi-Unit Common Bargaining Agents: A Next Phase in Teacher-School Board Bargaining in Michigan?, *Proceedings of the 1976 Annual Spring Meeting,* Industrial Relations Research Association, Madison, Wisconsin, p. 521, 1976.
21. J. P. Begin, Multilateral Bargaining in the Public Sector: Causes, Effects, Accommodations, J. W. Sutherland (ed.), *Management Handbook for Public Administrators,* Van Nostrand Reinhold, New York, 1978.
22. R. Pegnetter, *Multiemployer Bargaining in the Public Sector: Purposes and Experiences,* International Personnel Management Association, Chicago, p. 15, 1975.
23. M. L. Moore, Productivity Improvement in Government: The Effects of Departmental v. Occupational Bargaining Unit Structures, *Journal of Collective Negotiations in the Public Sector, 8:*4, 1979.
24. J. Alutto and J. A. Belasco, Determinants of Attitudinal Militancy Among Nurses and Teachers, *Industrial and Labor Relations Review, 27:*2, January 1974.
25. T. P. Gilroy, Management Labor Relations Structure in State Government, *Journal of Collective Negotiations in the Public Sector, 3:*3, pp. 10-11, Summer 1974.

Discussion Questions

1. Discuss the pros and cons of coordinating contract expiration dates with state or municipal budget processes and fiscal years.
2. Do you consider the Pennsylvania situation, where no line-item budget exists, favorable or unfavorable to employees? Why?
3. Explain multi-tier bargaining and discuss some of the problems inherent in this technique.

Reprinted from Journal of Collective Negotiations in the Public Sector Vol. 10(1), 1981

CHAPTER 10

Multi-Employer Bargaining in the Public Sector in Hawaii

JACK E. KLAUSER

Hawaii adopted a unique approach in its public sector collective bargaining law in that it specified the bargaining units in the legislation itself and established all of them on a statewide basis, with state and local government employees in the same bargaining units [1]. The designation of bargaining units in the basic legislation itself and limiting them to a small number has avoided the chaos overfragmentation of bargaining units caused in other states and cities and has facilitated a rational approach to negotiations. Jurisdictional conflicts among the unions are minimized—jurisdictional conflicts that do arise are more over the issue of who should be considered a public employee as established by law and thus falling within the jurisdiction of one of the established units than over which unit has jurisdiction over what occupations. Administration is simplified, and bargaining on a statewide basis, with both state and local government employees who do similar work in the same bargaining units, has made "leapfrogging," "end-runs," and the use of "whipsaw" tactics by unions difficult.

The success of the experience of Hawaii with statewide collective bargaining is in large part explained by the governmental structure of Hawaii.

Governmental Structure

OF THE STATE OF HAWAII

The governmental structure of Hawaii is unique in that the state consists of only five governmental units: The state government, headed by a governor; and four counties—the city and county of Honolulu, the county of Kauai, the county of Maui, and the county of Hawaii—each headed by a mayor. Within each governmental unit, the chief executive enjoys wide powers. The county governments can be characterized as providing for a strong mayoral form of government and the state government for a strong governor. The Hawaii Constitution gives the governor wide powers over every facet of the government. Although the Department of Education and the University of Hawaii have their own controlling boards, the first elective and the second appointive, the money for both school systems comes out of general revenues, thus giving the governor a controlling voice.

The State of Hawaii is also very centralized in the services provided to the people. Many of the functions performed by county and city governments elsewhere are conducted at the state level in Hawaii. Administration and operation of schools, public hospital and health facilities, district and higher courts, public housing and economic assistance and welfare aid, are all state functions. Services such as police and fire protection, public works and sanitation, ordinarily within the purview of city governments on the mainland, are handled by county governments.

The highly centralized nature of the state is also reflected in the number of public employees on the rolls of the state government. Out of a total of 38,787 public employees in 1975, 74 per cent were employed by the state government. The next biggest public employer was the city and county of Honolulu, absorbing 19 per cent of all public employees. The other three counties together accounted for only 7 per cent of all state and county employees [2].

FOR COLLECTIVE BARGAINING

Considering the uniqueness of Hawaii's governmental structure, Hawaii's approach to public sector collective bargaining is both innovative and logical. The law established the following bargaining units covering employees throughout the state:

1. nonsupervisory employees in blue collar positions;
2. supervisory employees in blue collar positions;
3. nonsupervisory employees in white collar positions;
4. supervisory employees in white collar positions;

5. teachers and other personnel of the department of education under the same salary schedule;
6. educational officers and other personnel of the department of education under the same salary schedule;
7. faculty of the University of Hawaii and the community college system;
8. personnel of the University of Hawaii and the community college system, other than faculty;
9. registered professional nurses;
10. nonprofessional hospital and institutional workers;
11. fireman;
12. policemen; and
13. professional and scientific employees, other than professional nurses.

The legislation seeks to prevent confusion by defining "public employer" as the governor in the case of the state; the respective mayors in the case of the counties; the board of education in the case of the Department of Education; and the Board of Regents in the case of the University of Hawaii; and any individual who represents one of these employers or acts in their interest in dealing with public employees [3]. The law further specifies that for the purpose of negotiations the public employer for bargaining units 5 and 6 shall mean the governor and the board of education; for bargaining units 7 and 8 the governor and the Board of Regents of the University of Hawaii; and for the other bargaining units the governor and the mayors of all the counties [4]. The designated employer representative for units 5, 6, 7, and 8 are provided with one vote each. For the other bargaining units the law provides the governor with four votes and the mayors of each of the counties with one vote each. Any decisions reached by the applicable employer groups is to be on the basis of simple majority.

Under these provisions it is clear that the governor's representative can prevent management decisions with which the governor does not agree.

The legislative provision giving the governor as many votes as those of the four mayors combined stems partly from the fact that state employees by far make up the bulk of public employees, and also from a desire to prevent the counties from settling with exclusive county employees, such as police, on terms that would upset comparability. Policemen, by virtue of the essential nature of their services, could bring tremendous pressure on the county employer for an advantageous contract that other bargaining agents would then have to imitate. It would be difficult to settle with other unions on terms that are much less advantageous than those received by one bargaining agent from the counties. Giving the governor a deciding voice in all negotiations reduces the possibility of any one union's being able to exploit its position and provides for a uniform approach to collective bargaining by the "employer."

Statewide Bargaining

PROBLEMS

While the inclusion of state and local government employees in the same bargaining unit seems logical given the unique governmental structure in Hawaii, a statewide merit plan, and a legal provision of equal pay for equal work for state and county employees, putting state and local government employees who do similar work in the same bargaining units does complicate the bargaining process. Both statewide and local issues have to be negotiated in the same unit. Some of the counties may have problems peculiar to them, or else the preferred solutions to a common problem may vary from county to county, depending on the preferences of management and employees [5]. Moreover, the several counties are not of equal financial strength. This problem was particularly noticeable during the reopener negotiations involving fire fighters in 1974 and during the 1976 contract negotiations involving policemen. Because of the legislated equal pay for equal work requirement, the three neighboring island counties that are financially the least well-off were pressured into acceding to the offer of the wealthier county of Honolulu, and their reluctance to do so exposed Honolulu to the risk of a strike by the union although it was willing and possibly able to meet the union's demand. On the other hand, bargaining on a statewide basis is beneficial to the employer in that a union cannot take advantage of a public employer who might be particularly vulnerable to union pressure (such as a mayor of one of the outer Island counties where unionization is more widespread than in Honolulu and where union support at election time is often critical in winning an election), and extract a very favorable contract to be used as a bargaining weapon in negotiations with other public employers.

EXPERIENCE

To date, bargaining on a statewide basis has worked remarkably well in Hawaii, with the employers having presented a surprisingly united front during the bargaining process. The employer decision-making process has worked primarily because of the existence of a commonality of interest: finances. Holding the line on costs has overridden political considerations. The public employers have realized the need and advantage of a common front at the bargaining table. Since what one public employer does in the area of collective bargaining affects all, an attempt by one to represent his interests separately would invite retaliatory responses from the others, in that they might not support an issue of particular importance to him. Each employer checks the other employers in the bargaining process. None of the employers can "play" politics and repay a political debt by openly advocating a position more favorable to the union than the position commonly agreed to without inviting the wrath of the other employers. Differing political relationships with unions by the various employers have also ensured that their "political debt" to unions is not the same.

The fact that joint decision making on personnel and wage policies predates collective bargaining also has an important bearing on the success of decision making under collective bargaining. Because the state's statewide merit plan and requirement of equal pay for equal work for all public employees—state and local—has a long history and existed before the establishment of collective bargaining, the state and counties are used to sitting together to formulate common personnel and wage policies. The principal officials involved in collective bargaining—the personnel directors of the state and the counties and the chief negotiator, who served as personnel director before the appointment to his current position—have established through years of personal contact a close personal relationship that greatly eases any strains that may arise during collective bargaining. Even if the principal political leaders of the state and the counties are not the best of friends, the professionals through whom the elected officials operate are able to work closely together.

The personnel directors have for many years held annually a Conference of Personnel Directors to classify and price all jobs in the state and counties in order to effectuate the state's merit plan and principle of equal pay for equal work. The state director of personnel, as chairman of the Conference of Personnel Directors and by virtue of the large role the state government plays in the Islands, has evolved as the official to whom the other personnel directors look for guidance, leadership, and direction. The need to achieve a common policy, which collective bargaining on a statewide basis necessitated, has therefore not been a new experience to the principal officials involved. It existed before collective bargaining was instituted. The adjustments the employers had to make to achieve internal agreement during collective bargaining were therefore eased considerably.

Structure of the Personnel System

The internal decision-making process is also facilitated by the structure of the personnel system. At the state level, the director of personnel reports directly to the governor and is the governor's chief advisor on policies and problems concerning personnel administration. The Civil Service Commission serves as an appellate body that hears department and employee appeals regarding classification, suspension, dismissal, and other civil service related actions taken by the Department of Personnel Services or any of the State's agencies.[1]

---

[1] The grievance system of the civil service commission operates primarily for issues that are not covered in the union-management contract or that involve employees not in any bargaining unit.

At the county levels, the mayors are the effective heads of authority to decide management's position on personnel issues and the directors of the civil service departments of the several counties represent the mayors at negotiations in which counties participate.

To further facilitate the collective bargaining process, an Office of Collective Bargaining within the Office of the Governor was established in 1975 to assist the governor in discharging his duties under the Public Employment Relations Act. The chief of the Office of Collective Bargaining has been designated as the spokesman for the employer's side, and he serves in that capacity in all negotiations. This arrangement has provided for a uniform approach to all negotiations.

Decision-making authority on personnel matters is thus centralized in the hands of the governor and the mayors, whose principal advisors on personnel matters are their representatives at the bargaining table: The chief negotiator, who serves as spokesman for the employer's side, and the Director of Personnel Services for the governor (plus a representative from the Department of Budget and Finance), and the directors of the civil service departments for the mayors. For units 5 and 6, in addition to the governor's representatives, two members from the board of education, and for units 7 and 8, two members from the Board of Regents, are also involved.

While these are the professionals actually doing the negotiating, the final say on policy decisions rests with the elected officials such as the governor and the mayors who, while relying for advice on their representatives, do establish the policy guidelines for the professionals. This has opened the door for unions to seek changes in the employer's position directly from elected officials. By and large, however, the collective bargaining process in the public sector of Hawaii cannot be characterized as one where unions have achieved through "back-door" politics or "end-run" tactics what they failed to achieve at the bargaining table. While union leaders have access to elected officials, the record does not bear out that any one union has been able to achieve significant concessions through political tactics. The political officials are quite aware of the consequences undercutting their representatives would have and that concessions made to any one unit, whatever the circumstances, can hardly be denied employees in all other units, except where a problem is limited to a particular unit.

Conclusion

Hawaii has the most centralized state and local government structure in the United States. This has greatly influenced the state's approach to public labor negotiations and how issues are handled. It has made possible collective bargaining on a statewide basis, with both state and local employees in the same bargaining units. With only five governmental jurisdictions and two educational authorities involved, and with the executive head of each jurisdiction having the authority to decide management's policy on personnel matters for his employees, achievement of a common approach to collective bargaining is made possible.

Collective bargaining in Hawaii has developed into a remarkably professional process. Although the elected political leaders—who establish guidelines for the professionals at the bargaining table—are of different personalities and are often political rivals, common interests have so far overcome political and personality differences. Financial necessity, historical relationship, and political convenience have conspired to make a process involving several independent "political actors" work.

REFERENCES

1. Section 89-6(a), *Act 171*, HRS, 1970.
2. State of Hawaii, Hawaii Public Employment Relations Board, *Informational Bulletin,* No. 10, January 30, 1976.
3. Section 89-2(9), *Act 171*, HRS, 1970.
4. Section 89-6(b), *Act 171*, HRS, 1970.
5. J. Seidman, *The Hawaii Law on Collective Bargaining in Public Employment,* University of Hawaii, Industrial Relations Center, Honolulu, p. 17, 1973.

Discussion Questions

1. Discuss why Hawaii's centralized governmental structure would lead to its current method of handling public sector collective bargaining.
2. What are the pros and cons of giving the governor a deciding voice in all negotiations?
3. Why and how would financial considerations pose problems in statewide bargaining?

Reprinted from Journal of Collective Negotiations in the Public Sector Vol. 6(1), 1977

CHAPTER 11

An Empirical Investigation of Comprehension of the Right-to-Work Law among Residents of the State of Virginia*

MARC G. SINGER
HAROLD L. DURRETT
KENNETH C. WILLIAMSON
KATHY L. SHANNON

INTRODUCTION

Section 14 (b) of the Labor Management Relations Act of 1947 (Taft-Hartley) provides enabling power to the states to enact Right-to-Work laws. These laws prohibit employers and labor unions from negotiating provisions into labor agreements requiring membership or nonmembership in labor unions as a condition of employment. Union shops had previously been permitted, and unions have continually been required to represent all employees in a prescribed

* This research was conducted as part of a senior's research project at James Madison University.

bargaining unit, for which they are certified, by the National Labor Relations Act of 1935 (Wagner Act). This provision has probably generated more persistent and animated controversy than any other feature of our national labor policy, as that policy is embodied in several complex labor laws and myriad rulings of the National Labor Relations Board. As Keller stated, "The mere mention of Right-to-Work laws causes an immediate and intense emotional reaction." [1, p. 5] While feelings run strong on both sides of the issue throughout the country, sentiment in favor of the Right-to-Work principle seems strongest in southern and midwestern states [2, p. 195], while opposition is most prevalent in other areas of the country. Most of the twenty states that enacted such legislation are found in the south and midwest. *Business Week* indicates that the existence of Right-to-Work tends to deter organizing, as does 'Southern cultural bias.' [3] Additionally, Moore and Newman found that location in the south, coupled with Right-to-Work laws, tends to have a restrictive influence of mandatory and comprehensive bargaining laws for public employees [4].

Numerous, varied, and imaginative arguments have been advanced by both sides in this controversy, but they can all be fairly well capsulized in what have been dubbed the "Free Rider" and "Captive Passenger" arguments. Labor unions and others who oppose the Right-to-Work notion contend that since unions are legally required to represent all bargaining unit employees in the collective bargaining process and considerable costs are entailed in providing such representation, it is only fair that every employee enjoying the benefits of representation should pay his fair share. They feel that those who would shirk such responsibility under the aegis of a Right-to-Work law are "free riders" or parasites. They believe such laws weaken unions, lower wage and salary levels, and hamper unions in living up to agreements the unions have negotiated.

Proponents, on the other hand, maintain that those who opt, for whatever reason, to decline union membership, are really "captive passengers" when compelled to join a union in the absence of Right-to-Work protection. Supporters believe the right to freedom of association of such people is violated, and only they can judge whether union representation is actually a benefit deserving their support. "Captive passengers" in unions are represented as the only group of citizens in the country legally compelled to financially support a private organization with whose aims and objectives they disagree. Proponents also contend that permitting only voluntary union membership will make union leadership more responsive and responsible. Finn indicated that proponents of Right-to-Work laws maintain that compulsory unionism violates freedom, unions do not deserve to enjoy greater strength than their voluntary support will sustain, and that Right-to-Work laws provide a stable workforce [5]. Miller recapitulated these arguments under the concept of "worker freedom." [6]

Since controversy over Right-to-Work laws has been so persistent and widespread, research examining attitudes concerning the matter would appear inevitable. In surveying managers, *Industry Week* concluded that managers feel

Right-to-Work laws lessen the control union leaders have on the workforce, which can indirectly benefit management [7]. Additionally, in a study conducted by the National Right-to-Work Committee, and reported in *Industry Week,* 69 per cent of those surveyed nationally indicated they would vote for Right-to-Work laws if given the opportunity [8].

In light of the foregoing studies, the obvious strength of attitudes on the matter, and more than thirty years of continuous, much-publicized controversy on the subject of Right-to-Work, one could reasonably conclude comprehensive knowledge of the provisions of Right-to-Work statutes should have thoroughly permeated nearly every American household.

In fact, that was precisely the defense erected by representatives of the AFL/CIO and affiliated unions in opposition to legislation introduced in the Virginia Senate in 1979 and again in 1980 (Senate Bill No. 125, Sec. 40.1-58.2). This legislation would have required the posting of the provisions of the state's Right-to-Work law in all covered places of employment. Patrons of the bill (Senators Miller, Schewel, Gray, Truban), the State Chamber of Commerce, The Virginia Manufacturer's Association, nonunion employers, and two covered employees, alleged that rights conferred by the laws are routinely and systematically violated in the state by employers and unions who conspire to force employees into union membership involuntarily. They contended, as suggested by Reynolds, "Employers who want good relations with their unions have usually winked at the law." [2, p. 195] They also maintained most bargaining unit employees forfeit their rights in such circumstances because of their ignorance of the specific provisions of the law, and the inaccessibility of a suitable and appropriate remedy when violations do occur.

Both bills were defeated in the Senate Labor Committee, and failed to reach the floor. This was apparently because a majority of committee members were persuaded that such legislation was unnecessary because a majority of workers affected were indeed familiar with labor laws.

Without delving into the desirability of Right-to Work laws or the validity of arguments for and against them, the present study was undertaken to determine the extent to which the populace of Virginia understands the provisions of the Right-to-Work law existing in the state.

METHOD

Subjects

The subjects for the present study consisted of 500 residents from the state of Virginia (201 males and 299 females). All of the subjects were aged eighteen or older, and were equally representative of both urban and rural areas. The age breakdown was 110 between ages 18-25, 136 between ages 26-35, 91 between ages 36-45, 46 between ages 46-55, and 117 between ages 56-70. Of the 500 subjects, 36 were self-employed, 168 were employed by a nongovernmental organization, 109 were employed by the state or federal government, 15 were actively seeking employment, and 172 were classified as "out of the workforce" (retired, not seeking employment).

Procedure

Initially, the population of the State of Virginia, and each city and county within the state was obtained through the use of 1970 census information. The population of each city and county was then proportioned based on the total population of the state. Using an N of 500 as the target figure, the number of subjects to be sampled from each area was determined based on the percentage of the state's population which it represented. Thus, an area that represented 10 per cent of the total Virginia population was targeted for fifty subjects (10% of 500).

Secondly, a questionnaire was designed consisting of eight questions regarding provisions of the state's Right-to-Work law. Each question was formulated in statement form, and required either an answer of "true," "false," or "not sure." Additionally, demographic data that included sex, age, and employment status was incorporated. (See Figure 1.)

Prior to its actual use, the questionnaire was reviewed by three experts on labor law to determine any biases that may have been introduced, and whether the questions represented an actual sample of Right-to-Work law content. Thus, through the use of expertise, content validity was obtained.

The third phase required the acquisition of the various area codes and first three digits of the telephone exchanges for use of the target areas. Additionally, a table of random numbers was obtained to generate the last four digits [9].

Since the survey was to be conducted by telephone, calls were placed in the evening between the hours of six and nine. This time period was selected to minimize the number of businesses that might be called (since random phone numbers were used), and to equalize the possibility of obtaining both male and female respondents. Since many specific phone numbers called did not exist, a total of 779 calls were placed to obtain the N of 500.

Each subject was read a standardized introduction to insure uniformity of administration. The experimenter was trained in survey techniques, and the same investigator was used for the total survey. Each subject was told the purpose of the survey was to sample "knowledge of Virginia labor law." At no time were the subjects informed that the purpose of the study was to investigate Right-to-Work knowledge.

Lastly, each subject's responses were recorded, and the data were analyzed through the use of a Statistical Package for the Social Sciences program [10]. Frequency data were obtained for the eight questions, sex, age, and employment status. Additionally, chi square analyses were conducted to determine differences between the sexes for the eight questionnaire items.

1. If he wants to, your boss can legally fire you for joining a union.

2. Government employees (teachers, firemen, policemen, sanitation workers) can be fired for striking.

3. If the company and union agree, they can require all employees to join the union and/or pay union dues.

4. It is legal for an employer to hire only persons who are already union members.

5. You can be refused a job because you are a member of a union.

6. If the union calls a strike, it cannot legally prevent you from working.

7. If you are fired for joining a union, your boss must pay you for any losses you incurred because he fired you.

8. If you work in a business where a union has negotiated for benefits such as life, medical, and hospital insurance, you must join the union to receive these benefits.

Male_____   Female_____

Age: 18-25_____   26-35_____   36-45_____   46-55_____   56-70+_____

Employment Status: _____

NOTE: Questions 1-8 required either a "true," "false," or "not sure" answer.

Figure 1. Questions used to sample knowledge
of Virginia Right-to-Work laws.

RESULTS

Table 1 indicates the frequency of responses for the eight questionnaire items. For all the questions, except numbers one and four, more than 40 per cent of the general population either answered the questions incorrectly or indicated that they were unsure. The question that elicited the most correct answers was question one, with 65.6 per cent of the population answering correctly. The most incorrect response was to question seven, where only 39.2 per cent of the population knew the correct answer.

Examining the breakdown of male and female responses again indicates that the most correct responses were for question number one, with 70.6 per cent of the males answering correctly, and 62.2 per cent of the females selecting the correct response. The most incorrect responses were obtained on question seven, with only 42.3 per cent of the males selecting the correct answer, and 37.1 per cent of the females selecting the correct alternative.

Of the 4,000 responses obtained (8 responses from each of 500 subjects), only 50.6 per cent were correct.

Table 2 indicates the chi square analyses between the sexes for the eight questionnaire items. All of the chi squares obtained were significant except for questions one and two. For all of the questions, males had a greater percentage of correct responses than females.

Table 1. Frequency Responses for the Eight Questionnaire Items

Question		True Response	True % of Population	False Response	False % of Population	Not Sure Response	Not Sure % of Population
1	Total N	98	(19.6)	[a]328	(65.6)	72	(14.8)
	Male	37	(18.4)	142	(70.6)	22	(10.9)
	Female	61	(20.4)	186	(62.2)	52	(17.4)
2	Total N	[a]213	(42.6)	192	(38.4)	95	(19.0)
	Male	92	(45.8)	80	(39.8)	29	(14.4)
	Female	121	(40.5)	112	(37.5)	66	(22.1)
3	Total N	179	(35.8)	[a]223	(44.6)	98	(19.6)
	Male	67	(33.3)	107	(53.2)	27	(13.4)
	Female	112	(37.5)	116	(38.8)	71	(23.7)
4	Total N	97	(19.4)	[a]306	(61.2)	97	(19.4)
	Male	52	(25.9)	125	(62.2)	24	(11.9)
	Female	45	(15.1)	181	(60.5)	73	(24.4)
5	Total N	109	(21.8)	[a]297	(59.4)	94	(18.8)
	Male	41	(20.4)	137	(68.2)	23	(11.4)
	Female	68	(22.7)	160	(53.5)	71	(23.7)
6	Total N	[a]257	(51.4)	150	(30.0)	93	(18.6)
	Male	124	(61.7)	57	(28.4)	20	(10.0)
	Female	133	(44.5)	93	(31.1)	73	(24.4)
7	Total N	[a]196	(39.2)	137	(27.4)	167	(33.4)
	Male	85	(42.3)	65	(32.3)	51	(25.4)
	Female	111	(37.1)	72	(24.1)	116	(38.8)
8	Total N	206	(41.2)	[a]205	(41.0)	89	(17.8)
	Male	71	(35.3)	106	(52.7)	24	(11.9)
	Female	135	(45.2)	99	(33.1)	65	(21.7)

[a] Denotes correct response

Table 2. Chi Square Analyses for the Eight Questionnaire Items Between the Sexes

Question No.	X^2	Probability
1	4.92	NS
2	4.66	NS
3	12.72	.001
4	16.95	.001
5	14.32	.001
6	20.75	.001
7	10.29	.005
8	20.59	.001

DISCUSSION AND SUMMARY

Considering the emotion-laden, controversial nature of the Right-to-Work issue that spawned this research, it seems prudent to put this investigation and its findings in perspective. The present investigation did not address, or pretend to shed light on, the underlying questions as to whether Right-to-Work laws are economically or socially desirable, whether abuses of such an existing law in Virginia actually are prevalent as alleged, or whether legislative proposals to require posting of the Virginia law in covered places of employment would affect, correct, or diminuate such abuses if they do exist. The focus of the present study was confined to determining, empirically, the extent to which Virginians understand the provisions of the Right-to-Work law existing in their state.

Results confirm that a large percentage of the population, ranging from 34 per cent on Question 1 to 61 per cent on Question 7, are indeed uninformed or misinformed about the provisions of a Right-to-Work law that has presumed to affect their working lives for over thirty years. Additionally, as Table 2 indicates, females, who are entering the workforce in greater numbers, appear to be significantly less informed than males. There have been numerous attempts in the state in recent years to repeal and/or modify this law, as well as nearly successful attempts at the federal level to repeal Section 14(b) of the Taft-Hartley Act, which enables such legislation. Each of these attempts has failed amidst strident and emotion-charged controversy.

The enigmatic question naturally arises: How can people so passionately defend or oppose legislation they do not really understand? Perhaps the answer is to be found in Lumsden and Peterson, who found that while states with Right-to-Work laws have a significant percentage of the workforce organized, the difference reflects the tastes and preferences of the population rather than the actual impact of the laws [11]. They concluded that Right-to-Work battles appear to be more symbolic than substantive. Further substantiation of this view may be found in Aebi and McClean, who concluded that these laws have no significant impact on states' industrial growth [12].

A variation of this viewpoint would be that workers to whom the law applies are not only largely oblivious to its provisions, but are also disinterested and indifferent, and that the raging controversy is really generated by a struggle between employers and union officials. In this view, employers defend the Right-to-Work principle because they believe their workers will be more docile and tractable out of unions, and union officials oppose such laws because their power and economic existence depend on recruiting dues-paying members. The plausibility of this hypothesis is enhanced by a review of the identities of witnesses testifying before the Labor Committee of the Virginia Senate when the previously cited posting bill was heard in 1980. All witnesses, except two, represented either labor union or employer organizations. Those two were bargaining unit employees who testified that their employers and unions had illegally conspired to force them into union membership involuntarily. Further support for this contention was provided by Hirsch [13], who found that the existence of a Right-to-Work law had little effect on collective bargaining coverage, but did substantially decrease union membership. Research by Warren and Strauss [14] and Moore and Newman [4] also appeared to confirm that Right-to-Work laws are a deterrent to union activities.

It appears that in attempting to persuade the general population to their respective viewpoints, both opponents and proponents of the Right-to-Work principle may have missed the mark. By relying on emotional appeals and propaganda, both sides seem to have generated commitment without comprehension. Committed, but uninformed, partisans in a dispute produce more controversy than converts.

As a point of conjecture, it appears the primary reason for the widespread ignorance concerning Right-to-Work laws is the lack of advocates with communication access to normal working people. There is no forum in which objective information may be imparted. Very little information on the subject is taught in schools; unions have a vested interest in preventing dissemination of such information; nonunion employers have no need to discuss it; and unionized employees can inform their employees only at peril of worsening their labor relations and facing the accusation that they are attempting to undermine a legally certified bargaining agent. The National Right-to-Work Committee has apparently not been able to accomplish its goal of informing the public on the matter, probably because of its strong advocacy position, which is viewed by many as biased, and its lack of a communication delivery mechanism that can reach those who are uninformed.

It is interesting to contemplate what the effect would be on the nature and resolution of the Right-to-Work controversy if the voting and working public were objectively and thoroughly informed. It is probably not possible to achieve that in the present contaminated atmosphere, but it appears to the present authors that is precisely what is needed. An informed public could then make the necessary value judgments and exercise its collective will such that the law would correspond to majority opinion.

Toward that end, the present authors sincerely hope this study will stimulate interest and further research into the matter addressed. Perhaps knowledge of Right-to-Work laws will take the controversy from the realm of symbolism into the world of reality.

REFERENCES

1. E. A. Keller, *The Case for Right-to-Work Laws: A Defense of Voluntary Unionism*, The Heritage Foundation, Illinois, 1956.
2. L. G. Reynolds, *Labor Economics and Labor Relations*, Prentice-Hall, Inc., New Jersey, 1970.

3. Labors New Southern Strategy, *Business Week*, No. 2469, pp. 28-31, February 7, 1977.
4. W. J. Moore and R. J. Newman, A Note on the Passage of Public Bargaining Laws, *Industrial Relations, 10*:3, pp. 364-370, 1975.
5. E. Finn, The Case Against Right-to-Work Laws, *Labour Gazette, 77*:10, pp. 446-449, 1977.
6. R. L. Miller, Right-to-Work Laws and Compulsory Union Membership in the United States, *British Journal of Industrial Relations, 14*:2, pp. 186-193, 1976.
7. What Managers Think of Right-to-Work Laws, *Industry Week, 192*:7, pp. 17-19, 1977.
8. Big Labor May Have an Image Problem too, *Industry Week, 182*:2, p. 21, 1974.
9. M. G. Kendall and B. B. Smith, *Tables of Random Sampling Numbers*, Cambridge University Press, London, pp. 2-5, 1939.
10. N. H. Nie, C. H. Hull, J. G. Jenkins, K. Steinbrenner and D. Bent, *Statistical Package for the Social Sciences*, McGraw-Hill, New York, 1975.
11. K. Lumsden and C. Petersen, The Effect of Right-to-Work Laws on Unionization in the United States, *Journal of Political Economy, 83*:6, pp. 1237-1248, 1975.
12. T. Aebi and R. A. McLean, Right-to-Work Laws and Industrial Expansion, *Indiana Business Review, 53*, pp. 7-10, 1978.
13. B. T. Hirsch, The Determinants of Unionization: An Analysis of Interarea Differences, *Industrial and Labor Relations Review, 33*:2, pp. 147-161, 1980.
14. R. S. Warren and R. P. Strauss, A Mixed Logit Model of the Relationship Between Unionization and Right-to-Work Legislation, *Journal of Political Economy, 87*:3, pp. 648-655, 1979.

Discussion Questions

1. In what ways can or do Right-to-Work laws undermine the power held by union leaders?
2. Discuss the reasons why a Right-to-Work law might have little effect on collective bargaining coverage, even while substantially decreasing union membership.
3. Do you agree with the reasons suggested by the authors as to why the respondents were so uninformed about Virginia's Right-to-Work law? Why or why not?

CHAPTER 12

The Impact of Proposition 13 on Public Employee Relations: The Case of Los Angeles*

GENE SWIMMER

The passage of Proposition 13 (also known as the Jarvis-Gann initiative) had tremendous repercussions on all aspects of the California public sector. The initiative drastically reduced property tax collections available to local governments by 60 per cent (about $7 billion) as of July 1, 1978. The state legislature, faced with an embarrassing budget surplus, passed a series of laws that bailed out local governments by providing $4.2 billion extra revenue for these jurisdictions in the 1978-1979 fiscal year and $4.8 billion for the subsequent year.[1] This paper concentrates on the impact of Proposition 13 and the subsequent state bailouts on employee relations in the City and County

* This paper was written while the author was on sabbatical leave at the Institute of Industrial Relations, U.C.L.A.

[1] For a discussion of the causes and possible effects of Proposition 13, see references [1] and [2].

of Los Angeles. Employment effects, if any, are examined on a "before and after" basis. The impact of the proposition on the collective bargaining process is then discussed. This section relies on interviews with labor and management principals. The paper concludes with some predictions about future employment relations in Los Angeles.

EMPLOYMENT EFFECTS

Table 1 presents Los Angeles City and County average quarterly employment levels for three eighteen-month periods:

1. July 1975 – December 1976;
2. January 1977 – June 1978; and
3. July 1978 – December 1979.

The first two periods encompass the three years prior to Proposition 13 and the final period corresponds to the "post-Prop. 13" environment. Employment statistics have been reported on total and disaggregated bases. Los Angeles City employment could only be divided between the "department of water and power" (which generates revenue) and "all other departments" (which are tax supported). County data could be disaggregated further. Individual tax-supported departments were placed into one of the six categories based on their budget classification:

- general (mainly central administration);
- protection (mainly policing);
- health (hospitals);
- social services;
- recreation and culture; and
- road maintenance.

The seventh category, "county districts and courts," includes all revenue-supported jurisdictions.

Even a casual glance at Table 1 indicates that almost all categories of city and county employment were declining before *and* after the passage of Proposition 13. Average city employment fell by 4.5 per cent between periods 1 and 2 (before the initiative was an important issue) and an additional 3.1 per cent between periods 2 and 3 (eighteen months before and after Proposition 13). The county's aggregate employment decreased by 5.4 per cent and 4.1 per cent for the same periods. Over the last four and one-half years, public employment has decreased by about 3500 for the city and about 6800 for the county.[2]

The picture of long-run decline is apparent in the disaggregated results as well. Somewhat surprisingly, employment in the department of water and power declined at a faster rate (8% each period) than in tax-supported city departments (about 2.5%), but in both cases the cutbacks were greater before Proposition 13. Five of the seven county categories declined throughout the 1975-1979 period.

---

[2] These results are even more impressive considering that during 1975-1979 population in both the city and county of Los Angeles increased by about 2.5 per cent [3].

Table 1. Average Quarterly Employment Levels For
The City and County of Los Angeles

	Period			% Change Between Periods:	
	July 75– Dec. 76	Jan. 77– June 78	July 78– Dec. 79		
	(1)	(2)	(3)	(1) & (2)	(2) & (3)
CITY OF LOS ANGELES					
Total Employees	47013	44904	43500	–4.5%	–3.1%
Water and Power[a]	11472	10471	9743	–8.7%	–7.0%
All Other Departments[a]	38780	37684	36766	–2.8%	–2.4%
COUNTY OF LOS ANGELES					
Total Employees	73379	69439	66587	–5.4%	–4.1%
General Administration	11205	10211	9997	–8.9%	–2.1%
Protection Services	15889	15943	15586	+0.3%	–2.2%
Health Services	21925	21671	21229	–1.2%	–2.0%
Social Services	14039	12482	11864	–11.1%	–5.0%
Recreation & Culture	2977	2673	2353	–10.2%	–12.0%
Road Maintenance	1753	1472	1346	–16.0%	–8.6%
County Districts & Courts	5580	5874	5433	+5.3%	–7.5%

[a] Employment data include all employees hired under the Comprehensive Education and Training Act (CETA); disaggregate city data excluding CETA employees were unavailable.

SOURCES: (1) "City Work Force" prepared by The Personnel Department, City of Los Angeles (Xerox), and (2) "Employee Population" prepared by the Office of the Director of Personnel, County of Los Angeles (Xerox).

Largest cuts in staff occurred in the recreation and culture (20% overall), the road maintenance (20%), and the social services (15%) areas. At the other extreme, health and protection services, as well as revenue-generating districts, experienced only slight net decreases. It would be unfair to say that the County of Los Angeles was concerned with maintaining its bureaucracy at the expense of providing services. The general administration category decreased substantially before and after Proposition 13 (about 11% overall).[3]

Overall, there was no apocalyptic impact of Proposition 13 on employment, partially because state funds replaced much of the lost property tax revenues.[4] Equally important is the fact that both the City and County of Los Angeles were trying to reduce the size of government long before July 1, 1978.

---

[3] By contrast, between the 1975 and 1978 fiscal years, City of Los Angeles full-time authorized employees increased by 5.4 per cent for "overhead departments" as opposed to only 1.2 per cent for "service departments." [2, pp. 39-41]

[4] The 1978-1979 state bailout generated the equivalent of $638 and $82 million for the county and city respectively. The 1979-1980 bailouts were $682 million and $69 million [4, pp. 4-5].

Collective Bargaining Impacts

Collective bargaining in both the City and County of Los Angeles exists within the framework of enabling legislation: the Meyers, Milias, Brown Act. Both jurisdictions require employers to "meet and confer" with employee organizations, negotiate written agreements (memoranda of understanding) and provide for resolution of unit determination and unfair labor practice cases by a quasijudicial body. Strikes are technically illegal, but have occurred on occasion. By 1975 about 90 per cent of city and county employees were represented by certified bargaining agents and covered by memoranda of understanding [5, p. 209].

By far, the largest unions representing city and county employees are Local 347 and Local 660 of the Service Employees International Union (SEIU). They represent most outside and inside nonprofessional employees. Separate independent associations represent police and fire personnel. This discussion concentrates on municipal personnel other than police and firefighters, because these associations could not be interviewed.

Until its repeal by the county in 1978, both jurisdictions had charter provisions requiring the payment of "prevailing wages." The difference between the city and county is probably unimportant because the city management and unions have generally agreed that any wage settlement negotiated would be considered consistent with the prevailing wage doctrine. One management negotiator referred to it as a "legal fiction."[5]

Before a description of the 1979 collective bargaining round, it is useful to discuss the impact of Proposition 13 on the attitudes of the parties to the bargaining relationship.

Right after the passage of the initiative, there was a rapid decline in public employee morale, resulting from a repudiation by the public. The unions lost some members due to voluntary attrition. But then the mood among rank and file shifted toward antagonism against an unfair stereotype that public employees did not work as hard as private sector employees (particularly as work loads across the city and county were simultaneously increased). This antagonism crystalized into greater interest in union activities.

Thus, indirectly, Proposition 13 has been beneficial to the Los Angeles local government unions in consolidating their internal organization. Although bargaining units have shrunk, the percentage of union membership in these units have increased dramatically. One local experienced a 10 per cent increase in members during 1979.

Most important are new rank-and-file militant attitudes, particularly among county workers. A spokesperson for the union representing county social workers said that members across the state have been ready to authorize strikes

---

[5] The only exception applies to city police and fire personnel, whose wage increases are determined by a strict formula tied to construction trades.

(which are illegal) to back up their demands.[6] Though both the Los Angeles County and City employees settled without strikes in 1979, the county workers were ready to go out.

One of the most interesting responses of the union members has been in relation to the possibility of work sharing. County union officials polled the rank-and-file (before the initial bailout bill was enacted) about wage cuts and work sharing.[7] Members were unwilling to trade wages for fewer layoffs. This was even true for those employees with the highest probability of being laid off. The county union leadership has since made it clear that its first priority is a decent wage for its members and if layoffs result, so be it. The government may have the responsibility of being employer of last resort, but the union does not. In this regard the union is clearly moving toward a private sector bargaining stance.

The rise in rank-and-file militancy is clearly a "double edged sword" for union leaders. While a united and determined membership increases the union's power at the bargaining table, it probably also increases the union leader's accountability to the membership. A contract inconsistent with employee expectations would generate greater political costs. One management negotiator interviewed conceded that though bargaining was going to be more difficult for everybody, it would probably be toughest for union leaders.

At the same time, the passage of Proposition 13 profoundly changed the attitudes of Los Angeles County and City management. Managers interviewed stated that Proposition 13 gave them a mandate to be tough at the bargaining table. Wage changes would have to be small, and some previously negotiated fringe benefits would have to be reduced to bring them in line with the private sector. They also felt that the political costs of a strike had decreased in the abstract, although it would be difficult to predict how politicians and the public would respond to the actuality of a city- or county-wide strike.

THE 1979 BARGAINING ROUND

It was within this generally antagonistic mood that the first big round of post-Proposition 13 collective bargaining negotiations for both the City and County of Los Angeles commenced (during spring 1979).

Three other events that occurred in late 1978 and 1979 (two of which were directly related to Proposition 13) contributed to the fragile bargaining environment. First, the temporary State Bailout Bill (SB 154) required municipalities who wished to receive the special revenue to limit their employees'

[6] There were thirty-three strikes or sickouts in California cities, counties, and special districts between January and August 1979 [6].

[7] Union leaders for the City of Los Angeles said they have purposely not addressed this issue with the members because they were afraid that both the rank-and-file and negotiators would become hooked into that way of thinking by management.

wage increases to the state employees wage increase (which was 0%). Many city and county employees in the middle of multiyear contracts did not receive interim wage increases. After almost nine months, a court ruled that the bailout bill did not take precedence over a labor agreement and the money had to be paid [7, p. 2].

President Carter issued wage guidelines calling for maximum increases of 7 per cent across the economy. The mayor and city council (for the city) and the county board of supervisors immediately adopted resolutions calling for compliance with the guidelines.

Finally, during the summer of 1979, the California State Legislature was working on a new (permanent) bill. The final bill passed (AB-8) included a deflater clause that would reduce state aid to municipalities and special districts if state revenues did not reach a specified target.

The participants in the city and county reacted differently to the same collective bargaining environment, probably because of greater historical union militancy in the county [5].

The City of Los Angeles' management took the view that, given the uncertainty of future state financing, the city would be unwilling to negotiate anything longer than a one-year contract. For their part, the unions were generally happy to accept the offer because they did not want a repetition of a state-imposed freeze on a nonnegotiable, long-term contract.

The county SEIU locals took the opposite view. With the Supreme Court of California having validated collective agreements, these unions felt that longer contracts with interim increases provided the best insurance against pending voter initiatives (Proposition 4 — which subsequently passed in November 1979 and Proposition 9 — which failed in the June 1980 election).[8] The county negotiators were willing to continue the long-standing practice of two-year agreements on the basis that, aside from greater financial control and stability, a longer contract that guaranteed wages increases would probably strengthen the county's power in bargaining about future bailout funds. Legally committed increases could not simply be cut, even if the state required across-the-board expenditure cuts as a prerequisite for future funding.

In all 1979 negotiations there was confusion as to the size of the city (and county) budget. Management negotiators in both jurisdictions were content to "stonewall" at the bargaining table in the hopes that wage negotiations would be delayed until the permanent bailout bill was legislated in Sacramento. (AB-8 became low on July 24, 1979.) This behavior simply generated greater hostility among union members, many of whom had to wait nine months to receive the previous year's wage increase. This frustration was expressed in limited job

---

[8] Proposition 4 (The Gann Initiative) limits growth in state and local government spending to increases in population and inflation. So far it has not been a binding constraint on either the City or County of Los Angeles. Proposition 9 would have cut the state income tax in half.

actions, one-day walkouts and sickouts, by various county groups between June and mid-July.

City and county unions also reacted differently to the president's wage guideline. City union locals generally zeroed in on the 7 per cent wage increase as soon as Los Angeles' Mayor Bradley said he would be bound by the president's request. Instead, they hoped to negotiate additional benefits on top of a 7 per cent wage increase. Considering the environment, the bargaining proceeded on what both parties perceived as a reasonably cooperative basis. There was no real threat of strikes. The major contracts, signed in early August, called for improved life insurance and dental plans and a delay of increased pension costs (the city would pay them until phased in), plus a 7 per cent wage increase, retroactive to July 1, 1979.

The county unions took a much more offensive stance. They argued that the guideline figure was unrealistically low, given that the previous year's average wage increase across the county was only 4.3 per cent. All county unions agreed on a strike deadline of August 1, 1979 to back up their demands. Bargaining continued through July in a highly antagonistic environment. One management negotiator described it as follows: "People were just kind of wild. They felt they were getting harpooned from every direction. Nobody felt anything was reasonable." Fifteen minutes following the strike deadline, agreements were reached with the major unions that called for total compensation increases of about 9 per cent per annum for two years. Wage increases were phased in as follows (to be more consistent with the president's guideline): 6 per cent retroactive to July 1, 1979; 2 per cent on January 1, 1980; and 7 per cent on July 1, 1980. In addition, some wage inequities were corrected (up to 2% pay increases), and the employer agreed to increase its pension contribution to improve the actuarial soundness of the plan (equivalent to about a 2.5% across-the-board wage increase). At the same time, management was able to "take away" some existing sick leave provisions, mainly on accumulation.

FUTURE EMPLOYEE RELATIONS

The future of employee relations at the city and county level is clouded by two issues: contracting out and the size of the state budget surplus.

Both the City and County of Los Angeles amended their charters in 1978 to give management the unilateral right to contract out work currently performed by government employees to the private sector, where economically feasible. Both jurisdictions would be required to "meet and confer" with the unions involved over the specific employment effects of contracting out, but not over the decision itself. Though no major contracting has yet occurred, city employees are faced with the biggest threat. A report from the chief administrator officer of the city identified over 7000 jobs that might be eliminated by contracting, the bulk of these being in sanitation, maintenance, and custodial services. The first political fight will probably be over residential refuse collection. A number of city council members want this service contracted to private companies. Local 347 of SEIU is waging a counterpropaganda campaign, arguing that service quality will fall and many of the city jobs will wind up in the hands of illegal aliens, often hired by the private contractors at low wages [8]. Although the city unions have not been strike-prone in the past, massive contracting out might push them into illegal job actions.

The move toward contracting out has progressed more slowly in Los Angeles County. The most vulnerable groups appear to be security officers and food and laundry service workers at some hospitals. Still, it remains a potential strike issue and the pace at which contracting out occurs will depend on the size of future state bailout funding.

The state revenue surplus, which exceeded $6 billion when Proposition 13 took effect, is estimated by drop to $2.1 billion by the end of the 1979-1980 fiscal year (June 30, 1980), and could be virtually wiped out one year later. Part of the decline stems from the $10 billion expenditures to aid local jurisdictions over the past two years. In addition, AB-276 has indexed state income tax schedules for 1980 and 1981, thus removing extra tax revenue generated by inflation pushing incomes into higher marginal tax brackets. Finally, the present recession is now projected to further reduce 1980 income tax revenues further by $130 million. If Governor Brown's proposed budget were adopted, the remaining surplus would be a mere $600 million [9]. It seems likely that across-the-board cuts in bailout funds will be required by the 1981-1982 fiscal year, at the latest. Current state aid to Los Angeles County and City represent 16 per cent and 6 per cent of their respective total budgets. Obviously, the county will be more vulnerable to future cutbacks.

THE 1980-1981 ROUNDS OF COLLECTIVE BARGAINING

The most recent collective bargaining round in the City of Los Angeles occurred during the summer of 1980. Forty-one contracts, the largest number ever, expired July 1, 1980. Scale increases of most city employees were 5 per cent and 7 per cent over the previous two years, leaving the workers with wages almost 18 per cent behind inflation for the period (based on changes in the Los Angeles-Long Beach area Consumer Price Index for urban wage earners between July 1978 and June 1980). Nonetheless, it seemed unlikely that the city would violate the President's 1980 wage guideline of 9.5 per cent. Given the unions' past record of militancy, it is not surprising that after an extremely protracted negotiating period (ending in mid-October), one-year agreements calling for 10 per cent wage increases were reached without strikes.[9] With the

[9] The contracts also call for medical and other benefits equivalent to an additional 3 per cent increase.

threat of Proposition 9 removed and healthy sales tax revenues generated by high inflation rates, the City should be able to pay for these settlements without requiring additional employment decreases.

The county does not bargain with its employees again until July 1981. By then wages of most employees will have fallen 18 per cent behind the rate of inflation for the previous three-year period [10, p. 3]. Nonetheless, the county's proposed budget for the 1980 fiscal year calls for additional cuts of about 1300 employees, most coming from the Health and Protection areas [11]. Next year the unions will undoubtedly demand large wage increases even if it means more layoffs. At the same time, the deflater clause in AB-8 will likely take effect, reducing state bailout funds to the county. Taken together, these facts point to another tough (perhaps the most difficult ever) round of negotiations. It will likely require spectacular effort on both sides to avoid a county-wide strike.

In sum, the worst effects of Proposition 13, as they apply to Los Angeles public employees, have yet to occur, but are probably no more than one year away.

ACKNOWLEDGEMENT

The author wishes to thank the Social Science Research Council of Canada for financial support.

REFERENCES

1. Proceedings of a Conference on Tax and Expenditure Limitations, *National Tax Journal, XXXII:*2, Supplement, June 1979.
2. A. Pascal, *et. al, Fiscal Containment of Local and State Government,* Rand Corporation Study No. R-2494-FF/RC, Rand Corporation, Santa Monica, 1979.
3. *California Department of Finance, California Statistical Abstract, 1979,* Sacramento, California, 1979.
4. The Proposition 13 Impact Reporter, July 31, 1979.
5. D. Lewin, Local Government Labor Relations in Transition: The Case of Los Angeles, *Labor History, 17,* Spring 1976.
6. M. Taylor, A Special Report: Disputes in Local Government, *California Public Employment Relations Magazine,* No. 42, pp. 23-32, September 1979.
7. M. Taylor, Court Ruling, Funding, Pay Standards Muddle Bargaining Scene, *California Public Employees Magazine,* No. 40, pp. 2-7, March 1979.
8. Union To Fight Private Trash Collection Plan, *Valley News,* November 20, 1979.
9. W. B. Rood, Brown Aide Predicts Near End of Surplus, *Los Angeles Times,* pp. 3, 26, May 30, 1980.
10. The UCLA Business Forecast 1980-1983, March 27, 1980.
11. D. Shuit, Higher County Costs, Fewer Services Seen, *Los Angeles Times,* pp. 1, 29, April 29, 1980.

Discussion Questions

1. Do you agree that unions gained members because public employees resented being characterized as less hard-working than private sector employees? Why or why not?
2. Why do you think workers were unwilling to trade wages for fewer layoffs? Discuss the short and long-term implications of doing so.
3. Discuss "contracting out" versus in-house-work from the point-of-view of a) management; b) taxpayer; c) an affected employee; d) the employee's union president; e) a client of the public agency involved.

Reprinted from the Journal of Collective Negotiations in the Public Sector Vol. 11(1), 1982

CHAPTER 13

Proposition 2½: The Massachusetts Tax Revolt and Its Impact on Public Sector Labor Relations*

GARY D. ALTMAN

On November 4, 1980, the people of Massachusetts passed the most sweeping tax cut proposal of the 1980 election year. More than 1.4 million voters, 59 per cent of the voting electorate, approved Referendum Question Number 2. Popularly known as Proposition 2½, the referendum mandated a drastic rollback in property taxes. It was predicted that without an infusion of state aid, cities and towns would have to cut an estimated $575 million during the 1982 fiscal year.

The first year of Proposition 2½ deeply affected the number of public employees and the level of public services. Statewide the Massachusetts Teachers Association estimated that 12,000 teachers had received layoff notices. The State Division of Employment Security reported for the period of November 1980 to November 1981 the municipal work force shrank by 30,400, an 11.8 per

* The views expressed in this article are those of the author and do not necessarily represent the views of the Massachusetts Labor Relations Commission.

cent reduction in the total municipal work force. During the same period, the state government reduced its staff by 6,200, a 6.2 per cent reduction in total work force. The State Division of Employment Security computed that almost 19,000 individuals filed for unemployment compensation, claiming that their jobs were lost because of Proposition 2½.

Two factors have contributed to these effects. First, Massachusetts heavily relies on personal property tax as a source of revenue. Local property taxes are the principal revenue source for cities and towns, and account for an average of 65 per cent of local expenditures. Second, Massachusetts, unlike California during the first two years after Proposition 13, did not have a budgetary surplus in the state treasury to take up the slack caused by the lost revenue of local governments. In fact, the governor's 1982 fiscal budget proposed an increase in state aid to the cities and towns of only $37 million. This fell far short of the amount necessary to bail out the localities for the anticipated loss in revenue caused by Proposition 2½.

With this scenario in place, a protracted budget battle ensued in the state legislature this past summer. Because there was no agreement on the amount of local aid, no state budget was passed when the 1981 fiscal year ended. Nor were there any temporary resolutions passed to provide welfare recipients their benefits nor state workers their paychecks. For almost a month state employees went without their paychecks. In protest of these payless paydays a statewide strike was called and an estimated 1,000 workers in the state hospitals set up picket lines.

Finally, a state budget was passed that increased the amount of local aid from the governor's proposal of $37 million to $265 million, almost cutting in half the losses to the cities and towns caused by Proposition 2½. Nonetheless, because of the budget uncertainties, many cities and towns could not set their final budget for the year until November and December.

WHAT IS PROPOSITION 2½

The main features of Proposition 2½ are the provisions calling for the reduction of local property taxes. The proposition was so named because it proposed that the total taxes assessed on real and personal property by any city or town be limited to no more than 2½ per cent of full and fair cash value. The House of Representatives Committee on Taxation reported, before passage of the referendum, that this provision would cost the cities of Boston and Chelsea 70 per cent of their property tax revenues, the City of Worcester would lose 52 per cent, and Springfield 39 per cent.

The law also mandates that if a municipality's level presently exceeds the 2½ limit, the municipality must reduce the levy by at least 15 per cent a year until its levy is 2½ per cent of the full and fair cash value. If a municipality's present property tax levy is below 2½ per cent, its tax rate will be frozen at that level.

Proposition 2½ also imposes a limit on how fast local property taxes can be increased to keep up with inflation. Once the 2½ per cent limit is reached (for the majority of cities this will occur in approximately four years), the property tax levy may then be increased by no more than 2½ per cent annually, regardless of the growth of full and fair cash value of property in the community or the current rate of inflation.

Under the original provision of the law, municipalities can override the provisions of Proposition 2½ by a two-thirds vote in a local referendum, which can only take place during a November biennial election, or by a special election called by the legislature. Moreover, under the original law there appear to be no exemptions for court-ordered costs, debt service, or pensions from the property tax levy limit.

In addition, Proposition 2½ rolls back the automobile excise tax by 66 per cent. The excise tax is a personal property tax on automobiles, also payable to the cities and towns. Before Proposition 2½ the rate was $66 per $1,000 of valuation. Now it is $25 per $1,000 valuation. This provision took effect January 1, 1981 and immediately cost the cities and towns over $150 million. The loss of excise tax revenue is significant because, other than the property tax, it is the only other revenue source that goes directly to the cities and towns.

Proposition 2½, while drastically reducing the municipalities' revenue sources, also alters the balance of power between the state and municipalities. For example, one controversial provision of the law prevents the state from mandating programs and imposing those costs on local governments. Under Proposition 2½ any future state laws that increase the localities' financial burdens can only become effective if the state reimburses the local governments for the costs it has imposed or the municipalities' governing bodies accept the program.

THE ORIGIN OF PROPOSITION 2½

There was no dispute that the state overly relied on property tax as a revenue source. Nonetheless, not one of 126 proposals to limit or reduce property taxes and local spending was enacted between 1932 and 1980. After public protest against taxes erupted in California, a small number of Republican members of the Massachusetts House of Representatives filed a bill to limit property taxes. Although the bill died, the genesis of "cutback politics" was created in Massachusetts. The Republican representatives then merged their efforts with a grass-roots organization, "The Citizens for Limited Taxation" (C.L.T.). C.L.T. is a statewide taxpayers association with over 5,000 members.

This coalition first sought to put a tax-cutting initiative on the ballot in 1978. This referendum contained most of the sweeping provisions of what ultimately became Proposition 2½. In addition, this proposal drastically restructured the balance of power between state and local governments and would have amended the public sector collective bargaining law. This referendum, however, was disallowed by the Massachusetts Attorney General's Office and was never placed on the ballot.

In 1979 several bills to reduce or limit local property taxes were before the legislature. Only one, however, became law, a stop-gap measure designed to limit city and town spending increases to no more than 4 per cent of the previous year's tax levy.

Frustrated by the legislature's inaction, various interest groups decided to place the issue directly before the public. Nine tax limitation initiatives were filed with the State Attorney General's Office. One was Proposition 2½, sponsored now only by the Citizens for Limited Taxation.

This time the petition, without some of the earlier proposals, was approved by the Attorney General's Office. C.L.T. then gathered the 60,000 signatures necessary to put the petition before the legislature. The legislature had a real opportunity to change the drastic provisions of Proposition 2½. Although there were a number of tax reform bills before the legislature, they refused to act on any of them. (Even today they have not adopted any meaningful tax reforms or any alternative to the regressive property tax.) Instead, the House of Representatives defeated the proposal by a vote of 146 to 5. The sponsors then were required to collect another 10,000 signatures to put the referendum directly before the voters, a task which they easily accomplished.

The pre-election debate was particularly vigorous.

The Pre-Election Debate

In addition to Citizens for Limited Taxation, supporters of the proposition included two notable business associations, the Associated Industries of Massachusetts and the High Technology Council. The High Technology Council's support proved crucial, because the group raised more than $250,000 in support of passage. Proponents of the referendum focused their arguments on the crushing property tax burden and claimed that localities' education payments and the state's welfare payments were excessive. They asserted that the only way to eliminate waste in government and limit spending was to force local governments to become more efficient and responsible. Proponents further claimed that a large tax cut would stimulate the state's economy, resulting in commercial expansion and new jobs.

Opponents, including the League of Women Voters, the Massachusetts Municipal Association, the Massachusetts Teachers Association, and other public sector unions, described the referendum as a "meat-ax" resolution to the complicated problems of municipal finance and tax reform. Opponents argued that passage of Proposition 2½ would be a disaster; they projected huge cuts in statewide service and a large-scale layoff of public employees. The 2½ opponents claimed that the proposition was misleading and would provide large tax breaks for business, with minimal, if any, financial relief for homeowners.

On election day 81 per cent of the voters turned out to approve the measure by almost a 2-1 margin.

Post Mortem Analysis

In the author's opinion, the harshness of the Bay State property tax scheme served as the catalyst for Proposition 2½. In relation to income, and in relation to population, Massachusetts property taxes are presently the highest in the United States. Factors that account for this rate include the following:

1. under state law the property tax is the only revenue tax that municipalities can impose;
2. municipalities have not imposed user fees; and
3. the state finances a very low percentage of local expenditures.

The practical effect of these factors is that Massachusetts residents pay almost twice as much property tax as the national average; approximately 4.7 per cent of their property value is paid annually to the property tax. Residents of Boston pay almost three times the national average. Indeed, adding to voter frustration, in some localities property taxes were raised an average of 11 per cent only two weeks before the voters went to the polls.

A study was completed by two professors at Harvard's Kennedy School of Government analyzing the Proposition 2½ vote [1]. The researchers concluded that a large portion of the voters believed that Proposition 2½ would reduce government inefficiency and corruption. Specifically, 80 per cent of all the respondents perceived at least some government inefficiency and corruption and 74 per cent were convinced there is much of it.

The study also indicated that people believe governments can spend less without making large-scale cuts in services. In fact, those interviewed after the election wanted to maintain state-provided services and some, particularly the residents of the cities, even favored certain increases. This, however, has not happened. Not surprising, the study found:

> Those who voted for 2½ were more likely than those who voted against it to believe that someone else's services, not the ones used by their households, would be the ones to be cut back . . . [1].

These beliefs turned into action during the spring and summer when municipalities, notably Boston, cut back on public services. The City of Boston closed neighborhood fire and police stations. In an amazing display of well-organized civil disobedience, the citizens took to the streets. The residents of those Boston neighborhoods affected by the service cuts actually walked onto and took control of the city's streets. Their actions snarled rush hour traffic and blocked commuters from coming into the city. Because of a diminished number of police, police officers still employed but sympathetic to the mounting protests over the loss of their fellow employees' jobs, and a mayor who was willing to use these protests to dramatize the city's need for increased state aid, the protests continued for weeks.

What Does It All Mean

In the author's opinion, through Proposition 2½ the public has voted its dissatisfaction with the business of government, i.e., the effective managing of public employment and efficient allocation of public services.

The Harvard study found that nearly one-half of the respondents thought local employees are overpaid and two-thirds thought public employees do not work as hard as their counterparts in the private sector. It is therefore not surprising that through two specific provisions of Proposition 2½, the public has bypassed the public managers and has demanded and obtained greater access to the public sector collective bargaining process. Specifically, Proposition 2½ abolished fiscal autonomy for school departments and binding arbitration for police and fire fighters. Thus, the referendum has shifted the mood of local labor management relations to provide the public with more accountability and influence in the actual bargaining process.

Proposition 2½ Affects Statutory Procedures for Police and Fire Fighters

Throughout the country many states have begun to establish forms of binding interest arbitration as the final step in public sector bargaining impasses. This trend has taken an unprecedented turn in Massachusetts. Proposition 2½, by its very provisions, repeals the law that originally provided for binding interest arbitration for police and fire fighter impasses.

In 1973, Massachusetts police and fire fighter labor organizations sought a statutory mechanism to resolve impasses over terms of new collective bargaining contracts. The device chosen by the legislature was last-best-offer binding arbitration. The binding arbitration bill was controversial and was passed over the veto of the governor. The provisions became effective on July 1, 1974, for a three-year period. In 1977, the police and fire fighter associations strenuously lobbied to continue last-best-offer arbitration. The management organizations for the cities and towns, convinced this method was counterproductive, argued for major revisions or repeal of the law. Again, last-best-offer arbitration was enacted by the legislature over the governor's veto.

The cities and towns, unwilling to give up the fight against last-best-offer, started a referendum drive to put the repeal of binding arbitration before the voters. While the signatures were being gathered, representatives of municipal management and employee groups sought the assistance of John Dunlop, former U. S. Secretary of Labor, in an effort to develop a different method of resolving impasses. An agreement was reached between the parties, which was later incorporated into a bill and passed by the legislature. The legislation established the Joint Labor Management Committee (JLMC), whose membership consisted of individuals from police and fire fighter employee organizations and municipal management.

Now, when an impasse is reached, either party petitions the JLMC, and it decides whether to assume jurisdiction over the impasse. If it assumes jurisdiction, the JLMC will encourage mediation and voluntary settlement by employing a variety of settlement devices in contrast to the single form of last-best-offer arbitration. If attempts at voluntary settlement do not work, the committee may initiate binding arbitration.

From September 1978 to January 1980, the committee was involved in 221 cases, of which only seven have proceeded to last-best-offer arbitration. Before the JLMC was established, between 1975 and 1977, ninety seven cases were resolved by last-best-offer arbitration. In other words, the JLMC through its existence encouraged the resolution of disputes without having to go the full route of final interest arbitration.

Proposition 2½, as originally drafted by Citizens for Limited Taxation in 1979, called for elimination of the JLMC. The group later amended its petition by dropping the statutory reference to the JLMC and adding a provision that repealed the statutory provision authorizing last-best-offer arbitration. Thus, in November of 1980, the voters repealed last-best-offer arbitration. The JLMC, however, will continue to exist. The Massachusetts Attorney General stated that in his opinion interest arbitration could still be used; however, any such award cannot bind a legislature (the appropriating body of a municipality). Town managers considered the repeal a major victory. Now, for police and fire negotiations there is no closure mechanism to end negotiations.

Proposition 2½ Abolishes
School Committees' Fiscal Autonomy

Dating back to 1647, local school committees in Massachusetts have had final authority to decide on the financial needs of the schools under their charge. Once the school committee determined the annual school budget, the city council or town meeting was legally required to appropriate the full amount. Proposition 2½ abolished the fiscal autonomy of local school committees. Under Proposition 2½ the final school budgets are now voted on by the city or town governing bodies.

Under the Massachusetts Collective Bargaining Law (Chapter 150E) the local school committee is the designated representative of the public employer charged with the statutory duty to bargain with school employee organizations. Accordingly, school employee unions and school committees must collectively negotiate and settle with each other. Prior to Proposition 2½, once a collective bargaining agreement was reached, the local legislative body was obligated to fund the cost items of the collective bargaining agreement, pursuant to the school committees' fiscal autonomy.

The abolition of fiscal autonomy has introduced a stranger into the customary relationship between school committees and employee organizations. Although school committees and unions must still negotiate, and school committees must still seek appropriate budgets, now another government entity will be involved. The introduction of this new party into the public school negotiating process will undoubtedly result in new bargaining tactics and engender new bargaining complexities.

The provisions of Proposition 2½ that repeal fiscal autonomy and binding arbitration, as well as the method of enactment of the entire referendum have been legally challenged by police and teacher unions, as violating the state constitution. The State Supreme Court recently upheld the law against all challenges.

Proposition 2½: The Initial Impacts

The actual reduction of services and layoffs caused by Proposition 2½ has varied greatly among the various cities and towns within the state. In fact, the impact of Proposition 2½ has been compared to a tornado, capricious in its action, devastating those communities in its path, yet only brushing the other areas. Many communities have kept layoffs to a minimum through such efforts as hiring freezes, negotiated attrition, and early retirement incentives. In addition, the impact has been softened by the increased state aid and the revaluation of local property to 100 per cent of full and fair cash value.

Between November 1980 and November 1981, public sector employment in Massachusetts fell by more than 36,600 positions, a 10.2 per cent reduction in the public sector work force.[2]. Almost 19,000 public employees filed claims for unemployment [2]. A survey conducted by the Massachusetts Municipal Association of its members demonstrated the extent to which cuts were made in particular departments [2].

Percentage of Work Force vs. Percentage of Cuts

% of Total Work Force	Department	% of Total Cuts
8	Fire	3.9
9	Police	3.7
66	Schools	66.5
7	Public Works	9.9
10	Other	16.0

The survey demonstrates that cuts in school personnel were proportionate to their percentage in the total work force. Public safety personnel cuts, however, were disproportionate, suggesting that cities and towns attempted to maintain their level of police and fire fighters at pre-2½ levels.

The Massachusetts Municipal Association Survey also attempted to ascertain the specific areas in which budgets were cut. Among the severe impact communities[1], appropriations for schools fell 9.9 per cent, public works by 10.8 per cent, libraries by 14.6 per cent, and recreation by 25.8 per cent. The study also compared departments' share of the total budget cuts. Again, police and fire department budget cuts were smaller than their share of the budget. School budgets, however, were cut disproportionately higher as a result of Proposition 2½. The survey report stated that the data indicate "the municipalities, either because they believed such cuts were publicly acceptable, because they saw the greatest potential for cost reductions, or for some other reason, turned to their school departments for somewhat greater expenditure reductions than their proportional share." [2, p. 7] The severe impact on public schools was demonstrated by a report from the Massachusetts Department of Education:

> In the last five years an average of forty-eight schools closed each year. This year, with Proposition 2½, there were 225 closings [3].

The reduction of teachers was proportionately much higher than the decline in student enrollment. For example:

City of Worcester	—	3% decline in students
		14% drop in staff
		6 closed schools
City of Quincy	—	9% decline in students
		31% drop in staff
City of Pittsfield	—	2% decline in students
		18% drop in staff
City of Boston	—	6% decline in students
		20% drop in staff
		27 schools closed

Budget cuts have also caused these changes in local school systems:

- Teaching staffs tend to be older and have more experience because many young teachers have been laid off.
- Many specialized and enrichment programs as well as library services have been eliminated.
- Athletics have been curtailed or abandoned and many localities now charge a fee for student participation.
- Students must be more careful walking to and from school because several communities have cut back bus service and school crossing guards have been laid off.

---

[1] Severe impact communities were defined by the Massachusetts Municipal Association survey as those communities that had to roll back their property tax levies by 10 per cent or more and that made significant personnel cuts.

Finally, municipalities delayed needed capital improvements. Cities and towns finance major construction, capital acquisitions, and major reconstruction through the issuance of bonds. In 1981, bond sales in Massachusetts came to a virtual halt. Massachusetts communities issued a total of sixty-four bonds in 1980; in 1981 they issued only six. The total dollar value decreased from 263 million in 1980 to 10 million in 1981. The postponement of much-needed capital expenditures and a continued delay in maintenance and replacement may well constitute a threat to public safety and economic growth [2, p. 10].

Year 2 Under Proposition 2½

After the first year of Proposition 2½, the Massachusetts property tax is still substantially above the national average. Specifically, Massachusetts cities and towns rely on the property tax for 44.5 per cent of their revenue, whereas the national average is 28.2 per cent [2, p. 13]. The second year of Proposition 2½ may be more severe for certain communities. Proposition 2½ requires municipalities whose tax levy is above 2½ per cent of full and fair cash value to reduce their levy by another 15 per cent until the 2½ level is reached. It has been estimated that in the second year of Proposition 2½ the City of Boston will have to reduce the tax levy by $66.1 million dollars, City of Cambridge by $10.1 million, City of Worcester by $10.7 million, and the City of Quincy by $8 million [4]. In addition, the communities of Chelsea, Fall River, Fitchburg, Lynn, New Bedford, Revere, and Springfield must again reduce their property taxes by the full 15 per cent required by the law. The effects of the second year will be concentrated on the older communities, in which over one-third of the state's population resides. Still, there has been no legislative action to reform the Massachusetts tax structure.

So called "corrective" legislation to Proposition 2½ was passed this year. The amendment to Proposition 2½ repeals the provision that allows a municipality's voters to override only at biennial elections with a two-thirds vote approval. The new provision allows the voters to override the tax limitation at any time as long as it pertains *only* to the current fiscal year's budget. A majority vote is necessary to increase the budget by 5 per cent instead of 2½ per cent if the locality's assessments are already at or under the 2½ limit. Communities over the 2½ limit, if the override passes, can now slow their tax losses by 7.5 per cent instead of the previously required 15 per cent. A two-thirds vote is still necessary if the locality wants to go beyond these limits. At the time of writing this article only the city of Cambridge obtained a two-thirds vote to completely override the tax limitations for the fiscal 1983 year. Another provision allows a majority of voters to waive the pre-2½ debt service from the 2½ per cent property tax limit. This last provision caused much confusion with the voters. After many towns had placed the debt exemption on the ballot, the Massachusetts Department of Revenue stated that debt override would hurt municipalities already at the 2½ limit. These communities would end up with a lower levy limit if they exempted debt service. Public officials then had to urge voters to vote against the proposal even though they had originally supported the override and had themselves put the issue before the voters. With this confusion in the mind of the voters and public officials and despite a recent poll indicating that Proposition 2½ would not now pass, no community, with the exception of Cambridge, has voted to override the tax limitations.

THE COLLECTIVE BARGAINING CLIMATE TODAY IN MASSACHUSETTS

Public sector unionization in the late 1960's and early 1970's burgeoned at unprecedented levels. To a large extent public union demands for higher wages were always met by public employers via tax increases. By the mid-1970's, fiscal stability of the major cities was threatened. The example taken from New York City, where 60,000 public sector jobs were lost between 1976 and 1978, was that public sector employees could no longer take employment security for granted.

Proposition 2½ is somewhat different from the fiscal crises that confronted New York. Of course, the issues of job security and preservation of wages are paramount for public employees and public managers. It must be remembered, however, that the fiscal crisis generated by Proposition 2½ is self-imposed. In other words, the tax-cutting referendum was imposed on the public sector not because of an inability to pay, but because of the public's unwillingness to pay any more taxes. This difference is affecting the climate of public collective bargaining negotiations in Massachusetts. Many public officials interpret the referendum as a mandate that shifts support from public unions to local managers and requires them to be more efficient. One public official stated:

> Any politician should realize that in light of Proposition 2½ that it is good politics now to be a good manager. If you fail as a manager, you're going to fail as a politician [5].

Indeed, state mediators have reported a noticeable change of attitude of employers at the bargaining table. For example, one public official stated that Proposition 2½ provides

> . . . an opportunity to make fundamental changes in the management of the town which has been needed and otherwise impossible, and a substantial opportunity to regain lost power [6].

To the extent that public managers believe a mandate exists shifting public support to them at the expense of public unions, bargaining will be more abrasive, and it will be that much more difficult to reach a negotiated settlement. This is especially true for police and fire fighter negotiations, where final and binding arbitration has been eliminated.

In California, as a result of Proposition 13, it was reported that unions became more militant and that public employee strikes, sickouts, and slowdowns were commonplace [7]. In Massachusetts this has not been the case; in fact, for the first year of Proposition 2½ the opposite has occurred. Although there were a number of job actions during the spring and summer of 1981, this fall the Labor Relations Commission had only one strike petition filed, involving the Boston teachers, and it did not result in an actual strike [8]. This is significant since there were over 200 teacher contracts that were not settled by the beginning of September 1981.

Once teachers in Boston decided not to strike, in the author's view, this lessened the possibility of teacher strikes throughout the state. The teachers in Boston had a no-layoff provision in their contract. Nonetheless, the city laid off more than 700 tenured teachers, in violation of the contract.

The union executive board recommended to the membership to vote "yes" to a strike. Support for the strike within the membership was thin. The core of support was from the 1000 or so laid-off, tenured and nontenured teachers. Black teachers, most of whom were protected from layoffs by federal court intervention, were against the strike. Teachers were also concerned with School Superintendent Spillane's threat that striking teachers would be dismissed. Finally, the membership had little support from the residents of Boston for a strike, the membership, believing that such action would be striking against the Boston electorate, who overwhelmingly voted for Proposition 2½.

The strike never materialized. Local teacher associations throughout the state may have similarly assessed the mood of the community and thus decided not to strike in the fall of 1981.

Relatively decent wages and job security were previously the norm for public sector employees. Now, through the fiscal constraints of Proposition 2½, difficult choices exist for both unions and management. The decision of whether to accept wage reductions in return for no layoffs is the predominant question. A survey of selected Massachusetts communities shows that no unions agreed to reopen their contracts to trade jobs for wage concessions [9].

When large numbers of layoffs were actually planned in spring 1982, unions attempted to avoid having to make these trade-off decisions. Unions this year have turned to the courts in unprecedented numbers, to enjoin the projected layoffs. Although the union occasionally succeeded, the majority of judges refused to enjoin the layoffs. When injunctions were issued they were later vacated. Legal protests over the layoffs also occurred at the Civil Service Commission and the Massachusetts Labor Relations Commission, with both agencies reporting unprecedented increases in caseload. Political tactics were also used to attempt to prevent the layoffs. In one city, a fire fighter's union publicly demanded that the mayor reopen a closed fire station by cutting patronage appointments. At the same time, the public, with informal union backing, took over the closed fire station. Unions also went to town meetings in an effort to restore service and personnel lost in the localities' budgets.

The foremost instance of job layoffs occurred in the City of Boston, over the layoffs of Boston teachers. The matter is now before the Supreme Judicial

Court, the highest Court in Massachusetts. Since 1975, the Boston Teachers' Union has had a job security clause in its collective bargaining agreements. In the 1980-1983 agreement, the school communitie and union agreed that for the first two years a no-layoff clause would be effective. The clause reads:

> Effective September 1, 1980 through June 30, 1982 any teacher or nurse with tenure or permanently appointed shall continue to be employed. This provision expires June 30, 1982.

The contract was fully funded by the school committee and city council for its first year. The school committee operated the 1981 fiscal year at a deficit of 26 million dollars. Accordingly, the schools were going to be closed in April. Only upon court order did the schools stay open the statutory 180 days. For the fiscal 1982 year the mayor told the school committee to live within its budget. To accomplish this the school committee had no choice but to violate the no-layoff clause and dismiss over 700 tenured teachers.

The battle then moved to the courts. The union argued that the contract, including the no-layoff clause, was already agreed upon and in fact the first year funds were appropriated. This contract should be no different than any other multiyear contract that requires legislative approval for the first year, but after which the city must live up to the remaining years, the union argued. (Indeed, an arbitrator agreed with the union that the city violated the contract.) The judge, however, saw the issue differently [10, 11]. The judge declared the job security provision of the contract was not specifically enforceable. Further, the determination of overall staffing levels is within the school committee's exclusive managerial prerogative, the judge ruled [10, 11]. Curiously, the trial court judge did not hold that all no-layoff clauses were illegal. Rather, they are unenforceable when there are insufficient funds. Because there were not sufficient funds in the 1982 budget, the trial judge did not order the city to appropriate additional funds. In other words, there was no obligation to live up to the remaining years of the contract with respect to the no-layoff provision.

The trial judge's ruling is significant in two ways:

- First, the legality of no-layoff clauses in the face of fiscal constraint is put into question in Massachusetts. The judge appeared to be saying that such clauses are enforceable only when sufficient funds exist. If this is true, it will offer little comfort to public employees in times of fiscal hardship. Moreover, unions will be unwilling to offer wage concessions in return for unenforceable job security clauses.
- Second, and more importantly, the validity of multiyear collective bargaining agreements is called into question. Under Massachusetts law, parties can enter collective bargaining agreements for three years. The law requires a public employer to submit the cost items of the contract to the appropriate legislative body during the first year. The judge's ruling appears to allow the employer to alter the terms of the collective bargaining

agreement during the second and third years. Thus, there may be no incentive to enter into multiyear agreements.

On May 12, 1982, the Massachusetts Supreme Judicial Court issued a unanimous decision on the appeal of the Boston Teachers Union's lawsuit. The Court held that collective bargaining agreements that call for salary increases for second and third years of a multiyear contract are enforceable. Specifically, the Court held that when the legislative body appropriates money for the first year of the contract, it has put its seal of approval on the cost items for the second and third year of the contract. Therefore, a public employer cannot renege on salary increases in the later years of a multiyear contract. The uncertainty over future wage increases has now been clarified in Massachusetts.

It appears, however, that the teachers' salary raises will be paid by laying off more teachers. Specifically, the Court did not enforce the job security clause that was contained in the parties' agreement. The Court ruled that no layoff clauses are valid only for time periods that do not span longer than one fiscal year. The job security provision in the parties' collective bargaining agreement was for the first two years of the agreement, and the layoffs occurred after the first year. The Court held that the job security provision intruded on areas that are reserved to the managerial prerogatives of the school committee and could not be bargained away. Therefore, the layoff of over 700 tenured teachers was not unlawful.

The Public Sector Collective Bargaining Law in Massachusetts gives public employees the right to organize and collectively negotiate [12]. The law requires that the employers and the representatives of employees to bargain in good faith over wages, hours, standards of productivity and performance, and any other terms and conditions of employment [6, 12]. The Massachusetts Labor Relations Commission has the primary responsibility for determining the scope of bargaining in the public sector and enforcing the legal requirement that the parties negotiate in good faith. As a result of Proposition 2½, the Labor Relations Commission experienced a dramatic increase in its unfair labor practice caseload.[2] Most Proposition 2½-related cases involved the bargaining relationship, specifically, the duty and extent of bargaining over layoffs.

The Labor Relations Commission has designated topics of negotiations as either mandatory, permissive, or illegal subjects of bargaining [13]. The public employer in Massachusetts can decide without bargaining over the decision whether to reduce the level of services and the size of its work force. The means of implementing any reduction in work force, whether through layoff, attrition, early retirement incentives, etc., is a mandatory subject of bargaining [14]. Other impact matters that are mandatorily negotiable include such topics as severance pay, continuation of health insurance coverage, and workload and safety of remaining unit members [15].

---

[2] The Labor Relations Commission caseload for the period of April to June 1981 increased by 40 per cent over the same period in 1980.

The commission in 1981 and 1982 had several cases in which the union alleged that a city or town implemented a reduction in force without bargaining to impasse on mandatory subjects [16]. In these cases the public employer raised as a defense the argument that a good faith impasse was not necessary before laying off personnel because of the fiscal constraints of Proposition 2½. One such case is New Bedford School Committee and the New Bedford Educator's Association [16]. The New Bedford School Committee decided to reduce the level of services of the city's school system. The association raised as bargaining topics:

1. teacher preparation time;
2. layoff of teachers who had failed to pay agency service fees;
3. placing of teachers slated to be laid off in long-term substitute positions;
4. elimination of extracurricular activities such as school swimming pool;
5. voluntary forfeiture of personnel time; and
6. a written recall provision.

Not all of these topics are within the scope of mandatory subjects of bargaining. Topics that were mandatorily negotiable were placing of teachers in long-term substitute positions instead of laying them off, and the written recall procedures. "Resolution of these issues," the commission determined, "could have resulted in the indefinite retention of all the terminated employees." [16, at 1480]

The commission found that the school committee laid off the teachers before reaching a good-faith impasse on these issues. In ordering reinstatement and backpay, the commission rejected the employer's defense that Proposition 2½ created an emergency situation beyond the city's control that required immediate action.

The commission stated:

> Finally, we note that Proposition 2½ was passed by voters in early November, 1980, and that the School Committee was on notice from that date onward that losses in excise tax revenues would result. Nothing, in the record indicates why, despite this knowledge the School Committee made no attempt until January 9, 1981 to inform the Association that a reduction in force during fiscal year 1981 might be necessary. We will not allow an employer to avoid its obligation to bargain to the point of resolution or impasse when it has established neither a commitment to fully maximize the time available for negotiations, nor the necessity of choosing a particular date for cutting off the negotiation process [16, at 1479].

Unions have also sought to broaden the scope of bargaining that presently exists under the law. Unions argue that a public employer's priorities are strictly financial: the public employer is attempting to save money as would a private employer. Because the unions contend that public managements' decisions are based less on public policy considerations and more on monetary issues, they argue they should be more directly involved in the decision of how and where to distribute public resources. Indeed, in one case the union demanded negotiations over whether the municipality should use free cash to reduce the number of fire fighter layoffs.[3] The commission, however, has not expanded the scope of bargaining on matters of resource allocation even though the decisions are based on economic considerations. In some instances, department heads have aligned with union leaders to seek higher appropriations from the governing bodies [18]. On the whole, however, public management has been unwilling under Proposition 2½ to relinquish the power to exercise its traditional managerial prerogatives.

Another significant issue that arose is whether the employer has the duty to bargain with the union over the revocation of civil service protections for municipal employees and other statutes that presently offer municipal employees specified benefits. A feature of Proposition 2½ is the provision that allows towns and cities the option of overriding certain state laws that regulate municipal business. State "optional laws," such as civil service and educational incentive pay provisions, were enacted by the state, and municipalities had the option of providing these benefits and protections to their employees. Now, under Proposition 2½, cities and towns are attempting to get out from under the provisions of these optional laws. The unions have argued to the commission that the towns must bargain before they set in action the revocation process, because these provisions directly affect the terms and conditions of employment of bargaining unit members. The public employers, on the other hand, argue that such decisions are to be decided by the electorate and because of their political nature they are not within the mandatory scope of bargaining. A commission hearing officer held that the town violated its duty to bargain in good faith by placing the matter on the town warrant before bargaining with the union. The case is now on appeal to the full commission [19].

Subcontracting issues have also been seen more frequently. Specifically, the Massachusetts municipal survey reported that subcontracting as a means to offer more services at a reduced cost has increased over the first year of Proposition 2½ [2, p. 11]. The Labor Relations Commission's precedent is that when the decision to subcontract will directly impact the bargaining unit, the decision is a mandatory topic of negotiation [20]. A novel variant of the subcontracting issue involves the use of volunteers. A commission hearing officer indicated that in his opinion the decision to use volunteers to perform work previously done by displaced teachers would be a matter that would first require bargaining [21]. His decision was not appealed to the commissioners.

Another bargaining matter decided by the commission involved the bargaining obligation concerning administrators who bumped into the teachers' bargaining unit [22]. The commission held that the school committee had to

---

[3] The commission dismissed, without issuing a formal complaint, the union's charge involving, among other things, its demand to bargain over allocation of the town's free cash reserves [17].

bargain with both the union representing teachers and administrators over the method of calculating seniority rights. Once an employee enters a new bargaining unit, his or her terms and conditions of employment are governed by the existing contract of the new unit — not by arrangements made with the employer outside the scope of that contract. In other words, it is within management's discretion to hire displaced administrators as teachers. Once the displaced administrator is put into the teachers' bargaining unit, the administrator's seniority is determined by provisions in the teachers' collective bargaining agreement.

Finally, complicated conflicts arose statewide between EEO, affirmative action requirements, and reductions in force. In Boston, teacher, police, and fire fighter unions have provisions in their contracts that call for layoffs to be scheduled according to seniority. The schools of Boston are still under the federal district court's jurisdiction because of a previous determination of unlawful racial discrimination. Judge Arthur Garrity, Jr. of the U. S. District Court, disregarded the seniority provision in the teachers' contract and ordered that 20 per cent of the teaching staff must remain minority. Similarly, Judge Andrew Caffrey, overrode the seniority provisions in police and fire contracts. He held that the police department could not reduce the percentage of minority police below 11.7 per cent and that the fire department must maintain a level of at least 14.7 per cent minority. The U.S. Court of Appeals recently affirmed the district court's orders, and the U.S. Supreme Court has agreed to hear arguments in this case.

Association of Worcester violated its statutory duty of fair representation by refusing to proceed to arbitration with a grievance of minority teachers who were laid off [23]. In the collective bargaining agreement there were provisions for layoff by reverse order of seniority within a discipline. Also in the agreement was a provision stating the intent that the affirmative action plan, already agreed upon, would apply to reductions in force. The association and the school committee agreed to interpret these provisions by laying off by seniority and agreeing that affirmative action guidelines would be used in case of a tie. As a result, nineteen minority teachers were laid off. The minority teachers filed a grievance, without the assistance of the association. The grievance was denied by the school committee. The association refused to proceed to arbitration with the minority teachers' claim. The minority teachers then went to court. The superior court held that the association's actions were arbitrary and discriminatory and the association had breached its duty of fair representation. The court ordered arbitration with the minority teachers participating. In particular, the superior court appeared to hold that the association had violated its duty by insisting on straight seniority as a means to implement layoffs. The threat of future duty of fair representation violations before the state's courts is now a serious concern for all public sector unions.

DISCUSSION

The patient has survived the first year of Proposition 2½'s tax-cut surgery. Layoffs and service cutbacks, although significant, were not as severe as first predicted, primarily because of increased state aid. The vote has been analyzed and described by many researchers. The message of the voters, however, remains elusive. What is certain is that Proposition 2½ has and will revolutionize the business of government.

The severe restriction on public spending has altered the relationship between public employers and public sector unions. The predominant question this year and in the foreseeable future for both public employees and public management is whether to trade jobs for wages. In 1981, because of the uncertain legal validity of job security provisions, uncertainty of the localities' financial conditions, and management's unwillingness to surrender responsibility in budget-making decisions, public union givebacks did not occur. It is too early to predict whether, in the second and third years of Proposition 2½, public unions will follow their private sector counterparts and negotiate wage concessions. The loss of final and binding interest arbitration will undoubtedly draw out contract negotiations for police and fire fighters. Finally, under the first year of Proposition 2½, the legal system, including the courts, the Labor Relations Commission, and the Civil Service Commission, were called on in unprecedented numbers to resolve public sector labor disputes.

CONCLUSION

The Labor Relations Commission anxiously awaits whether the second year of Proposition 2½, with deeper cuts expected, will bring more employee militancy and public sector strikes, as occurred in California after Proposition 13, and whether negotiations will be protracted and heated, causing the commission's caseload to again swell.

REFERENCES

1. H. Ladd and J. Boatright Wilson, Proposition 2½: Explaining The Vote, cited in *Impact: 2½,* Mass. Inst. Tech. Dept. of Urban Studies and Planning, May 1, 1981 (*Impact: 2½* is published twice a month and monitors the impacts of Proposition 2½).
2. *Report on the Impact of Proposition 2½,* Massachusetts Municipal Association Survey, January 1982.
3. Statements of Ann McHugh, Chairman of the Massachusetts Board of Education, reported in *Impact: 2½*, October 15, 1981.
4. Massachusetts Department of Revenue, as reported in *Boston Globe,* March 5, 1982.
5. Statement, Samuel Tyler, Associate Executive Director, Boston Municipal Research Bureau, *Boston Globe,* September 13, 1981.

6. Interview with Chip O'Hare, Town of Belmont Selectman, quoted in *Proposition 2½ and Public Sector Union Response — The Case of Belmont,* R. Black, Masters Thesis, M. I. T., Department of Urban Studies, 1981.

7. Tax Revolt Digest, *Public Employees Hurt by Proposition 13,* October 1979.

8. Massachusetts Labor Relations Commission, S. I. 140, 1981.

9. *Impact: 2½,* Massachusetts Institute Technology Department of Urban Studies and Planning, 1981 and 1982 (Survey of cities and towns reaction to Proposition 2½ is reported on a bi-weekly basis).

10. *Boston Teachers Union v. Boston School Committee,* Suffolk Superior Court, CA. 48184, June 1981.

11. *Boston Teachers Union v. City of Boston,* Suffolk Superior Court C. A. 48228, June 1981.

12. Massachusetts General Laws, Chapter 150E (G. L. ch. 150E).

13. *Town of Danvers,* 3 Massachusetts Labor Cases (MLC) 1559, 1977.

14. *Newton School Committee,* 5 MLC 1016, 1978.

15. *City of Boston,* 8 MLC 1419, 1981.

16. *New Bedford School Committee,* 8 MLC 1472, 1981; *City of Malden,* 8 MLC 1620, 1981.

17. *Town of Belmont,* MUP-4174, March 1981.

18. *Impact: 2½,* Survey of Town of Burlington, March 1, 1982.

19. *Town of South Hadley,* 8 MLC 1609, Hearing Officer, 1981.

20. *City of Boston,* 7 MLC 1975, 1981.

21. *Town of Georgetown,* 8 MLC 1031, Hearing Officer, 1981.

22. *Saugus School Committee,* 7 MLC 1849, 1981; *Chelmsford School Administrators Association,* 8 MLC 1515, 1981.

23. *Concerned Minority Educators of Worcester et al. v. Worcester School Committee, et al.,* Worcester County Superior Court, C. A. 81-20388, July 1981.

Discussion Questions

1. How realistic do you judge Massachusetts' 2½% property tax limit to be under varying conditions of the nation's economy?

2. Compare the effect of the working class of the Massachusetts' original tax laws versus Proposition 2½.

3. How do you account for the shift in attitude on the part of public managers after passage of Proposition 2½? Do you believe it will continue?

PART IV
FEDERAL EMPLOYEES

The Tennessee Valley Authority collective bargaining relationship with its employees is frequently held up as a paradigm of public sector unionism. Brookshire describes TVA as "the first public employer in this country to engage in meaningful collective bargaining with unions of its blue-collar, white-collar, and professional employees, beginning in the 1930's." Brookshire attributes the success of the TVA experience to its bargaining structure, which is described in some detail in the paper. He also describes an "outstanding weakness of centralized bargaining [that] has . . . surfaced in the TVA experience and should be considered by others."

The second chapter in this part describes a study made to determine whether workers in the public and the private sector are motivated to join unions for the same or for different reasons. Imundo also examined government workers' attitudes toward their own right to strike and received some interesting responses, which are thought-provoking, to say the least. Sulzner reviewed twenty federal bargaining units to examine the impact of labor-management cooperation committees on personnel policies and practices.

The reader is left to ponder the implications for the nation in the future, if workers in service occupations on the federal level, such as air-traffic controllers, exercise a right to strike.

CHAPTER 14

Bargaining Structure in the Public Sector: The TVA "Model"

MICHAEL L. BROOKSHIRE

Bargaining structure may be defined as the organization of parties for collective bargaining and the location(s) of decision-making power within these organizations. In the private sector, the pronounced trend in union structures over the last several decades has certainly been the centralization of these structures, both in the sense that negotiators have come to speak for larger groups and that decision-making power has flowed away from rank-and-file union members. This centralization has been vertical and horizontal. Decision-making power has moved upward from local union levels to national union levels, and, at the same time, separate unions have come together horizontally to coordinate their bargaining at local, intermediate, and national union levels.

Within the past few years, bargainers in government have given increased attention to structure, especially on the union side, because of the fragmented structures and relatively decentralized bargaining that have characterized the public sector. The groundwork for fragmentation was laid prior to Executive Order 10988 and similar orders and statutes dealing with the recognition and bargaining privileges of unions in state and local governments. Since recognition did not entail meaningful bargaining privileges, many government agencies were inclined to recognize bargaining agents for units that were small, potentially overlapping with other units, and otherwise inappropriate. Few agencies anticipated the problems that occurred after the early sixties when they faced a proliferation of bargaining units, often fashioned along illogical lines. Of course, the 10988 approach actually intensified the problem of dealing with a multitude of bargaining agents, as a union could consult with management after establishing a meager following of only 10 per cent of the members of a unit.

Adding to the problem was the fact that the scores, and even hundreds, of bargaining agents that faced government agencies showed little propensity to coordinate their bargaining, and thus centralize their own structure, in contrast to the activities of many unions in the private sector. Public employers quickly realized the sheer inefficiency and high cost in management resources of separate dealings with a multiplicity of bargaining agents. Morale and productivity problems also surfaced when negotiated benefits varied significantly among work groups in the same governmental jurisdiction or department. Furthermore, government employers faced the whipsawing action and high wage inflation produced when each union attempts to improve upon the economic package gained by the last union that has reached a settlement with a common employer.

The response in the late sixties by New York City and by the State of New York was indicative of the response by many cities and states that had suffered the difficulties of fragmented bargaining. The city and state moved toward centralized bargaining by fashioning broader bargaining units. Agencies in charge of appropriate unit determination were directed, in effect, to give significant weight to the efficiency advantages of larger units, and affirmative actions were taken to consolidate existing units.[1] In Michigan, Pennsylvania, New Jersey, Kansas, and other states, the problem of overfragmentation became an important consideration as appropriate unit determinations were made. Hawaii went even further in creating thirteen statewide units for its employees by statute, thereby precluding decentralized bargaining [2].

The federal response began with Executive Order 11491 of 1969, which mandated exclusive recognition as the only form of recognition in the federal government. However, decentralized bargaining had already been introduced at the federal level. By the mid-seventies, the Department of Defense had a duty to bargain in almost 2,000 units. A 1974 survey of 52 federal agencies, including the Department of Defense, revealed that 3,483 exclusive recognitions had been granted by these agencies and that the average exclusive bargaining unit contained 327 employees [3]. Executive Order 11838 of 1975

---

[1] See the brief discussion of the activities of the New York City Office of Collective Bargaining and of the Public Employee Relations Board under the Taylor Law of New York State by E. Rock [1].

was a further federal response to fragmented bargaining, for a primary aim of the order is to facilitate the voluntary consolidation of units and to promote elections designed to consolidate units. Yet, considerable debate exists over whether the order will accomplish significant defragmentation at the federal level [4].

With concern for the structural aspects of union-management relations reaching a new peak in the public sector, it is instructive to look at the experience of the Tennessee Valley Authority with bargaining structure. TVA was the first public employer in this country to engage in meaningful collective bargaining with unions of its blue-collar, white-collar, and professional employees, beginning in the 1930's. Many observers have labelled union-management relations at TVA the model for the public sector, and the TVA experience with collective bargaining was studied by the first "Hoover Commission" on federal personnel policies, the commission reviewing the federal experience under Executive Order 10988, the U.S. Postal Service and its unions, the New York State Public Employee Relations Board, the California State Personnel Board, Canada's Preparatory Committees on Collective Bargaining in the Public Service, and many other government agencies and U.S. municipalities.

Much of the efficacy of the TVA experience is attributable to the structure of bargaining at TVA, on the union side and on the management side. In particular, the TVA approach to the determination of bargaining units, to the centralization of union structures, and to management's organization for negotiations and contract administration offers much of value to public sector bargainers elsewhere. Moreover, the outstanding weakness of centralized bargaining has also surfaced in the TVA experience and should be considered by others.

TVA and Trades and Labor Unions

The Tennessee Valley Authority was created by a May 1933 Act of Congress as a government corporation charged with electricity generation and flood control for the Tennessee River Valley. In general, it was directed to foster the development of an entire region. TVA was removed from civil service regulations by the 1933 Act, so that the agency would have great discretion in formulating personnel and labor relations policies. The agency was directed to pay trades and labor employees not less than the prevailing wage for similar work in the vicinity, and due regard was to be given to negotiated labor agreements in the multistate "vicinity" as prevailing rates were determined. A final, important labor provision of the Act designated the Secretary of Labor as the final arbiter of disputes over what constituted prevailing wages [5].

These labor provisions became important when the TVA Board of Directors made an early decision that TVA should perform its own construction and other work, instead of contracting out the work. A large work force would therefore emerge under the agency's direct control. The total work force would peak at almost 30,000 during World War II, decline substantially, and climb again above the 20,000 level in the 1970's.

The discretion given TVA in personnel matters also became important because of the relatively liberal attitudes toward labor unions exhibited by top TVA management. In consonance with the New Deal spirit that had created the agency and implicitly favored unions through the labor provisions of the TVA Act, management chose not to interfere with the AFL craft unions that had begun almost immediately to organize TVA's trades and labor employees. Yet, management wished to develop a formal statement of labor relations policy and entered a two-year period of decision making and consultation with employee groups.

This process culminated with the issuance in 1935 of the *Employee Relationship Policy* (ERP). The ERP gave all employees the right to form and participate in labor organizations, without fear of coercion or discrimination on the part of management. It committed the agency to collective bargaining with recognized employee representatives over annual revisions in wages, and it provided employees with a grievance procedure. The ERP also resolved some important problems of unit determination and union structure.

As the ERP was being developed, sentiment existed in the Personnel Department for accepting a craft unit structure for trades and labor employees. The AFL craft unions were working out such a structure according to jurisdictional precedent. A few agency officials also proposed that the craft structure be supplemented by an overall organization to represent craft workers in collective bargaining. Some members of management felt quite strongly that AFL unions should not be recognized as bargaining agents because nonemployees should not be able to speak for TVA's workers in dealings with management. A more serious controversy existed over "minority rights". The chairman of the TVA Board of Directors, and others, wished to allow all representatives of employees in bargaining units to confer with management, even if the representatives did not speak for a majority of employees in a unit.

With significant help from outside consultants, management reached a decision on these issues in the ERP. The "majority rule" principle was adopted, as a designee of a majority of any "professional group, or craft, or other appropriate unit" was given the exclusive right to represent all employees in that unit [6]. Any organization or person, including an AFL union, could represent employees. Furthermore, the reference to craft units represented an endorsement of the organization of blue-collar employees along craft lines, and fourteen AFL unions were quickly recognized to represent agency-wide craft units.

The first wage conference was held in 1935, with various locals of the recognized AFL unions submitting wage proposals based on their conception of prevailing wages. Management had already considered the inefficiency of separate bargaining with over a score of unions, and it recoiled at the independent demands of several locals of the same craft union. Therefore, TVA took the position that a consolidated union organization for bargaining would facilitate the development of meaningful collective bargaining, and it reiterated its desire for a horizontal union centralization during the second wage conferences of 1936.

The response of the fourteen AFL-affiliated craft unions was to form the Tennessee Valley Trades and Labor Council in 1937. A president, vice president, and secretary were elected for the Council, and an Executive Board was constituted of one international union representative from each of the affiliated organizations. The Council presented itself to TVA as the overall bargaining agent for trades and labor employees, and management accepted the structural scheme without hesitation.

Of course, management had wanted to face a single entity in negotiations primarily for efficiency reasons. Evidence also exists that some members of management foresaw, and wished to avoid, the whipsawing and wage inflation that may result from separate bargaining with craft unions.

Significantly, the craft unions did not resist TVA's pressure for a consolidated bargaining structure, developing their centralized organization for bargaining rather quickly. In the depressed economy of the 1930's, the various craft unions were willing to form an alliance and speak with one voice. Prosperity would have led the stronger local unions in the TVA area to demand separate bargaining. Furthermore, the national craft unions wished to cooperate with TVA in building a viable bargaining relationship, for the establishment of collective bargaining at TVA was an inroad to the organization of craft workers in the South generally.

The AFL, itself, had strongly lobbied for the creation of TVA and anticipated the establishment of similar agencies throughout the country. By quickly developing a stable system of union-management relations at TVA, the AFL hoped to lay the groundwork for its affiliate unions to organize any new federal agencies and government workers in general. One indication of the federation's support for its unions at TVA was the fact that the Trades and Labor Council was allowed to exist as a multistate superstructure and, through the affiliate unions, to organize workers in the seven states of TVA operations. The power of AFL federations in each of these states to coordinate organizational activity was largely usurped.

The formation of the Trades and Labor Council was a prerequisite for top management's decision to authorize the negotiation of a written labor agreement. In 1940, after lengthy negotiations, TVA signed a general agreement with the Council, rather than with the individual unions.

Concentration of decision-making power in the Council *vis-a-vis* the fifteen (and later sixteen) craft unions was consummated.

The general agreement was without parallel in the public sector. It provided for annual wage negotiations between TVA and the Council to be based on prevailing wage data, and it allowed fringe benefits and work rules to be included in the scope of bargaining. Management refused the Council's demand for a union shop provision, but language encouraging union membership was included in the agreement. The Council could take a grievance brought by any member union to binding arbitration, and the Council could send any bargaining impasse over prevailing wages to the Secretary of Labor for final resolution.

Meaningful bargaining would occur year after year over wages, benefits, and terms of employment. Each international union representative utilized input from local union delegates during negotiations and led the Council's deliberations over wage rates particular to his craft. Significant power lay with each international representative, for the general agreement disallowed membership referenda over contract terms. Yet, more power attached to the international representatives collectively, for the Council's executive board took positions on the subject matter of bargaining in concert, participated in the written agreement as a single entity, and made decisions on impasse and grievance appeals together. Decision-making power was truly centralized.

TVA and Unions of Salary Policy Employees

TVA's experience with unions of its white-collar and professional employees (labelled salary policy employees) is even more interesting because, in its dealings with these unions, TVA was breaking ground for both the public and private sectors. As management formulated the ERP and demonstrated its willingness to deal with AFL craft unions, various unions aimed organizational efforts at salary policy employees. The American Federation of Government Employees (AFGE), an AFL affiliate, began to organize office employees in TVA's Knoxville headquarters as early as 1934 and quickly established several loosely-connected locals throughout the Tennessee Valley. The National Federation of Federal Employees (NFFE) also established a few locals of white-collar employees.

After its establishment in 1935, the CIO set up the United Federal Workers of America (UFWA), and this union quickly replaced the AFGE as the primary organizer of TVA's white-collar workers. These organizational efforts also spurred engineers and subprofessional technicians throughout the valley to form their own local associations. Members of these associations wished to avoid representation by any of the unions competing for other salary policy employees.

Some of the competing groups unrealistically demanded recognition to bargain for all salary policy employees, who ranged from accountants and engineers to guards and janitors. Other groups requested recognition to bargain for employees of particular departments, one containing as few as fourteen workers. The potential for allowing the creation of a plethora of bargaining units, with overlapping boundaries, became evident to management. The ERP called for exclusive representation rights for designees of a professional group, craft, or "other appropriate unit". But management had little precedent for determining appropriate units of white-collar and professional workers. Therefore, the TVA response to union demands for recognition was, until the early 1940's, simply to deny recognition to any of the competing unions who claimed majority support among various groups of employees.

In 1942, the TVA personnel department elaborated TVA's position on appropriate bargaining units for salary policy employees. No organization would be recognized if its jurisdictional boundaries with already existing organizations were unclear. The personnel department would assume a quasi-judicial role in resolving appropriate unit issues and would give great weight to desires of employees. It would also consider two other factors in determining bargaining units: the suitability of proposed units for collective bargaining and any unit determination precedents established by the National Labor Relations Board.

By the end of 1942, two organizations had proven their majority status in units that TVA found appropriate according to its stated guidelines, and the organizations were recognized as bargaining agents. The Public Safety Service Employees' Union had proposed to represent a valleywide unit of all TVA guards, and the American Federation of Office Employees had likewise proposed a single, valleywide unit of office employees. TVA approved this scheme of dividing units along occupational lines and having each unit extend over all TVA locations, for such a plan meant that bargaining units would neither overlap nor proliferate. Other organizations, including associations of professional employees, quickly began to consolidate locals that were strung across the valley, so that a valleywide unit could be proposed. Seven organizations were recognized by the end of 1943 to represent valleywide, nonoverlapping units; the units encompassed virtually all salary policy employees who were not considered to be closely connected with management.

Each organization had presented evidence of majority support in its proposed unit and, in one case, the personnel department had held a representational election, allowing employees to choose between two competing unions. Two units contained both professional and nonprofessional employees, in consonance with the desires of the employees involved. Professional chemists and chemical engineers located at TVA's Muscle Shoals, Alabama, operations desired not to be included in a unit with nonprofessionals, and their wishes were respected (see Table 1).

Even as the bargaining units were being established, management was taking action to drive the various employee organizations into a single, centralized

Table 1. The Original Bargaining Agents and Bargaining Units for
Salary Policy Employees

Public Safety Service Employees' Union (PSSEU),[a] AFL-affiliate: to bargain for employees in the Public Safety Service, e.g., guards.

American Federation of Office Employees (AFOE),[b] AFL-affiliate: to bargain for subprofessional and professional employees whose duties are closely identified with office operations and related specialized and general clerical functions, such as accounting, planning, editorial, statistical, office procedural, and secretarial.

Chemical Workers' Union (CWU), AFL-affiliate: to bargain for subprofessional technicians involved in chemical and chemical engineering activities.[c]

Hotel and Restaurant Employees' International Alliance (HREIA), AFL-affiliate: to bargain for employees engaged in the preparation and serving of food at TVA's projects.[c]

Building Service Employees' International Union (BSEIU), AFL-affiliate: to bargain for employees engaged primarily in cleaning and servicing of TVA-operated buildings.

TVA Association of Professional Chemists and Chemical Engineers (TVAAPCChE), independent organization of TVA employees: to bargain for professional employees engaged in chemical, chemical engineering, ceramic, and metallurgical work.

TVA Engineers Association (TVAEA), independent organization of TVA employees: to bargain for subprofessional and professional employees engaged in engineering, geological, architectural, and closely related activities; but excluding those involved in chemical, ceramic, and metallurgical work.

---

[a] In 1962, the PSSEU would become Directly Affiliated Local Union #3033 of the AFL-CIO.

[b] The AFOE at TVA would help form the Office Employees International Union in 1945. This union would later become the Office and Professional Employees International Union (OPEIU) and would continue to represent subprofessionals and professionals at TVA.

[c] Employees in these units would later be absorbed into units represented by the TVAEA and by the Office Employees' Union, respectively, so that by the 1950's and thereafter, salary policy employees would be divided into only five bargaining units.

Source: Adapted from the TVA Administrative Code, III Union Relations, Recognition, November 29, 1943.

structure comparable to the Trades and Labor Council. Each of the employee organizations was granted a very limited form of recognition—to bargain over matters affecting employees in their unit only. Since the classification system and salary schedule, the hours of work, and most important personnel policies affected all salary policy employees, TVA refused to bargain with any one of the recognized groups on these matters. The implication was that a meaningful scope of bargaining depended upon a centralized bargaining structure on the union side. Furthermore, management openly expressed its desire for all of the salary policy employee organizations to come together.

In response, the five AFL affiliates formed a council, and the council was recognized to bargain for the combined memberships. Yet, this recognition was of the same, limited nature. TVA wanted the two independent organizations included in a single, overall structure. Therefore, the seven organizations reluctantly formed a Salary Policy Employee Panel in 1943. Their combination might be termed a "shotgun wedding", for the organizations represented heterogeneous groups with disparate backgrounds and interests. The Panel did not elect common officers, but rather chose for years to speak with the three voices of the Council of AFL affiliates, the independent TVAAPCChE, and the independent TVAEA. Recognition to bargain over matters affecting all salary policy employees was, however, granted to the Panel as an entity, and cooperation among its member organizations became a necessity.

Despite its recognition to bargain for all salary policy employees, the Panel was frustrated in its attempts to engage in meaningful bargaining during the 1940's. TVA chose to tie salaries and fringe benefits of salary policy employees to those of comparable employees in the classified federal service. Employees represented by the Panel did not receive increases in compensation unless and until Congress increased pay or benefits for federal employees covered by the civil service.

In 1950, the Panel did persuade TVA to sign a written agreement, but the articles of agreement contained general principles of agreement only and did not broaden the scope of bargaining. A profound change in the relationship occurred the succeeding year, when TVA agreed to the Panel's demand that compensation for salary policy employees no longer be tied to prevailing federal practice. Instead, TVA agreed to begin basing wages and benefits on prevailing practice in the multistate area of TVA operations. Just as did the Trades and Labor Council, the Salary Policy Employee Panel would participate in the prevailing wage determination process and engage in meaningful bargaining over the exact wage and benefit levels to be extracted from the ranges provided by prevailing practice data.

The 1951 broadening of bargaining scope exacerbated the other serious problem that had been facing the Panel—the discomfort of the member organizations with the structure that had been forced upon them. Since wage bargaining was finally to become meaningful, the two independent organizations representing professionals took a close look at the situation of their members *vis-a-vis* the nonprofessionals represented by the Council of AFL affiliates. A single salary schedule covered all of the salary policy employees, and some of the salary grades contained both top-level subprofessional positions and entry-level professional positions. If the salary levels for these grades were to be based on some average developed from a prevailing wage survey of subprofessional and professional positions, then the prevailing wage determination process would pull down the salaries of professionals and pull up the salaries of nonprofessionals. Further, the prevailing practice survey was confined to southern states, whereas the independent organizations claimed that the salaries of professionals should be based on national surveys.

Thus, the TVAAPCChE and TVAEA demanded that they be able to bargain separately over separate salary schedules for professionals. They asked that the Panel be voided as an entity. Although the Council of AFL affiliates had no strong desire to continue in a centralized structure with the independent groups, it did ask for the continuance of a single salary schedule.

TVA kept the Panel intact by refusing to bargain with any entity but the Panel as originally constituted. Since the single salary schedule was maintained for several years, the independent groups were forced to participate in a structure and a salary-determination process that they felt worked to the disadvantage of their members. Panel members worked together in annual wage negotiations with great difficulty. The TVAAPCChE openly displayed its displeasure with the centralized union structure and, on occasion, simply refused to work with the other groups.

By the mid-fifties, management had agreed to begin a joint study of multiple-schedule salary plans. The employee groups pushed for a plan that divided salary schedules according to union jurisdiction; they envisioned separate bargaining by each union over its own salary schedule and an effective dissolution of the Panel. When management accepted the principle of multiple schedules, it successfully insisted upon its own alternative scheme of dividing the salary schedules according to related work.

Final agreement was reached on the management proposal for a five-schedule plan in 1957. Salary schedule A included classes of positions involving administrative, management-service functions, such as accounting; schedule B covered clerical positions; schedule C encompassed a hodgepodge of building service, safety service, printing, and other functions; schedule D involved professional engineering and scientific functions; and schedule E included subprofessional, technical positions. Management insisted that the Panel bargain as an entity over all salaries and over all other matters; but, in effect, the various employee organizations were able to lead the Panel's deliberations over the salary schedules relating to their members. The Office and Professional Employees' Union, through the Council of AFL affiliates, would lead bargaining over schedules A and B; the Council would bargain for all of the three AFL affiliates representing workers covered by schedule C; both independent groups would be concerned with schedule D, and the TVAEA would direct the Panel's actions concerning schedule E.

The multiple-schedule plan alleviated the major source of tension among Panel members and stimulated the rapid development of the Panel as an effective vehicle for collective bargaining. Significant membership gains were made by the five employee organizations, such that nearly 90 per cent of eligible salary policy employees would become union members. The larger organizations developed good professional staffs. The Panel and its member organizations also became increasingly aggressive in negotiations and in processing grievances toward binding arbitration.

In 1964, the Panel succeeded in obtaining management's agreement to a comprehensive *Articles of Agreement and Supplementary Agreements,* consisting of seven general articles and nineteen supplementary agreements on specific subject matter. A wide variety of topics, including classification, work scheduling, pay, selection, tenure, union security, and grievances, was covered in great detail. Furthermore, procedures for resolving bargaining impasses were included in the agreement; these procedures would later be revised so that final-offer arbitration would be specified for salary disputes.

Resolution of one remaining problem was necessary for the final solidification of the Panel structure. By the early sixties, the unions of guards and of building service employees had come to feel dominated by the significantly larger Office and Professional Employees' Union. The Council of AFL affiliates represented all three groups in leading negotiations over the hodgepodge salary schedule C and in grievance handling, and the two small unions claimed that the larger organization dominated the actions of the Council.

TVA and the Panel resolved this structural problem in 1966. Two additional salary schedules, for guards and for building service employees, were created so that the two smaller unions could lead negotiations over the salaries of their members. The Council of AFL affiliates was disbanded, and the three AFL affiliated unions assumed an independent status on the five-member Salary Policy Employee Panel. Also, the member organizations elected a common secretary to coordinate their activities—an act of cooperation and solidarity that had been performed by the Trades and Labor Council in 1937.

The five salary policy employee organizations have now grown quite comfortable with the centralized structure that was originally forced upon them by management. Each organization takes the lead in analyzing prevailing salary data and in negotiating on the salaries of those it represents. Yet, most benefits and negotiated policies apply uniformly to all salary policy employees. The employee groups cooperate closely and effectively in preparing for, and engaging in, bargaining over these topics, and the Panel's secretary coordinates these activities. Negotiators sitting on the Panel speak with authority, for the labor contract prohibits membership ratification of contract terms. Thus, management faces a structure that is stable and deals with negotiators who have the responsibility of binding their constituents.

Moreover, the Panel structure allows adequate union democracy, despite the fact that salary policy employees cannot vote to ratify agreements made by their representatives. Election controls provide employees with sufficient influence over their negotiators sitting on the Panel. For the three AFL unions, decision-making power in negotiations resides with union officers and executive bodies elected by the valleywide membership, and with appointees of these elected officials. Representatives from the international unions, beyond the direct control of TVA employees, have little or no power in the union-management relationship. Of course, the two independent organizations are exclusively responsible to the membership below, as they have no national organization or federation attempting to exert control from above. Thus, salary policy employees have felt able to control the positions of their negotiators through the device of frequent elections and have not complained that centralized bargaining has emasculated union democracy.

Current Reinforcements

Management has never ceased its efforts to reinforce centralized bargaining on the union side, despite the voluntary acceptance of centralization that is increasingly evident among Council and Panel members. TVA has continued to imply that any union leaving the Council or Panel would either not be recognized as a bargaining agent or would not be allowed to participate in a meaningful scope of bargaining. In the sixties and seventies, some unions challenged TVA, stating that Executive Orders 10988 and 11491 applied to the agency. The orders forced recognition of unions with majority support in a unit and mandated some minimum in bargaining scope.

TVA replied that the two presidential orders did not apply to TVA, even though the orders had actually excluded only TVA's existing labor contracts that were already in effect. To remove any doubt, however, TVA succeeded in obtaining a special Executive Order 11901 of 1976, removing the Authority from the labor-management framework applicable to virtually all other federal agencies. Clearly, TVA can now make good its threat to discriminate against any employee organization leaving either one of the two centralized structures.

Furthermore, TVA has continued to insist on provisions in its labor contracts that reinforce the concentration of power in the Council and Panel *vis-a-vis* their member unions. The labor contracts are with the Council and the Panel, not with individual unions. The Council and Panel decide as single entities to take grievances to binding arbitration and to send wage and salary disputes to arbitration. This is true even though the grievance or wage issue may involve only one of the member unions and not the general constituency of the Council or Panel.

Good Results

Management has maintained its preoccupation with union structure because of the good results that it feels have accrued from centralized bargaining. A major advantage of union centralization to management has been efficiency. TVA now bargains over two contracts covering 14,000 trades and labor employees (in 1974, contracts for construction employees and operating and maintenance employees were separated). The alternative would be separate bargaining for sixteen contracts covering craft units, some with less than 100 members. TVA is concerned with only one contract covering 6,000 salary policy employees, rather than with five contracts, a few dealing with less than 300 employees. Management representatives are involved in only one intensive period of wage negotiations annually for each of the two relationships, rather than twenty-one negotiating sessions with the individual unions of the Council and Panel.

Management also finds it easier to train supervisors in contract administration and to transfer supervisors when only three contracts cover all employees. Uniform, negotiated results from centralized bargaining have been found to obviate morale problems that may result when workers compare disparate results achieved by their respective unions. Furthermore, management has realized what it desired the most from the centralized union structures— responsibility. The union negotiators are somewhat removed from direct pressure and observation by the rank-and-file. They can move responsibly toward an agreement that is reasonable in social terms and that is not accomplished through strike threats or illegal slowdowns or work stoppages.

Of course, advantages from centralization have also accrued to the unions involved. They combine their strength and their staff support for bargaining. Uniform results on most of the subject matter of bargaining does not make some negotiators appear inept relative to others. At the same time, wage increases need not be uniform, and each union has the ability to lead the Council or Panel in bargaining over the wages or salaries of its members.

Yet, the key test of centralized bargaining at TVA lies in its social results. The record of wage settlements and the strike record at TVA can be examined to see whether the end products and the process of bargaining with centralized union structures in government are reasonable in social terms.

Has the centralization of unions at TVA boosted the collective power of the employee groups to obtain inflationary wage settlements? Or has centralized bargaining mediated against socially damaging wage settlements by eliminating the whipsawing demands of unions that face a common employer in decentralized bargaining? Table 2 presents the record of annual percentage increases in wages and salaries negotiated by the Trades and Labor Council and by the Salary Policy Employee Panel. Although wage comparisons are fraught with many difficulties, a few comparisons of TVA wage increases and wage increases elsewhere may be instructive.

Wage inflation in the building trades has been an acute social problem for the last decade and, therefore, the record of wage increases for the Trades and Labor Council versus building trades generally is particularly important. From 1960 to 1973, the average annual increase in hourly wages for a composite of U.S. building trades was 6.05 per cent [7]. The comparable annual average negotiated by the Trades and Labor Council was 5.58 per cent. The Bureau of Labor Statistics also publishes average annual increases in salaries for a composite of professional, administrative, technical, and clerical positions across the nation. From 1961 to 1975, annual increases for this group averaged 5.03 per cent [8]. Annual increases negotiated by the Salary Policy Employee Panel averaged only a slightly higher 5.40 per cent. The available evidence indicates that the wage and salary results of centralized bargaining have been reasonable in social terms.

Table 2. Average Wage and Salary Increases Negotiated Annually for
Employees Represented by the Trades and Labor Council and by the
Salary Policy Employee Panel

Year	Average wage increase negotiated by trades and labor council (per cent)	Average salary increase negotiated by salary policy employee panel (per cent)
1940	0.4	not available
1941	4.6	not available
1942	2.9	not available
1943	3.0	not available
1944	3.8	not available
1945	2.5	14.7
1946	5.3	14.5
1947	14.8	no increase
1948	10.5	flat $330
1949	12.2	average $140
1950	3.0	no increase
1951	10.5	11.6
1952	5.7	2.6
1953	5.3	2.9
1954	4.7	3.1
1955	3.3	2.6
1956	4.6	4.8
1957	5.4	5.2
1958	4.9	5.1
1959	4.7	4.5
1960	4.4	4.5
1961	4.3	3.5
1962	3.8	3.0
1963	3.6	4.2
1964	3.1	2.9
1965	3.0	2.9
1966	3.7	3.8
1967	3.9	6.7
1968	5.2	5.2
1969	6.5	5.7
1970	8.0	7.2
1971	10.1	6.2
1972	7.9	6.2
1973	5.1	5.3
1974	5.7	7.0
1975	8.9	9.3

Source: Adapted from personnel correspondence files of the Tennessee Valley Authority.

Work stoppages in the federal government have not appeared to be a severe problem since detailed reporting of government strikes began in the late 1960's; only two or three strikes have been reported at the federal level per year. However, strikes by state and local government employees, mostly illegal, have escalated to an alarming level since the early sixties. In 1968, man-days idle from government strikes were 5.2 per cent of man-days idle from all U.S. strikes. The comparable figures for 1972 and 1973 were also high—4.7 per cent and 8.2 per cent, respectively [7, pp. 407-410].

In the four decades of TVA's relationship with unions of trades and labor workers, only three strikes have occurred; a few other work stoppages did occur but were not designated by TVA as strikes. Each of the three strikes involved jurisdictional disputes between craft unions, rather than bargaining impasses. This is a low incidence of strikes in comparison to the public sector generally and especially in comparison to the level of strike activity for building trades unions in either the public or private sectors. Salary policy employees have never been involved in a work stoppage. Furthermore, the parties to bargaining at TVA have generally resolved impasses on their own. Very few wage disputes have been submitted by the Council to the U.S. Secretary of Labor, and the Panel has not yet used the final-offer arbitration machinery available for salary disputes. Centralized union structures at TVA have contributed greatly to a stable bargaining process and to the minimization of strikes that entail both private and social costs.

The Achilles Heel

In contrast to the overall good performance of the centralized union structures at TVA, the outstanding potential weakness of centralized structures has recently emerged in TVA's experience with the Trades and Labor Council. Members of local unions represented by the Council cannot vote in a referendum to ratify or reject the agreements made by the union negotiators on the Council. Neither do the rank-and-file union members have effective election controls over those who represent them in negotiations and in other aspects of the union-management relationship.

Many trades and labor employees of TVA belong to local unions that contain non-TVA employees. Thus, the local union officers and delegates to TVA wage negotiations may not be the majority choice of TVA employees in the craft locals. These locally elected officials only have an advisory role in negotiations anyway. The international union representative, sitting on the Executive Board of the Council, has the real decision-making power. Even then, the international representative can only appeal wage disputes if the whole Council agrees and can only influence nonwage issues by interacting with the other international union representatives on the Council. The election control over negotiators is clearly a weak and indirect one for the rank-and-file.

Their primary leverage is through their votes for the international union officers who appoint representatives to the Trades and Labor Council.

Prior to 1974, the locally elected officials could at least attempt to keep the international representatives in touch with rank-amd-file desires through their advisory role in negotiations, and the local union officers possessed some authority in grievance adjustment. However, the 1974 negotiations between TVA and the international representatives dominating the Council resulted in a further erosion of democracy in union decision making. Contract changes removed the duty of international representatives to invite local union delegates to the annual negotiations. The international representatives also assumed the authority, formerly exercised by local union officials, of day-to-day dealings with management over such matters as work assignment, the hiring of employees at new work locations, recall of workers, and grievance adjustment beyond the second step.

Many rank-and-file union members had already voiced concern over their inability to control the centralized union structure. With the new contract changes, rank-and-file frustrations with the Council became exceedingly visible. A number of operating and maintenance employees, for example, hired a law firm to represent their complaints to TVA. These workers claimed that the majority of operating and maintenance employees desired TVA to hold an election, so that they might withdraw support of the Trades and Labor Council as their representative. Alternatively, they requested that serious reforms be made to improve democratic controls within the centralized union structure. The group threatened to press its complaints in federal court, or push for an election under Executive Order 11491, if TVA refused to take action.

TVA did decline to act on the employees' complaints. Thereupon, the group brought suit in federal court, but the court eventually claimed that it lacked jurisdiction to act in the matter. Action under Executive Order 11491 was also forestalled early in 1976 when TVA was formally removed from the coverage of this order. The issue of inadequate union democracy was not resolved, and adverse private and social effects are continuing to accrue in the form of morale and productivity problems. Of course, the extreme of slow-downs and strikes by dissident employee groups is also possible when bargaining structures are not responsive to the constituency represented.

The lesson is clear for the public sector. Encouragement of structural centralization, either through larger bargaining units or through the vertical or horizontal flow of decision-making power, is efficient for management and can yield increased responsibility on the union side because negotiators are given some isolation from direct rank-and-file pressures. Yet, the centralization can be carried too far. Coupled with a lack of referendum rights and with ineffective election controls, it can mean employee inability to influence the structure that purports to represent them. Private and social costs of employee discontent can become so great that they exceed the efficiency and responsibility advantages of centralized structures.

The Management Structure

On the management side, structure is important for collective bargaining itself and for the administration of negotiated results and other personnel policies. In the years of rapid expansion following TVA's creation, top management was forced to rely on a highly centralized personnel staff. However, the Board of Directors foresaw the great diversity of operations that TVA would perform over a wide geographical area and committed itself to a path of decentralization for employee relations. The decentralization was not to be in a geographical sense only, where field personnel offices would have operated under the central personnel staff. Rather, the decentralization was to involve a shifting of responsibilities for personnel decisions and union-management relations from the personnel department to line management in the various operating divisions.

The process proceeded most swiftly in the management structure for collective bargaining. By 1937, two advisory groups of line management had been formed to join the personnel staff in wage and salary negotiations with unions of trades and labor employees and with organizations of salary policy employees. As TVA and its union-management relationships developed, the ability of these line managers to influence TVA's positions and goals in negotiations increased markedly.

A significant step in decentralization for personnel and contract administration was taken in 1953. The division personnel officers (DPO's), operating in each line division but under the control of the central personnel staff, were removed from the division of personnel and placed under the administrative control of the heads of the operating organizations they served. With the primary exception of the employment function, the personnel division would thereafter coordinate personnel activities of the other divisions and provide staff assistance. Day-to-day matters of personnel and contract administration would be left to the DPO's and to operating management, unless the aid of the central personnel staff was requested.

The spirit of management decentralization continues to be embodied in the activities of the advisory committees for bargaining and of the DPO's. The Trades and Labor Negotiating Committee and the Salary Policy Negotiating Committee are composed of top line managers appointed by TVA's General Manager upon the recommendation of the Director of Personnel. Operating offices and divisions that employ large numbers of trades and labor or salary policy employees are given greater representation on the appropriate committee. The committees work with, and use the staff support of, the employee relations branch in all aspects of the bargaining process, and both groups are under the direction of the second-ranking official in the division of personnel, the administrator of union-management relations.

Each negotiating committee begins its involvement with the bargaining process when union-management decisions are being made on the methods of conducting the prevailing wage and benefit surveys. When survey data have been collected, the line managers are active on the overall negotiating team in setting goals and positions for bargaining. During the actual bargaining sessions, the Manager of Union-Management Relations is management's spokesman. The TVA Code states that the negotiating committees can only "assist" the manager in establishing positions and making decisions. In fact, the line managers play a powerful role in establishing management's positions on wages, salaries, benefits, and other contract terms. Neither the manager nor members of the employee relations branch dominate the line officials in management caucuses. Decisions are normally reached by consensus, and the operating managers are quite vocal as issues and positions are debated.

Thus, management's organization for bargaining has been effectively decentralized away from dominance by a central employee relations staff. The decentralization has constituted a form of democracy on the management side, since operating management is a constituent of management negotiators, and it has also produced positive results in practical terms. The management negotiating team is assured of understanding problems of contract administration encountered by operating management and of appreciating recruiting, discipline, and other problems that should be addressed in bargaining. Operating managers better understand the negotiated policies they must administer. The negotiated policies are more likely to be administered in good faith because operating management plays a major role in their formulation. For the same reason, the operating divisions are unlikely to push the Board of Directors to repudiate a tentative agreement reached in negotiations.

The DPO's continue to be important actors in the decentralized management structure. They serve two masters, reporting administratively to the directors or assistant directors of the divisions they serve but having functional responsibilities to the director of personnel. On the one hand, these DPO's provide a vital upward flow of information from their division to the division of personnel. For example, they are counselors to employees and are able to discern how personnel policies are performing in practice. The central staff must have this feedback. The DPO's also are instrumental in developing and communicating positions that management in their divisions desires to have pressed in bargaining. They may be active both in prenegotiation and negotiation activities, working with the central personnel staff and the negotiating committees. They may prepare management's case in a grievance that will ultimately involve the central personnel staff.

On the other hand, DPO's play a critical role in the flow of policies downward from the central personnel staff to operating divisions. The DPO's are personnel generalists and become involved in administering most areas of negotiated, and other, personnel policies in their division: classification, pay, and staffing, for example. They must insure that operating managers and supervisors understand their own responsibilities in administering personnel policies. Negotiated policies, and other policies made centrally, must not be interpreted and applied differently in each division. The DPO's must not diverge significantly from the directions of the Division of Personnel, and they must not allow divergence to characterize their divisions.

Indeed, the possibility of inconsistent application of negotiated, and other, personnel policies is the greatest potential disadvantage of the management structure. Unions have charged that directors of operating divisions can induce the DPO's under their administrative control to "bend" personnel policies where the operating division may reap an advantage. The result would be large numbers of grievances and significant morale problems.

In fact, this problem has been avoided at TVA when the director of personnel has exercised sufficient power within the management hierarchy to enforce the relatively uniform administration of personnel policies. DPO's could not remain under the administrative control of line management in the absence of a strong-willed director capable of enlisting the aid of top management when divergence from centrally determined policies is threatened. At present, the TVA experiment in decentralizing its own structure for union-management relations and personnel administration is yielding positive net results. Significant inconsistencies in the administration of personnel policies are not evident.

Just as bargainers in government can learn from the achievements and from the weakness of centralized union structures at TVA, public employers should consider the success that TVA has realized from a formalized sharing of decision-making power between a central personnel staff and line management.

REFERENCES

1. E. Rock, Bargaining Units in the Public Service: The Problem of Proliferation, *Michigan Law Review, 67:*March, pp. 1001-1016, 1969.
2. F. Forbes and W. C. Clelland, Bargaining Units: A Management View from the City of Minneapolis, Minnesota, *Journal of Collective Negotiations in the Public Sector, 4:*3, pp. 198-201, 1975.
3. Compiled from data presented by the U.S. Civil Service Commission Office of Labor-Management Relations, *Union Recognition in the Federal Government,* November, pp. 20-21, 1974.
4. New Amendments to Executive Order 11491—Panel Discussion, *Public Personnel Management, 4:*6, pp. 348-364, 1975.
5. 48 Stat. 58, Public Law No. 17, 73rd Congress, 3.
6. Board of Directors, Tennessee Valley Authority, *Employee Relationship Policy,* Para. 6, p. 5, 1935.
7. Bureau of Labor Statistics, *Handbook of Labor Statistics 1975—Reference Edition,* U.S. Govt. Printing Office, Washington, D.C., pp. 229-230, 1975.
8. Bureau of Labor Statistics, *National Survey of Professional, Administrative, Technical, and Clerical Pay,* U.S. Govt. Printing Office, Washington, D.C. p.2, March, 1975.

Discussion Questions

1. Describe the bargaining structure of TVA and how it accounts for the agency's relationship with its employees.
2. Would you describe the TVA experience with employee relations as successful? Why or why not?
3. Discuss how the TVA's imposed centralized structure affected the salary policy workers during the 1940's and 1950's. How did the effects differ from those felt by the blue-collar workers?

Reprinted from Journal of Collective Negotiations in the Public Sector Vol. 5(3), 1976

CHAPTER 15

Why Federal Government Employees Join Unions: A Study of AFGE Local 1138

LOUIS V. IMUNDO, JR.

Although federal government employees have had the legal right to join unions since 1912, union membership among nonpostal government employees has historically been relatively low.[1] According to a Civil Service Assembly survey of 1939, only 19 per cent of the federal government's nonpostal employees were union members [1].

When Executive Order 10988 was issued in January 1962, it represented the first government wide official labor-management relations policy. Although the Order and its 1969 and 1971

---

[1] The Lloyd La Follette Act passed in 1912 gave postal employees the right to join unions. Interpretation of the Act expanded the right to join unions to nearly all government employees. The Act did not encourage government employees to join unions nor did it encourage the development of any system for the joint determination of terms and conditions of employment for government employees.

amendments are restrictive when compared to the statutes regulating labor-management relations in the private sector, they affected union growth among government employees. By 1963, 25 per cent of the government's nonpostal employees were union members. For the period 1963 to 1971 nonpostal government employees represented by unions increased from 180,000 to 1,038,000 [2]. As of November 1971, 53 per cent of the government's eligible nonpostal employees were represented by unions [3].

Historically, blue-collar workers have accounted for over 50 per cent of the government's employees. By 1971 white-collar workers numbered 1.9 million, accounting for nearly 70 per cent of the government's employees [4]. In the past decade white-collar workers have been responsible for the majority of the increases in union membership. Today, 42 per cent of the government's white-collar workers are union members. They account for nearly 60 per cent of total union membership [5].

The American Federation of Government Employees (AFGE), an industrial type union that represents only nonpostal federal government employees, has, over the past decade, experienced the highest growth rate of any union. In 1960 AFGE membership was 70,300. By 1970 actual membership had increased by over 400 per cent to 304,000. As of November 1972 government employees represented by the AFGE reached 606,391 [5]. White-collar workers accounted for most of the AFGE's growth over the past decade, and presently account for approximately 50 per cent of actual membership and 63 per cent of the government employees represented by the union. Today, the AFGE is the largest union in the government.

Local 1138 of the AFGE is the exclusive bargaining agent for the 5,004 civilian government employees employed at Wright Patterson Air Force Base's Logistic Command Center (AFLC), located in Dayton, Ohio.[2] These employees are covered under a two-year negotiated contract that expires November 15, 1974. The Air Force granted Local 1138 exclusive recognition for Wright Patterson AFLC employees in 1970 as the result of a union representation election in which the AFGE received a majority of the votes cast by AFLC employees. Since exclusive recognition was granted, Local 1138 has had sporadic growth. At the time that the study was conducted the Local had 707 active members.

---

[2] Wright Patterson Air Force Base, located in Dayton, Ohio, is headquarters for the Air Force Logistics Command (AFLC)—the logistics arm of the Air Force.

The rapid increases in government union membership, coupled with the relative decreases in private sector union membership have led people to speculate about why government employees join unions. Generalizations have been made that government employees join unions for the same reasons as workers in the private sector [6]. Yet, conditions of work in the government preclude many explanations about the reasons people join unions.

The first condition is the historical role of the civil service system. Since its inception, the philosophy underlying the civil service system has been the development and maintenance of policies designed to protect government employees from management or political attack. Many of the subjects covered within the scope of private sector collective bargaining were covered under civil service regulations and procedures before collective bargaining was widely adopted.

The second condition is the government's maintenance of the sovereignty doctrine, which is reflected in its labor-management relations policies. Meaningful collective bargaining does not exist because of the following: the legally sanctioned institutionalized belief in government sovereignty coupled with the legal sanctioning of management's rights appears to have reinforced a historically negative attitude toward collective bargaining on the part of government management. The government's legal and philosophical attitudes toward meaningful collective bargaining are manifested in Executive Order 11616 issued on August 26, 1971. This order specifically denies government employees the right to strike, establishes no provisions for collective bargaining over wages or hours, and strongly asserts management's rights.

The third condition is that the high proportion of white-collar union members in government contrasts sharply with the low proportion of white-collar union members in the private sector. It is also commonly believed that the traditional appeals of unions do not attract white-collar workers.

The purposes of the study were to test the following hypotheses: (1) the reasons the sampled blue-collar and white-collar Local 1138 members joined the union differed significantly from the reasons workers in the private sector join unions; (2) The sampled blue-collar and white-collar Local 1138 members joined the union for the same reasons.

The secondary research for the study included the following: an examination of the contributions of labor historians to the development of a unified labor theory, an examination of the empirical studies uncovered by the author that have been used to establish why workers join unions [7]; and last, an examination of the most widely accepted reasons pertaining to why white-collar workers in the private sector have not joined unions in significant numbers [8].

The primary research centered around a questionnaire that was sent to the homes of 384 Local 1138 members. The sample was established by selecting every other white-collar and every blue-collar member listed in the local's membership file. The sample consisted of 60 blue-collar and 324 white-collar members.

The questionnaire was sent to the sample group during June 1972. The sampled members were asked to respond to questions relating to the following: social background, job environment factors, AFGE membership and participation, reasons for joining the union, the civil service system, the scope of collective bargaining, and the right-to-strike issue.

The questionnaire was designed to allow only for discrete responses (yes, no, don't know) in all of the question categories except the last two, which were general response questions ("The main reason that I joined the AFGE was:" and "Is there anything else that you might tell me that might be helpful?").

The chi-square test was used in the two-part data analysis.[3] In the first part of the data analysis, the sampled members' responses to each question were tabulated by group and were tested for statistical significance, first by group response, then by total response.

The responses to the general background questions were compared by group and question categories with information known about all Local 1138 members and all Wright Patterson AFLC employees. The results were used to determine whether certain factors were present in the members' background that may have had either a positive or a negative influence on their joining the union. The results of the comparisons were also used as a check of the representativeness of the sampled union members to the union population and to all Wright Patterson AFLC employees.

The responses to the remaining questions were analyzed to establish the reasons why the blue-collar and the white-collar members joined the union. The reasons the sampled union members joined the union were compared to the reasons workers in the private sector join unions to test Hypothesis 1.

---

[3] Discrete data limits the statistical tests that can be used for analysis purposes. Because the chi-square test requires no assumptions about the shape of the parameter distribution, chi-square was used for analyzing the responses of the questionnaire.

In the second part of the data analysis the responses of the blue-collar and the white-collar members to each question were compared. The chi-square test was used to determine whether a statistically significant difference existed between the proportional responses of the sampled groups. Using this nondirectional method of statistical analysis, the results of this comparison were used to test Hypothesis 2.

Unless otherwise noted, the responses discussed in this paper are only those of the sampled union members who responded to the questionnaire. The usable responses and the response rate for the blue-collar and the white-collar members are shown in Table 1.[4]

Table 1. Number of Usable Responses and Response Rate by Employee Classification

Group	Usable Responses	Percentage of Sample Responding
Blue-Collar	32	50.3
White-Collar	162	50.0
Total	194	50.5

Findings

The findings of the study showed that 66 per cent of the blue-collar members and 49 per cent of the white-collar members were born and educated in Ohio. The distribution of the members who were born and educated in Ohio was comparable to the distribution for all Wright Patterson AFLC employees. An additional 8 per cent of the blue-collar members and 10 per cent of the white-collar members who were not born in Ohio were educated in Ohio between the ages of 7 and 18 years.

Based on the responses to the questionnaire, the AFGE has the highest proportional membership among Wright Patterson AFLC workers over 50 years old and lowest proportional membership among AFLC workers under 30 years old. These findings were determined by comparing the white-collar union members' age distribution with the age distribution of all AFLC employees.

Enough evidence existed to suggest that previous union

---

[4] Questionnaires sent to the homes of two blue-collar and seven white-collar members were not usable for various reasons.

membership had some influence on 33 per cent of the members joining the union. Statistically significant differences existed in the responses of the two groups. Fifty-nine per cent of the blue-collar members had been union members whereas only 28 per cent of the white-collar members had been union members prior to joining the AFGE. The possibility that a member may have joined the union because he had been influenced by one of his parents' experiences with unions was present in 27 per cent of the responses. The 53 members were probably influenced in their decision to join the AFGE by their parents' experiences.

The researchers who conducted studies in the private sector found that workers join unions for multiple reasons. However, Chamberlin, Rose, and Walker and Guest in each of their respective studies were able to conclude that a single reason was responsible for a majority of the workers joining the union [9]. Chamberlin concluded that "results" were the main reason for the workers joining the union. From the text of his study, "results" were construed to mean the satisfaction of economic needs. Rose concluded that a worker's joining the union was a function of social pressure, but the worker's perception of the union's function was the satisfaction of economic needs. Walker and Guest concluded that the workers joined the union for psychological reasons [10]. Bakke and Seidman, et. al., in their studies, were unable to conclude that a majority of the workers expressed a dominant reason for joining the union [11]. Bakke concluded that inter-related social, economic, and psychological reasons in that order were responsible for the workers joining the union. The strongest reasons centered around the need for economic gains. Seidman, et. al., concluded that the workers joined the union for social and psychological reasons. They did not join the union for economic reasons.

The findings of the study showed that nearly all of the sampled members joined the union for psychological and economic reasons. A maximum of 20 per cent of the members joined the union because of some form of social pressure. The 20 per cent response was small when compared to the members' responses to the psychological and economic related questions and the findings of the studies conducted in the private sector. For these reasons the presence of some form of social pressure as a primary factor for the members' joining the union was discounted.

Eighty per cent of the members believed in the purposes of unions and that membership in the union could personally benefit them. It was inferred that the members perceive the purposes of the union and the benefits from membership as psychological, i.e., protecting their rights, and economic, i.e., wage and fringe benefit increases. This conclusion was further validated by the members' responses to the questions that related to psychological and economic reasons for joining the union.

Seventy-three per cent of the members believed that management does not treat them fairly. Seventy-three per cent of the members believed that management does not give them a chance to participate in decision making.

Seventy-one per cent of the members believed that membership in the union was the best way to get wage and fringe benefit increases. Although statistically significant differences existed in the responses of the blue-collar and white-collar members, a clear majority of each group believed that membership in the AFGE was the best way to get wage and fringe benefit increases. Eighty-five per cent of the members believed that the union should have the right to collectively bargain with management over wages and fringe benefits.

The responses to the psychological questions were close enough to the percentage of responses to the economic questions to conclude that the sampled members joined the union primarily for psychological and economic reasons.

Based on the findings of the study, Hypotheses 1 and 2 were accepted. Hypothesis 1 was accepted because the findings of the study when compared with each of the findings of the studies conducted in the private sector indicated that the sampled workers did not join the union for the same reasons that workers in the private sector join unions. The small combined percentage responses to all forms of social pressure as a reason for joining the union and the close relationship between the psychological and economic reasons were not present in any of the findings of the studies conducted in the private sector. Hypothesis 2 was accepted because the reasons for the blue-collar and white-collar members' joining the union were the same.

The findings of the study showed that only 30 per cent of the members believed that since the union has exclusively represented Wright Patterson AFLC employees they have been treated more fairly. Only 25 per cent of the members believed that since they joined the union their personal relations with management have improved. Statistically significant differences in the responses of the two groups existed in both questions. In both questions the responses showed that a lower percentage of the white-collar members believed that membership in the union had helped to improve their general and personal relations with management. The reason for their feelings may be that initially their working conditions were better than the working conditions of the blue-collar members or that membership in the union has not benefited them.

Fifty-seven per cent of the members felt that the civil service system does not protect their rights. This response is important because the Civil Service Commission's operational philosophy has centered around the protection of workers' rights and sound principles of personnel management. Considering that another 13 per cent of the members "don't know" if the system protects their rights, it can be concluded that a large majority of the members have some doubts about the Commission's ability to meet one of its basic objectives.

The members' dissatisfaction with the Civil Service System was not deep enough for them to feel that the system should be discontinued. Twelve per cent of the members believed that the system should be discontinued, while 19 per cent indicated that they "don't know."

Forty-nine per cent of the members did not believe that they should have the right to strike. The data showed that slightly more than half of the blue-collar members believed that they should be allowed to strike while slightly over half of the white-collar members believed that they should not be allowed to strike. Considering the government's position on strikes, this response was important because it was not higher.

To examine the strength of the members' belief in having the right to strike, they were asked if they would participate in a strike. Only 45 per cent of the members indicated that they would not participate in a strike. Twenty-four per cent of the members did not know whether they would participate. This indicates that the members who did not know whether they would participate in a strike would have to examine the conditions leading to the strike before making a decision. The fact that a smaller percentage of the members indicated that they would not strike than those who did not even want the right to strike is somewhat inconsistent with logical expectations. The only explanation that is offered is that some of the members feel a deep sense of loyalty to the union. Even though they do not want the right to strike, some of the members are willing to consider participating in a strike.

The results are very important considering that government employees who participate in a strike are subject to very severe penalties under Public Law 330.

The responses to the opinion question were grouped into 6 categories. The responses were not significantly different from the expected distribution of responses. The majority of the responses paralleled the responses to other related questions in the question- naire.

Conclusion

Unions in the government cannot negotiate on wages, fringe benefits, work hours, management's rights as defined in the ex- ecutive orders, union security, nor do the members have the right to strike. In spite of these limitations on collective bargaining, extensive progress in labor-management relations has been made over the past decade. This progress has come about largely because of union activity.

Survival and growth of any organization where membership is largely voluntary is dependent upon the organization's ability to satisfy its members' needs as the members see them. Based on the findings of this study and a parallel study with similar findings con- ducted during 1971 on AFGE Local 916 (the AFGE's largest local) at Tinker Air Force Base, Oklahoma City, Oklahoma [12], it appears that the government unions will continue their efforts to further redefine the sovereignty doctrine that has permeated labor-management relations in the government from its inception.

REFERENCES

1. Morton R. Godine, *The Labor Problem in the Public Service: A Study in Political Pluralism* (Cambridge, Massachusetts: Harvard University Press, 1951), pp. 94-95.
2. United States Civil Service Commission, Office of Labor-Management Re- lations, *Union Recognition in the Federal Government* (Washington, D.C.: U.S. Government Printing Office, November 1971), p. 19.
3. United States Civil Service Commission, Office of Labor-Management Relations, *News Release*, March, 1972.
4. United States Civil Service Commission, *Annual Report*, 1971, Table A-1, p. 57.
5. United States Civil Service Commission, Office of Labor-Management Re- lations, *News Release*, March 1972.
6. For a detailed discussion, see H. J. Christrup, "Why Do Government Employees Join Unions," *Personnel Administration XI*, (September- October, 1966), pp. 49-54; W. D. Heisel and J. D. Hallihan, *Questions and Answers on Public Employee Negotiations* (Chicago, Illinois: Public Personnel Association, 1967). This material represents the only sources uncovered by the author that discuss why government employees join unions.
7. Discussions relating to the reasons why people join unions may be found in the following:

E. Wright Bakke, "Why Workers Join Unions," *Personnel*, XXII, No. 1 (July, 1945), pp. 38-46.

Edwin M. Chamberlin, "What Labor Is Thinking," *Personnel Journal*, XIV, No. 3 (September, 1935), pp. 118-125.

Arnold M. Rose, *Union Solidarity* (Minneapolis, Minnesota: University of Minnesota Press, 1952).

J. Seidman, J. London and B. Karsh, "Why Workers Join Unions," *The Annals of the American Academy of Political And Social Science*, CLXXIV, (March, 1951), pp. 75-84.

M. S. Viteles, *Motivation and Morale in Industry* (New York: John Wiley and Sons, 1962).

8. Discussions relating to the reasons why white-collar workers do not join unions may be found in the following:

H. M. Douty, "Prospects for White-Collar Unionism," *Monthly Labor Review*, XCII (January, 1969), pp. 31-35.

Bernard Goldstein, "The Perspective of Unionized Professionals," *Social Forces*, XXXVII (May, 1959), p. 325.

"Papers from Industrial Relations Research Association Meeting," *Monthly Labor Review*, LXXXVII (February, 1964), pp. 125-131.

R. L. Rowann and H. R. Northrup, (eds.) *Readings in Labor Economics and Labor Relations* (Homewood, Illinois: R. E. Irwin Co., 1968), No. 25, "New Union Frontier: White Collar Workers," p. 265.

Leonard R. Sayles and George Strauss, *Human Behavior in Organizations* (Englewood Cliffs, New Jersey: Prentice-Hall, Inc., 1966), p. 68.

Arthur A. Sloane, "Prospects for the Unionization of White-Collar Employees," *Personnel Journal*, XLVIII (December, 1969), pp. 964-971.

9. Edwin Chamberlin, "What Labor is Thinking," *Personnel Journal*, *op. cit.*

Arnold M. Rose, *Union Solidarity, op. cit.*

M. S. Viteles, *op. cit.*, p. 340, citing C. R. Walker and R. H. Guest, *The Man on the Assembly Line* (Howard University Press 1952).

10. M. S. Viteles, *op. cit.*, citing Walker and Guest, *op. cit.*, pp. 340-341.

11. E. Wright Bakke, *op. cit.*, p. 42.

Seidman, *et. al.*, *op. cit.*, p. 78.

12. Louis V. Imundo, "Why Government Employees Join Unions: A Study of AFGE Local 916," *Public Personnel Management* II, (January-February 1973), pp. 23-28; and Louis V. Imundo, *Why Government Employees Join Unions: A Study of AFGE Local 916* (Norman, Oklahoma: University of Oklahoma Bureau for Business and Economic Research, Monograph, 1972).

Discussion Questions

1. In view of the strictures on the scope of collective bargaining in the federal sector, how do you explain the growth in unionism among federal employees?

2. Lack of participation in decision making was cited by a large percentage of workers as a reason for joining a union. Do you agree that this issue is a realistic worker expectation? Discuss the issue from employer and employee perspectives.

3. Compare the civil service system to unions with regard to the concept of protecting workers' rights.

Reprinted from Journal of Collective Negotiations in the Public Sector Vol. 4(3), 1975

CHAPTER 16

The Impact of Labor-Management Cooperation Committees on Personnel Policies and Practices at Twenty Federal Bargaining Units

GEORGE T. SULZNER

SETTING

Joint labor-management cooperation committees have been receiving increasing attention in public sector labor relations as the public demand for more effective governmental services while maintaining or reducing the costs of government grows. In a recent issue of the former *Civil Service Journal* (now entitled *Management*) devoted entirely to the topic of productivity improvement in the federal government, both Alan Campbell and Anthony Ingrassia noted the role that joint labor-management committees might perform in improving productivity and enriching the work life of Federal employees [1]. Moreover, a 1979 study of *Labor-Management Committees In The Public Sector*, by the

Midwest Center for Public Sector Labor Relations observed that, "The public sector, stymied by inflation, limited budgets, and the growing popularity of Proposition 13 legislation, might. . . find joint labor-management committees helpful in solving its problems." [2]

Generally, the proponents of labor-management committees stress their communication function as forums for discussing problems of mutual interest outside the adversarial climate of formal collective bargaining. Ingrassia wrote, "The practice of continuing dialogue, instead of start-and-stop consultation, encourages positive attitudes and relationships. . . . that dialogue can often be best served by union management committees." [3] This perspective is illustrated by the prevalent kinds of joint committees embodied in federal agreements. Martin pointed out that the executive orders creating and solidifying the federal labor-management relations system (10977 and 11491, as amended) encouraged the contractual establishment of joint committees [4]. A 1971 Bureau of Labor Statistics survey of a representative sample of 671 federal agreements reported that 44 per cent contained articles setting up some type of joint committee [5]. A November, 1979 survey of over 3,000 federal contracts disclosed that 75 per cent instituted safety or safety policy committees; 30 per cent called for the formation of EEO committees, more than 25 per cent provided for general purpose labor-management cooperation committees; and while relatively few agreements contain productivity clauses *per se*, approximately eighty contracts set up joint committees that specifically deal with productivity issues [6].[1] According to Strauss, the absence of a productivity focus would place federal joint committees clearly within the mainstream of formal worker participative bodies currently functioning in the United States and elsewhere [7].

Evidently, joint committees are more likely to operate in the federal labor-management setting when they are focused on areas that are subject to what Walton and McKersie have labeled as "integrative bargaining" concerns; i.e., topics that are responsive, as organizational development specialists would claim, to "win/win" rather than "win/lose" interchanges [8]. Driscoll's recent survey of joint committee operations, however, raises doubts even about their effectiveness in dealing with "integrative bargaining" issues. Rather, he concludes their impact is most visible on the subprocess of bargaining Walton and McKersie identified as "attitudinal structuring." [9]

It would appear, therefore, that federal joint committee experience is not

---

[1] Executive Order 12196, which went into effect in July 1980 and establishes occupational health and safety standards in the federal sector, provides incentives for federal managers to establish joint health and safety labor-management committees. This puts presidential exhortation in line with Congress which passed legislation in 1978 directing the Federal Mediation and Conciliation Service to encourage the formation of joint committees in the private sector. P. L. 95-524 (October 27, 1978), 92 Stat. 1909 et. seq.

particularly relevant to handling problems of governmental productivity and delivery services. John A. McCart, the former executive director of the Public Employee Department of AFL-CIO, provides a convincing explanation for the existence of only a handful of federal joint labor-management productivity committees. "In the absence of suitable bargaining relationships," he writes, "such approaches as joint committees will not be effective. . . . Until government managers realize that role of collective bargaining, greater productivity will remain a goal, not a reality." [10] Moreover, Driscoll observed that three key circumstances affecting the effectiveness of joint committees are outside pressure to take action, equality of union-management bargaining power, and maturity of the labor-management relationship. None are present typically in the current federal practice [9, pp. 7; 10].

Realistically, it is difficult to imagine that joint productivity committees will become common and effective instruments of employment policy as long as federal unions are prohibited from bargaining about wages and hours of work. General purpose labor-management cooperation committees, which are established usually to foster regular communication about labor relations and working conditions, would, as Ingrassia observed, seem to have the most potential for dealing with work life and other operational job issues [3, p. 45]. Unfortunately, as previously noted, they are absent from about three quarters of all federal labor-management dealings.

The impact of general purpose labor-management cooperation committees on personnel policies and practices and related matters of working conditions at twenty federal bargaining units is the subject of this paper. Martin conducted two studies of joint committee functioning at six federal units in a midwestern Metropolitan area, and several of his findings were confirmed by the present and more extensive investigation [4, 11]. The current analysis, however, produced more guarded conclusions about their effectiveness in encountering the employment perplexities facing federal managers and union officers.

RESEARCH METHOD

The examination of the impact of labor-management cooperation committees on federal personnel policies and practices is part of a larger study sponsored by the office of Labor-Management Relations of the United States Civil Service Commission (now the Office of Personnel Management), of which some findings have been reported previously in this journal [12]. Eighty-one management and sixty-one union respondents were asked to assess the statement that "general labor-management cooperation committees will impact on personnel policies and practices." Their answers, which touched on, as well, closely related areas of working conditions, form the basic data for the analysis. It is supplemented, wherever possible, by the relevant results from other studies.

FEDERAL LABOR-MANAGEMENT
COOPERATION COMMITTEES

A 1975 survey of federal agreement clauses instituting joint cooperation committees reported that 93 per cent of the provisions prescribed membership on the committee (usually equal representation for the parties); 90 per cent specified subject matter (53 per cent excluding discussions of individual grievances and disputes, and 25 per cent excluding negotiatons by the representatives); 79 per cent contained scheduling (typically monthly, quarterly, and by request of the parties); 58 per cent provided for written minutes or summaries of the meetings; and 55 per cent prescribed a premeeting agenda [13].

The committees established by the agreements governing the units studied here are representative of the typical entities described in the survey, What is unusual is the fact that three-quarters of the units examined contained agreements that created formally general purpose labor-management cooperation committees, a ratio that is certainly disproportionate for the entire federal sector. It is a sign, however, of the unique vigor of the agreements included in this study.

FINDINGS

A slim majority of respondents, 52 per cent of the 61 per cent for whom the joint committee proposition was relevant, indicated that general purpose cooperation committees impacted on personnel policies and practices. Moreover, if one regards the 29 per cent who could not answer because no formal committee existed in their units as a recognition of limited need for them at the activities (a reasonable assumption) the narrow majority is transformed into a sizeable minority (42%) of interviewees who saw impact.

The strongest impression received from a scan of interviewee comments is that the size of the unit is a key to utilization of the committees. This point is vividly illustrated in Table 1 but it is important to note its significance here. Only one respondent from the five units with fewer than 700 employees which had committees provided an assessment of significant impact. The typical remark was that an open door policy was in place in these smaller units and in an organizational setting where face-to-face contact is important and feasible, the formality of the committee structure seemed to be dysfunctional and where committees existed they seldom met. Martin reported also that the size of the unit is a key variable in committee effectiveness [4, p. 278; 11, p. 349].

Moreover, as Martin and Driscoll have commented elsewhere, relationships between the parties were important determinants of committee success. [4, p. 281; 9, p. 7; 10; 11, p. 7]. Deterioration at the lower and middle level of contact in the installation meant that great emphasis was placed on the unit-wide committee meetings. Some union officials observed that end runs around operating managers were common practice in this situation. On the other hand, if the parties were working together smoothly throughout the installation, the unit-wide meetings were treated more casually. Deterioration of top-level relationships usually meant that the committees were abandoned and placed in storage. Union commitment to the committees' continued functioning seemed to be a little stronger than management's because, as an experienced union president observed, "in the federal sector the union has to participate to be effective."

Several of the variations in impact appraisals portrayed in Table 1 have been noted already. A majority of union representatives (61%) perceived a committee impact compared to a minority (45%) of management officials. Since unions have a larger stake in the committees' effective operation, this assessment is not surprising. The most pronounced contrast is associated with the size of the bargaining units. Respondents in units containing fewer than 700 employees were almost unanimous in this assessment of negligible impact. This finding takes on an added dimension when it is recognized that 88 per cent of the units

Table 1. Perceptions of Impact of General Purpose
Labor-Management Cooperation Committees Analyzed by
Selected Respondent and Unit Variables[a]

Respondent and Unit Variables	Significant (%)		Somewhat Significant (%)		Not Too Significant (%)		Insignificant (%)		Total (%)	
Affiliation										
Union	12	(32)	11	(29)	4	(10)	11	(29)	38	(100)
Management	10	(21)	12	(25)	6	(12)	20	(42)	48	(100)
L-M Relations Experience										
Inexperienced	5	(29)	3	(18)	2	(12)	7	(41)	17	(100)
Moderate Experience	9	(35)	5	(19)	4	(15)	8	(31)	26	(100)
Experienced	8	(19)	15	(35)	4	(9)	16	(37)	43	(100)
Size of Unit										
Below 700	1	(3)	0		4	(14)	24	(83)	29	(100)
700 to 1,099	10	(56)	4	(22)	2	(11)	2	(11)	18	(100)
1,100 to 3,500	8	(38)	7	(33)	2	(10)	4	(19)	21	(100)
Above 3,500	3	(17)	12	(67)	2	(11)	1	(5)	18	(100)
No. of Agreement in Unit										
1st Agreement	0		2	(13)	2	(12)	12	(75)	16	(100)
2nd Agreement	5	(16)	11	(35)	3	(10)	12	(39)	31	(100)
3rd Agreement	13	(65)	5	(25)	1	(5)	1	(5)	20	(100)
4th & 5th Agreement	4	(21)	5	(26)	4	(21)	6	(32)	19	(100)
All Respondents	22	(26)	23	(26)	10	(12)	21	(36)	86	(100)

[a]Fifty-six interviewees did not answer this question; one unit is under the 5th agreement.

in the federal sector are in this category [14]. Thus, it would appear that general purpose labor-management cooperation committees are not likely to be important assemblages in the typical federal labor-management setting. Impact seems to be greatest at the largest units surveyed, which nationally comprise just 6 per cent of the federal total [14].

A weaker but parallel tendency is evident in the distribution of responses according to the number of agreements negotiated in the units. Driscoll has already been cited as reporting an association between joint committee effectiveness and mature relationships defined by the number of contracts negotiated. This study also indicates that working committees are linked to the actions of experienced labor and management practitioners operating within a setting that has a labor-management history. A mature labor-management relations climate, however, is not typical of the federal sector.[2]

In brief, what we have seen so far is a confirmation of impact on joint committees of bargaining unit and labor relations variables that have been observed by other researchers. What is distinct about this study is the verification of their relative absence in the federal sector.

At bargaining units where committees operated, an unusual situation in the federal sector, most participants regarded the two-way flow of communication worthwhile, even though union messages tend to be specific and management's general. Management can obtain a quick temperature reading of employee and union morale from these meetings. Moreover, as one manager observed, they can serve as an additional channel of information about the performance of lower-level management from the employee's perspective. One union president said the meetings gave the union a "regular opportunity to make a dent on working conditions." Union officers can use them as an early warning device to prepare employees for any "bad news" that is coming down the pike. One union steward stressed the educational value of the meetings for relaying messages to the employees. The communication flow on the union side does put pressure on management, however, to develop an effective internal communication network to the supervisors. One supervisor related how she was often embarrassed by the fact the stewards knew what top management was planning before it had filtered down through the ranks to her. Unions definitely want to be brought into the larger operational picture. This was stressed repeatedly, not only for its symbolic effect on the union's image but also because communication in and of itself can have an ameliorative impact on labor-management relations. In fact, Driscoll reported that half of the beneficial changes attributed to joint committees by the respondents in his study lie,

---

[2] A majority of the federal workforce was not covered by negotiated agreements until 1975, and one quarter of the respondents in this survey, focused on units operating under what seemed to be unusually robust federal agreements, were governed by the first negotiated contract. It seems to be a reasonable conclusion that labor-management relations have not yet reached a mature stage of development in most federal settings. See [12, p. 145].

"in the interpersonal relationships between committee members, most frequently, improved communication and trust." [9, p. 5]

While a number of managers seemed to think that the usefulness of the committees improved when subjects become more general and less narrowly focused on labor-management relations, an evaluation that matches Martin's findings, one particularly reflective manager indicated that "nit picking specifics raised by the union representative were not troubling because they were a sign that the basics of the employment situation were healthy." [4, p. 280; 11, p. 13]. This is a perspective that has also been observed in other environments where joint committees are functioning [15]. Union representatives were more hesitant to move from problem-oriented topics to larger-scope issues at meetings because the resulting understandings were much less susceptible to measurement on a win/lose scale and therefore not as rewarding politically for the union.

Committee particulars such as regular attendance by important management and union representatives, the exclusion of individual grievances and disputes from discussion, semimonthly or monthly meetings, the development of a premeeting agenda, seemed to be features of productive joint committees. These characteristics of a functional joint committee situation appear also to have some general applicability [11, p. 4; 13]. Again, where committees operate usefully, many of the ingredients that are associated with success are found outside the federal sector as well. What is unique about the federal sector is the relative unlikelihood that joint cooperation committees will be established formally, or if established, remain viable for an extended period of time.

CONCLUSION

General purpose labor-management cooperation committees appear to be uncommon entities in federal labor-management relations. They are present mainly in bargaining units with more than 1,500 employees, which represent a very small fraction of the total federal bargaining units. At those larger sites, committees appear to keep channels of communication between the parties open and provide each with a regular opportunity to examine the state of their mutual relations in a fairly relaxed, noncompetitive atmosphere. This pattern of accomplishment is similar to that for joint committees operating at other levels of government and in private industry. Results there as well as in the federal sector indicate that substantive contributions seem focused on improvements in working conditions ranging from safety to flexitime and that increased productivity was seldom a product of committee interaction [9, p. 6].

At smaller bargaining units surveyed, which are representative of the vast majority of organized federal workplaces, committees either have no formal existence or they are not utilized regularly where they exist. At these smaller organized settings, labor-management relations do not seem to be as dependent on formal structure to assure systematic contact. Regardless of where committees exist, their performance is affected by the labor-management relations climate at the activity. The experience level of the parties' representatives and the messages transmitted by them throughout the areas of dealing in an installation have an impact on the functioning of labor-management cooperation committees.

Federal joint labor-management cooperation committees seem to have limited promise, therefore, as vehicles for dealing with government productivity and cost concerns. They are like their private sector counterparts in this regard. Joint committees seem most effective when they are concerned with "integrative bargaining" issues that concern specific aspects of working conditions or engaged with matters that relate to the mutual attitudes of the parties.

Surely, commitment to the idea of joint committees should not lead to an unreflective imposition of them into an environment where committee processes would appear to complicate rather than facilitate communication between the parties. Driscoll is on target in relating that the research on joint committees suggests a cautious diagnostic approach to the selection of locations for new committees. He wrote, "Rather than supporting committees in all geographic areas and bargaining relationships, the present study (his) suggests refining a selection methodology to identify the *subset* of situations with the optimal potential for effective committees." [9, p. 10] Certainly, the thrust of the analysis throughout this paper sustains the wisdom of Driscoll's suggestion as it pertains to the federal labor-management relations program.

REFERENCES

1. A. K. Campbell, A Challenge for Federal Managers, *Civil Service Journal* (now entitled *Management*), *19*:3, p. 36, January/March, 1979.
2. *Labor Management Committees in the Public Sector: A Practitioner Guide*, Midwest Center for Public Sector Relations, Bloomington, Indiana, p. 1, 1979.
3. A. F. Ingrassia, Productivity: The Neutral Ground in Labor-Management Relations, *Federal Service Labor Relations Review, 2*:2, p. 43, 1980.
4. J. A. Martin, Joint Labor-Management Meetings in the Federal Government: Results from Six Sites, *Journal of Collective Negotiations in the Public Sector, 6*:4, pp. 276-277, 1977.
5. Collective Bargaining Agreements in the Federal Service, Late 1971, *Bulletin 1789*, Bureau of Labor Statistics, Washington, D.C., 1973.
6. Labor Agreement Information Retrieval System (LIARS) survey, United States Office of Personnel Management, Office of Labor-Management Relations, Washington, D.C., November, 1979.
7. G. Strauss, Workers Participation: Symposium Introduction, *Industrial Relations, 18*:3, p. 253, Fall, 1979.
8. R. E. Walton and R. B. McKersie, *A Behavioral Theory of Labor Negotiations*, McGraw-Hill, New York, p. 5, 1965.

9. J. W. Driscoll, Labor-Management Committees in the United States: A National Survey, Massachusetts Institute of Technology, Cambridge, mimeograph, p. 9, August 1979.
10. J. A. McCart, Collecting Some Union Views, *Civil Service Journal, 19:3*, p. 38, January/March, 1979.
11. J. E. Martin, A Comparative Longitudinal Study of Joint Union-Management Committees, Wayne State University, Detroit, Michigan, mimeograph, 24 pp., September, 1979.
12. G. T. Sulzner, The Impact of Grievance and Arbitration Processes on Federal Personnel Policies and Practices: The View from Twenty Bargaining Units, *Journal of Collective Negotiations in the Public Sector, 9:2*, pp. 143-157, 1980.
13. *Labor-Management Cooperation Committees: Provisions in Federal Agreements,* United States Civil Service Commission, Office of Labor-Management Relations, Washington, D.C., pp. 1-4, August, 1975.
14. Labor Agreement Information Retrieval System (LAIRS) Survey, United States Civil Service Commission, Office of Labor-Management Relations. Washington, D.C., May 22, 1978.
15. H. M. Douty, *Labor Management Productivity Committees in American Industry*, National Commission on Productivity and Work Quality, p. 29, May, 1975.

Discussion Questions

1. Why might cooperation committees have little effect on governmental productivity and delivery of services?
2. Discuss the advantages and disadvantages of cooperation committees in small (under 700 employees) governmental units.
3. What is distinctive about the federal sector that might serve to discourage the formation of cooperation committees?

Reprinted from Journal of Collective Negotiations in the Public Sector Vol. 11(1), 1982

PART V
PROPOSED
NATIONAL LEGISLATION

In this concluding part Lieberman puts the issue of federal bargaining legislation into perspective, detailing its probable impact on state laws. Lieberman analyzes various state statutes dealing with public employee working conditions and benefits and identifies some alternatives available to Congress: 1) complete preemption of state legislation; 2) complete exemption of state legislation; and 3) preemption or exemption of some state legislation. Haughton presents the bargaining process from his own long experience step by step, providing practical pointers, constantly suggesting the concept of deadlines.

As a footnote to Lieberman's analysis, it should be mentioned that no federal legislation has been passed by Congress as this book goes to press. The reader is left to ponder the reasons for this, and to ask whether, from the public's point of view, this is beneficial or detrimental.

CHAPTER 17

Impact of Proposed Federal Public Employee Bargaining on State Legislation

MYRON LIEBERMAN

The following analysis of preemption problems arising out of proposed federal public employee bargaining legislation is excerpted from the principal investigator's study entitled Identification and Evaluation of State Legal Constraints Upon Educational Productivity. Although it raises several other issues, the final report for this study, which was funded by NIE (National Institute of Education), is now being completed; however, because of the urgency of pre-emption issues, a part of the study dealing with preemption issues is being disseminated at this time to interested parties.

It must be emphasized that the following analysis is not and was never intended to be a comprehensive or exhaustive analysis of preemption problems arising out of the proposed federal legislation. On the contrary, it is intended only to be illustrative and to highlight the need for a prompt and comprehensive study of preemption problems in connection with the proposed federal legislation.

This need is underscored by the pervasive neglect of preemption problems by interest groups and government bodies concerned about the proposed federal legislation. From June until early December 1974, the principal investigator interviewed a substantial number of national and state leaders in education. With only one exception, none appeared to be cognizant of the preemption problems discussed below, even though the problems have drastic implications for their interest groups, for educational governance, and for intergovernmental relations in this country. This was true regardless of whether the implications or potential consequences of the preemption issues were highly favorable or highly unfavorable to the particular interest group.

It should also be noted that the preemption problems considered below were not considered in the House and Senate hearings on H.R. 8677 and H.R. 9730. (These bills are identical to S. 3294 and S. 3295, introduced by Senator Harrison Williams. For editorial simplicity, the analysis will use the House numbers only.) These hearings devoted considerable attention to what would and/or should be the relationships between a federal public employee bargaining law and the various state laws providing bargaining rights for state and local public employees. Although this issue is extremely important, it is quite different from the issue of to what extent, if any, should state legislation on terms and conditions of public employment be preempted by H.R. 8677 or H.R. 9730? Whether or not state public employee bargaining laws, such as New York's Taylor Act, should be preempted by H.R. 8677 or H.R. 9730 is clearly not determinative of whether the state retirement or state tenure or state civil service laws in states without bargaining laws are to be preempted by a federal statute.

Another limitation of the following analysis is its emphasis upon the legal issues involved. The analysis does not raise all the public policy issues or present the major options with respect to these issues. Again, its purpose is only to demonstrate the need for a more comprehensive analysis which does raise all the issues and analyze all the options relating thereto. It is obvious, however, from the limited analysis that follows that the preemption policy problems which must be faced raise some very difficult issues not only for Congress but within as well as between the various groups directly affected by federal public employee bargaining legislation.

The analysis is not intended either to support or to oppose a federal public employee bargaining law, whether it be H.R. 8677, H.R. 9730, or some other. Instead, the analysis is an attempt to delineate some issues that should be resolved insofar as bargaining rights for state and local public employees are under consideration.

Both H.R. 8677 and H.R. 9730 raise important preemption issues. However, since H.R. 8677 appears to include a preemption policy and H.R. 9730 does not, it may be helpful to explain why the following analysis is formulated largely in terms of H.R. 9730.

The basic reason is that the interest groups supporting a federal bill appear to be uniting over H.R. 9730 as the vehicle for enacting federal legislation. This is an impression which may be erroneous now, or it may become erroneous as circumstances develop. It is, however, more than sheer speculation as evidenced by the NEA's shift from acceptance of H.R. 9730 to active support of it in November, 1974.

Another factor was the lack of attention paid to the preemption policy embodied in Section 13(b) of H.R. 8677, which reads as follows (italics added): "All laws or parts of laws of the United States inconsistent with the provisions of this Act are modified or repealed as necessary to remove such inconsistency, and this Act shall take precedence over all ordinances, rules, regulations, or other enactments of any State, territory, or possession of the United States or any political subdivision thereof. *Except as otherwise expressly provided herein, nothing contained in this Act shall be construed to deny or otherwise abridge any rights, privileges, or benefits granted by law to employees.*"

In effect, the policy set forth in Section 13(b) would prohibit preemption of any state statute providing employee rights, privileges or benefits. It is not clear to the principal investigator whether the lack of attention to this section of H.R. 8677 was due to lack of conviction that the bill would be a focal point of federal legislation, or whether it was due to the fact that the clause was not widely understood. At any rate, it is difficult to assume that Congress, in the absence of any public discussion of the matter, would specifically exempt all state legislation providing employee rights, privileges, or benefits, and preempt or remain silent on all other state legislation on terms and conditions of public employment. Clearly, state and local public management was not cognizant of the matter in 1974 and would have been certain to offer alternatives to 13(b) if it had been so cognizant. In addition, it might also be argued that preemption policies enunciated under the NLRA would not necessarily prevail under a separate federal law for public employees. Regardless, it appears that there has been virtually no public discussion of preemption problems under either H.R. 8677 or H.R. 9730 (again, it must be emphasized that the reference is not to preemption or possible preemption of state public employee bargaining laws, which has been the subject of considerable testimony before Congressional committees).

For these reasons, the fact that the following analysis is not as fully applicable to H.R. 8677 as it is to H.R. 9730 is not due to failure to recognize the differences between the bills, but results from the lack of discussion of the issues in the context of either bill.

Finally, no significance should be attached to the fact that some of the statutes cited are from states, such as New York, which might be exempt from federal coverage if it is decided to exempt states which have met certain criteria for exemption.

Virtually all of the statutes cited are intended to illustrate legislation which exists in a number of states, including states which do not provide bargaining rights for public employees.

Memorandum

Bills were introduced during the 93rd Congress (H.R. 9730 by Congressman Thompson and S. 3294 by Senator Williams) that would have extended the National Labor Relations Act to employees of state and local governments. Unlike P.L. 93-360, which, while extending NLRA coverage to health care institutions (see NLRA #2 (14)), made other changes in the NLRA (e.g., adding #8 (g)) and the Labor Management Relations Act (adding #213) to deal with the special problems of the health care industry, neither H.R. 9730 nor S. 3294 make any concessions to the special problems of public employment.[1] On the other hand, another pair of bills introduced during the 93rd Congress (H.R. 8677 by Congressman Clay and S. 3295 by Senator Williams) did assume a need for some concessions in this regard. H.R. 8677 would enact a National Public Employment Relations Act which would apply to states, territories and possessions of the United States and political subdivisions that vary from those of the NLRA. Moreover, H.R. 8677 would preserve state collective bargaining laws that are substantially equivalent to the federal legislation elsewhere included in H.R. 8677. The constitutionality and desirability of extending NLRA coverage to state and municipal employment were discussed at committee hearings on the two bills. These hearings, however, have

[1] The "# sign" is used to denote the section throughout this memorandum.

thus far failed to raise or deal with the following question: To what extent, if any, would and/or should federal legislation providing bargaining rights for state and local public employees preempt state legislation on terms and conditions of employment for state and local government employees? The purpose of this analysis is to illustrate the importance of this question and to underscore the serious problems that are likely to result if the question is not fully explored and resolved in any federal legislation along the lines of either H.R. 8677 or H.R. 9730.

At least since 1882 when New York State, the first state to do so, enacted its first Civil Service Law, the states have enacted a growing body of legislation governing terms and conditions of employment for state and local public employees. Undoubtedly a great deal of this legislation provides benefits and protections for public employees. Quite possibly, some of it was enacted partly because state and local public employees lacked bargaining rights. Regardless, it is crucially important to recognize that the legislation deals with matters that are mandatory subjects of bargaining under the NLRA. Were NLRA coverage extended to state and municipal employment and the prevailing doctrine of preemption of federal law to apply (see *Garner v. Teamsters Local 776*, 346 U.S. 485 (1953)), most, if not all state laws dealing with mandatory subjects of bargaining under the NLRA would be invalidated.[2]

The state laws potentially subject to preemption include some employer as well as some employee protections. They also appear to include a great deal of legislation which appears to favor, or could favor, either employers or employees, depending on the circumstances. Thus, in calling attention to the preemption issue, no claim is made that the statutory benefits and protections for public employees under state laws justify the exclusion of such employees from NLRA coverage or that such benefits and protections should be forfeited upon extension of NLRA to public employment. Neither is it argued that these benefits and protections should be preserved notwithstanding NLRA coverage. Rather, the intent is to urge prior and comprehensive consideration of the impact of a federal public employee bargaining bill upon state legislation on terms and conditions of employment for public employees. After judgments are made as to what should be done about the various state laws, proposed federal legislation can be drafted to reflect those judgments.

Moreover, in addition to the fact that extension of the NLRA

[2] See also *San Diego Building Trades Council v. Garmon*, 359 U.S. 236, (1959).

to public employment in conjunction with the preemption doctrine would force public employers and public employee unions to bargain over many matters which are now resolved by legislation (e.g., retirement benefits) such federal legislation may affect public employees in other ways. For example, some supervisory employees in the public sector who now enjoy collective bargaining rights under state legislation, as in Massachusetts and New Jersey, would appear to lose them under NLRA coverage.

State legislation on public employment is usually found in Civil Service and Education Codes, but it may appear anywhere within a state's statutory law. Similar provisions may appear as regulations of a state agency such as a civil service commission or an education commissioner; in some instances they may even appear in state constitutions. The extent to which such provisions would be preempted by the extension of the NLRA coverage to public employment is not altogether clear. In theory the duty of the parties "to meet at reasonable times and confer in good faith with respect to wages, hours and other terms and conditions of employment . . ." (NLRA #8 (d)) should require them to bargain over each such term or condition of employment notwithstanding the provisions of a state law dealing with such term or condition. Moreover, just as the public employer might be obligated to bargain about a demand that it provide benefits and protections in excess of those required by statute, so might a union be required to bargain over an employer's demand that benefits or protections be reduced to a substatutory level. Just as the union, after bargaining to impasse, could strike if its demands were refused, so could the public employer, after bargaining to impasse, choose to take a strike by standing on its position and telling the union that it can take it or leave it. The point made here is not that public employee unions should (or should not) be allowed to bargain for benefits above a statutory minimum. Nor is it that public employers should (or should not) be allowed to bargain for less than a state mandated minimum. It is that a clear resolution of these issues is needed in any federal legislation providing bargaining rights for state and local public employees.

Notwithstanding the view that extension of the NLRA to public employment without further amendment would preempt state enactments covering terms and conditions of public employment, two legal doctrines point in the other direction. Over a period of years, some of the protections contained in civil service type laws have been elevated to constitutional status. For example, the decisions of the United States Supreme Court in *Board of Regents v. Roth*, 408 U.S. 564 (1972) and *Perry v. Sindermann*, 408 U.S. 593 (1972) recognize that teachers may have property rights in their jobs, of which they cannot be deprived without due process (see also *Arnett v. Kennedy* 416 U.S.C. 134 (1974)).

A second consideration is that some of the statutes might be specifically authorized under federal law and thus not subject to preemption. For example, the Fair Labor Standards Act #18(a) provides: "No provision of this Act or of any part thereof shall excuse noncompliance with any Federal or State law or municipal ordinance establishing a minimum wage higher than the minimum wage established under this Act or a maximum workweek lower than the maximum workweek established under this Act, and no provision of this Act relating to employment of child labor shall justify noncompliance with any Federal or State law or municipal ordinance establishing a higher standard than the standard established under this Act."

Similarly, the Occupational Safety and Health Act (29 USC #667(a)) provides that "Nothing in this chapter shall prevent any State agency or court from asserting jurisdiction under State law over any occupational safety or health issue with respect to which no standard is in effect under section 755 of this title.", and OSHA does not apply to state or municipal employees (29 USE #652(5)).

A third classification of state legislation governing public employment that might not be preempted consists of *legislation applicable to employment generally*, such as the provision of workmen's compensation benefits. Even for some of this legislation, however, preemption issues may arise even though they may not have been settled in the private sector. For example, the provision of the Rhode Island Unemployment Insurance Law that gives unemployment compensation to strikers has recently been challenged as being preempted by the National Labor Relations Act, and the status of that law is now uncertain (*Grinnell Corp. v. Hackett*, 475 F. 2d 449, 1st Cir., 1973).

Some examples of the legislation affecting public employees that would appear to be subject to preemption should public employment come under the NLRA are listed below. The listing was compiled by reference to the laws of only a few states and is not comprehensive even for those states. The purpose in presenting it is to illustrate the pervasive nature of preemption problems and to underscore the need for a more comprehensive study of state legislation on terms and condition of public employment, especially such legislation which is potentially at least subject to preemption.

Preemption policy should be explicit in federal legislation, but such policy should be made with full knowledge of the statutes involved.

Although most of the state laws cited below specify benefits and protections to public employees, some are designed for the benefit and protection of public employers. There are also many laws that specify procedural or substantive terms and conditions of employment which may alternately benefit either governments or their employees, depending upon the particular circumstances of a situation. In any case, the laws cited are illustrative, not necessarily representative. Simply counting the number of statutes which appear to favor public management, public employees unions, or are "neutral" is apt to be misleading. Many public employee unions would gladly give up several statutory benefits for the right to strike, i.e., statutory benefits and restrictions are not of equal weight. Secondly, as a practical matter, members of Congress will probably want to know the impact of any preemption policy upon their district or state, not simply the impact in general. In the third place, preemption policies may well be affected by the number of states involved. Whether five states or fifty have a law may be crucial as to whether or not the law should be preempted by a federal statute. For these and other reasons, the examples should not be interpreted as supporting or opposing the preemption policy of any particular interest group.

JOB SECURITY

Tenure. Most civil service employees and teachers earn tenure after serving a probationary period. As tenured employees, they enjoy a high degree of job security. Job security, however, is a mandatory subject of negotiations, hence the tenure statutes would appear to be invalidated if the NLRA were extended to public employees. New York Civil Service Law #75 and 76 are typical of tenure statutes. Section 75 provides that no permanent employee in the competive class of the state or municipal civil service shall be removed or otherwise subjected to any disciplinary penalty "except for incompetency of misconduct shown after a hearing upon stated charges pursuant to this section." Section 76 provides procedures by which an employee, believing himself aggrieved by his dismissal or some other disciplinary penalty, may appeal to the Civil Service Law. A lower state court has ruled that this agreement deprives employees of a constitutionally protected right to judicial review of their discipline (*Antinore* v. *State of New York*, 79 Misc. 2d 8 (1974)) and the State has appealed from that decision.

In 38 states and the District of Columbia, some type of teacher tenure law applies to all school districts in the state. In four additional states (Kansas, Nebraska, Oregon, and Wisconsin), legislation provides tenure in one or more of the largest districts, while most districts are not covered. In three states (California, New York, and Texas) tenure is optional or optional in certain districts. Five other states (Georgia, Mississippi, South Carolina, Utah, Vermont) provide for annual or long term contracts but not for tenure, at least on a state-wide basis.

As will be illustrated briefly, this tenure legislation varies enormously on every important dimension of tenure: Who is covered, the length of the probationary period, the causes for dismissal, the procedures for challenging dismissals, and so on. In some states, preemption would be welcomed by teacher unions; in others, it would be supported by school management. Approximately 30 states provide some form of tenure for supervisory or managerial personnel. Both preemption and exemption pose a number of difficult problems just in the tenure area alone (see Research Division, *Teacher Tenure and Contracts, A Summary of State Statutes* (Washington, D.C.: National Education Association, 1972), for a comprehensive summary of the state tenure statutes as of September 30, 1972).

Notice and procedures. New Hampshire law illustrates a legislative approach to tenure which is typical of a number of states. In New Hampshire (RFA 189) a teacher who is not to be reappointed for the next school year must be notified by March 15 prior thereto if he has taught one or more years in a school district. Any such teacher who has taught for three or more years in a school district is entitled to a written statement specifying the reason that he is not being reappointed and a hearing before the school board. The hearing must comply with due process standards and the decision of a school board may be appealed to the State Board of Education. An additional hearing may then be held by an ad hoc review board. The review board must consider, either on the record or on the basis of its own hearing, whether the refusal to reappoint was:

   a. in violation of constitutional or statutory provisions;
   b. in excess of the statutory authority of the agency;
   c. made upon unlawful procedure;
   d. affected by other error of law;
   e. clearly erroneous in view of the reliable, prohibitive and substantial evidence on the whole record; or
   f. arbitrary and capricious or characterized by abuse of discretion or clearly unwarranted exercise of discretion.

This procedure points up a number of protections provided by the laws of many states. It requires notice before dismissal, the right to be given reasons for the dismissal and to a hearing, and the right to have the decision reviewed by higher authority.

Minnesota provides similar protections (Minnesota Law, #125.12 and 125.17). The Minnesota law (#125.12, subd. 6) also limits the grounds for which a teacher may be terminated to: "(a) Inefficiency (b) Neglect of duty, or persistent violation of school laws, rules, regulations or directives; (c) Conduct unbecoming a teacher good and sufficient grounds rendering the teacher unfit to perform his duties; or (e) Discontinuance of position, lack of pupils, or merger of classes caused by consolidation of districts or otherwise. . . ."

Paragraph (e) above illustrates a potential difficulty interpreting Section 13(b) of H.R. 8677. On its face, paragraph (e) above is a protection for teachers, hence not subject to preemption under 13(b). On the other hand, some teacher organizations have negotiated seniority clauses that provide job security for all members of the bargaining unit, regardless of declining enrollments or discontinuation of positions. Conceivably, paragraph (e) could be interpreted by employee unions in contradictory ways in the same state, perhaps even in different bargaining units under the same employer.

Layoff and reemployment. Section 2510 of the New York State Education Law, like the Minnesota law previously cited, deals with layoffs occasioned by the abolition of jobs. It provides for layoff in order of lowest seniority (see also New Jersey Ed. Law #18A:28-10). For this purpose, seniority is within a given tenure area and according to the courts (*Baer v. Nyquist*, 40 AD 2d 925 (197)) there are but few tenure areas and they cannot be subdivided by a school district. Consequently a complex system of bumping comes into play in the event of layoff. This system of bumping is unattractive to many school districts and some might seek to get rid of it through negotiations under the National Labor Relations Act. In the past, laws specifying the order of layoff were invoked chiefly in rural districts undergoing consolidation. In the future, they are likely to be invoked more often in urban and suburban districts experiencing a drop in enrollment, relatively little teacher turnover, and pressures to employ more minority teachers. Under these circumstances, whether these laws are preempted will become increasingly important.

Duration of probationary status. An important tenure consideration is the time that must be spent by an employee on probationary status. In education, the probationary period ranges from one to five years, with three years being the most common probationary period in state legislation.

Statutes specifying the length of a probationary term are another example of laws that may benefit employers in one situation and employees in another. As a matter of fact, enactment of H.R. 8677 could lead to some paradoxical situations relating to probationary periods. In the private sector, probationary periods are typically less than three years and there is no doubt that teacher unions would bargain for shorter probationary periods if they have the right to do so. Suppose a teacher union bargains for a one year probationary period in a state which has a three year probationary period as part of a tenure law otherwise highly supported by teacher unions. Could the teachers bargain for a less than three year probationary period under 13(b), i.e., could they legally maintain the position that only the probationary period in the tenure law was preempted, since it and it alone was no longer a right, privilege, or benefit granted by law to public employees? And if an employee union has the right to bargain on, and perhaps reduce the statutory probationary period of three years to a few months in a collective agreement, would the state courts uphold the other parts of the statute in the absence of a severability clause? That is, if one part of a tenure statute (the probationary period) becomes a mandatory subject of bargaining, what is the legal status of the statute in the absence of a severability clause?

RETIREMENT BENEFITS—AUTHORITY OF EMPLOYER TO NEGOTIATE

Retirement as a mandatory subject of negotiations raises questions that go beyond the problem of preemption. The preemption problem is nevertheless very important. To a large extent, pension rights are constitutionally protected. Employees with vested benefits could not lose such rights through negotiations, but new employees coming into public employment could find themselves covered by negotiated pension plans that would be less attractive than those currently provided by statute (for examples of state laws establishing pension systems, see New Jersey Ed. Law #18A:66-1 et seq.; Florida Statutes #238; Minnesota Law #354 et seq.; California Ed. Code #13801 et seq.; New York State Retirement and Social Security Law, and New York C.S.L. #154 and 155).

As in the case of the tenure laws, in some instances, the protections afforded by state laws and/or state constitutions may be greater than those of federal law and the federal constitution. For example, the New York State Constitution, Article V, #7 protects the pension rights of public employees most generously. It has been interpreted as precluding the diminution of the interest that is to be credited to the account of a member of a pension system for his contributions (*Cashman* v. *Teachers' Retirement Board*, 301 NY 501 (1950)). It may even protect a member's interest in having applied to him more beneficial mortality tables (*Matter of Ayman* v. *Teachers' Retirement Board*, 9 NY 2d 119 (1960)). One of the many issues raised by NLRB coverage is what happens to employee rights which are contractual by virtue of a state constitution which is itself preempted by federal statute?

Consideration of retirement benefits raises several important issues concerning the authority of public employers to negotiate. In many instances the powers of school districts, public benefit corporations and other governmental or quasi-governmental institutions are limited by the state legislature that created them. What happens when they are explicitly denied the power to perform an act, the performance of which is a mandatory subject of bargaining? Would extension of NLRA coverage to such governmental or quasi-governmental institutions invest them with powers that, by the terms of their corporate structures are *ultra vires*, or would their duty to negotiate fall short of the full range of mandatory subjects of bargaining by reason of limitations in the legislation creating them? Under NLRA coverage, would the state itself, as source of authority, have to be treated as a joint employer so that the full range of mandatory subjects of bargaining could be considered? If so, would the state be brought to the table at each negotiation or would some form of tiered bargaining emerge with bargaining on different terms of employment taking place in successive stages?

The difficulties are most acute in the area of retirement, where for actuarial purposes among others, many local government employees are covered by a single state retirement system. Under Minnesota Law #356.24, it is "unlawful for a school district or other governmental subdivision or state agency to . . . contribute public funds to a supplemental pension or deferred compensation plan which is maintained and operated in addition to a primary pension program for the benefit of governmental subdivision employees." New York State (Ret. and Soc. Sec. Law #444) establishes maximum retirement benefits available to employees who join the New York State Employees Retirement System on or after July 1, 1973 and denies to local governments the power to create their own retirement systems (Ret. and Soc. Sec. Law #113).

As a matter of fact, it appears that extension of NLRA coverage to public employment, at least without amendment, would lead to basic changes in the very structure of state and local government. This might be desirable, but such change should not happen fortuitously. On the one hand, if public employers and public employee unions have the right to negotiate retirement benefits, it is virtually certain that some will opt out of state systems or negotiate changes that would make it impossible to maintain state retirement systems as we have known them. On the other hand, treating the state as employer for retirement purposes raises a different set of problems. Would there be a state-wide bargaining agent for public employees? Would it be feasible to have public employees represented by one union at the local level, e.g., an AFT local, and a rival union at the state level, e.g., an NEA state affiliate?

Who would bargain for public management, in view of the diffuse nature of legislative and executive responsibility for retirement systems? Would it be feasible to limit state-wide negotiations to retirement benefits? How would the timing of state-wide bargaining on retirement be coordinated with local bargaining so that local employers could estimate their total personnel costs with a reasonable degree of accuracy? And so on.

These are not assumed to be insoluble problems. After all, some contracts in the private sector cover hundreds of thousands of employees dispersed over several states. The point is that the solutions may involve changes which go far beyond negotiations and/or personnel policy, and which therefore have to be fully understood if they are not to solve one problem by creating others which are more troublesome.

PROMOTION

Closely related to tenure are promotion rights of public employees. New York State's Constitution, Article V, #6 provides that:

> Appointments and promotions in the civil service of the state and all of the civil divisions thereof, including cities and villages, shall be made according to merit and fitness, to be ascertained, as far as practicable, by examination which, as far as practicable, shall be competitive;

Promotion within a bargaining unit, however, is a mandatory subject of negotiations. Public employers dissatisfied with the strictures of competitive examinations might try to avoid them through collective negotiations; so might unionized employees. Initial employment is less likely to be a mandatory subject of negotiations, at least to the extent that it would preempt state laws requiring competitive examinations (cf. *NLRB v. Laney & Duke Co.*, 369 F. 2d 859 (5th Cir., 1966)), but negotiations might deal with the establishment of hiring halls.

VETERANS BENEFITS

Many states have enacted statutes giving extra employment protections and benefits to veterans, a term typically defined as persons who served in the armed forces during specified wartime periods. Such protections fall into two categories. Applying for appointment or promotion, veterans may be given extra credits on civil service examinations (e.g., Minnesota Statutes #197.45; California Ed. Code #13735; New York C.S.L. #75). It would appear that veterans benefits, such as salary credit for military service, would be a mandatory subject of negotiations.

CONTRACT PERFORMANCE

The converse of job security legislation are laws designed to protect public employers against the loss of their employees at inopportune times. New Jersey Statutes #18A:26-10, provides that a teacher may not leave his position during the school year without permission from the board of education. The sanction for violation of this duty is that the teacher may lose his certification for up to one year. A number of states have enacted statutes designed to afford public employers similar protections, e.g., South Dakota (#13-43-9), Kansas (#72-5412) and Alabama (#361(L)).

SICK LEAVE AND PERSONAL LEAVE

Every state appears to have enacted some legislation on sick leave. Obviously, Congressional treatment of state minimums or state maximums will be of intense interest to public management and public employee unions. Certainly, all such legislation would appear to be preempted by extension of NLRA coverage to the public sector. To illustrate the kind of legislation involved, full-time civil service employees in the California educational system accumulate 12 days of sick leave per year (California Ed. Code #13651.1), as well as bereavement leave (California Ed. Code #13651.4). Teachers in California accumulate 10 days sick leave a year (California Ed. Code #13468) which, pursuant to rules of the state Board of Education, may be transferred to other school districts (California Ed. Code #13468.1). Moreover, such sick leave can be used not only for reasons relating to illness, but also whenever the teacher must appear in court as a litigant or as a witness under an official order (California Ed. Code #13468.5). Under Florida Education Law #231.40, a fulltime teacher is entitled to sick leave because of his illness "or because of the illness or death of father, mother, brother, sister, husband, wife, child, or other close relative, or member of his own household,". A teacher is entitled to 10 days of sick leave with pay as of the beginning date of employment and accumulates 10 days a year up to 120 days. One-half of his accumulated sick leave is transferrable if the teacher accepts employment in another school district within the state. Florida law also mandates personal leave without pay (Florida Ed. Law #231.43). On the other hand, Arkansas and Florida prohibit payment for unused sick leave, a provision frequently sought and sometimes negotiated in public employment.

MILITARY LEAVE

Minnesota (General Statutes #192.26) provides its state and municipal employees with 15 days military leave with pay while in the reserves or some branch of the state or national militia. In New York State, military leave with pay is mandated for up to 30 days (New York State Military Law #242; various other protections and benefits are accorded to employees on military leave by Military Law #243; see also New Jersey Ed. Law #18A:6-33). It is virtually certain that all states make some provision for military leave.

MATERNITY LEAVE

Maternity leave is of particular interest. It is required by the statutes of many states (see New Jersey Law Against Discrimination #10:5-1 et seq.), but some laws went so far as to mandate suspension or termination of employment to a degree that violated the federal constitution (*Cleveland Board of Education et al. v. La Fleur; Cohen v. Chesterfield County School Board et al.*, 414 U.S. 632 (1974)). In some instances, the protections afforded by state laws exceed constitutional requirements. For example, it is suggested in Footnote 13 of the *Cleveland* decision that school authorities may establish a fixed time during pregnancy for the commencement of maternity leave without violating the Due Process clause of the 14th Amendment to the United States Constitution. This can not be done under New York State Law (New York State Executive Law #296.1(a)) as interpreted by *Union Free School District No. 6 of the Towns of Islip and Smithtown et al.*

v. New York State Human Rights Appeal Board, 35 N.Y.S. 371, (1974). The *Smithtown* decision dealt directly with the question of whether a collectively negotiated agreement could diminish maternity leave benefits below those mandated by state law, but still sufficient to satisfy the due process requirements of the Constitution. The decision held that under state law, such reduction of maternity leave benefits was a prohibited subject of bargaining. Of course, whether it would be under H.R. 9730 is another matter.

LUNCH PERIODS

Several states have enacted a duty free lunch period for employees, either by statute or by state regulation. For example, the New Jersey Administrative Code (#6:3-1.15) provides for a duty-free lunch period for teachers, whereas California provides the same benefit by statute (California Ed. Code #13561 and 13561.1).

WAGES

As previously noted, the Federal Fair Labor Standards Act preserves states' rights to establish higher minimum wages than those contained in federal law. Under extension of the NLRA to public employment, it is an interesting question which, if any, of the following would service preemption on the theory that they constitute minimum wage laws.

Minimum salary schedules. New Jersey is one of many states that has enacted a minimum salary schedule for teachers (New Jersey Ed. Law #18A:29-70). It also requires yearly increments (#18A:29-8) and provides credit for increment purposes when teachers are in military service (#18A:29-11). Pennsylvania also mandates minimum salaries and increments (Pennsylvania Education Law #11-1142). Moreover, its laws require an additional increment when a teacher has a master's degree (#11-1114) and mandates extra compensation for teachers when they attend school meetings (#11-1188).

Prevailing wages. New York State has a prevailing wage statute for laborers, workmen and mechanics employed by the state and municipal governments if they are not allocated to civil service grade (New York State Labor Law #220). Civil Service employees in larger school districts in California must be paid wages "at levels at least equal to the prevailing salary or wage for the same quality of service rendered to private employees under similar employment when such prevailing salary or wage can be ascertained . . ." (California Ed. Code #13601.5).

Miscellaneous. Pursuant to Indiana law (Indiana Statutes #28-4505), a teacher may not have his compensation diminished because a school closes during the school year.

Under California law (California Ed. Code #13506) salaries must be uniform for teachers of various grades. Moreover, the school district may not decrease the annual salary of a person employed by the district in a position requiring certification qualifications for failing to meet any requirement of the district that such person complete additional educational units, course of study, or work in any college or university or any equivalent thereof (California Ed. Code #13511).

Procedures. A recent decision of a lower court in New York State (*Campbell v. Lindsay*, 78 Misc. 2d 841 (sup. ct., NY Co., 1974)) illuminates the relationship between wage benefits mandated by statute and collective agreements. Notwithstanding the salary scales contained in an agreement between police officers and the City of New York and the availability of arbitration to resolve grievances, police officers who worked out of title were held to be entitled to the benefits of the procedural and substantive provisions of the Administrative Code of the City of New York (#434a-3.0, subdivision c; #434a-15.0). This included the right to a higher salary and to have that right determined by a court.

UNION SECURITY

At least two states, Hawaii (Public Employment Relations Act, #3 and 4) and Rhode Island (State Government Employees Law #36-11-2) mandate service fee payments to the bargaining agent by employees who are not members. In Vermont (State Employee Labor Relations Act #941(k)), nonmembers must pay a service fee if they wish to avail themselves of the services of the union to represent them in a grievance. A number of states appear to have made the agency shop a mandatory subject of negotiations, whereas other states, e.g., Kansas, have specifically prohibited such agreements. Many state (including Alaska—Public Employee Relations Act #23.40.220; Kentucky—Firefighters Collective Bargaining Act #12; Minnesota—Public Employment Labor Relations Act #5; New Hampshire—State Government Employees Act #98-c;3; and New York—Taylor Law #208) mandate dues checkoff. On the other hand, under the National Labor Relations Act, union security is a mandatory subject of negotiations. Presumably, any employer under the NLRA could bargain not to grant a recognized or certified union the right to dues checkoff or to a service fee. Conversely, many states prohibit one or another form of union security.

Usually this is the effect of laws that prohibit the discharge of employees by reason of their refusal to pay union dues (e.g. New York C.S.L. #75) and that preclude checkoff without the employee's consent (e.g., New York Gen. Mun. Law #93-b). The duty to bargain over union security would appear to supersede these state limitations.

PERSONNEL EVALUATION AND PERSONNEL RECORDS

During the past ten years or so, there has been a considerable amount of state legislation devoted to personnel evaluation. Since 1963 in the field of education alone, 30 states have enacted statutes intended to encourage accountability in education. Thirteen of these statutes enacted since 1967 alone deal with teacher evaluation. The Kansas statute (House Bill 1042, enacted in July, 1973), is typical of these statutes, which appear to be prime candidates for preemption under the NLRA. As a matter of fact, the "accountability statutes" often include a number of enactments on other terms and conditions of employment. For example, the contracting out of educational services is not only authorized but is encouraged in the California and Colorado statutes. Legislation on in-service education is more frequent although the precise number of states which have legislated on the subject is not available. Furthermore, accountability legislation was introduced but not enacted in at least seven states in 1972-73, and it appears that the state legislatures could be enacting legislation while Congress is simultaneously preempting it. (Note Data on accountability legislation is taken from Cooperate Accountability Project, *Legislation by the States: Accountability and Assessment in Education* (Madison, Wisconsin: State Educational Accountability Repository, November, 1974).

It should be noted that legislation concerning personnel evaluation and personnel files is not always included or categorized as "accountability legislation." For example, Minnesota is not listed as a state with accountability legislation in the SEAR report cited above, but Minnesota law (125.12, subd. 6(3)) provides: "All evaluations and files generated within a school district relating to each individual teacher shall be available during regular school business hours to each individual teacher upon his written request."

RESIDENCY REQUIREMENTS

Residency requirements are a frequent concern in public employment. Minnesota law (#125.12, subd. 2) states: "No teacher shall be required to reside within the employing school district as a condition to teaching employment or continued teaching employment." By its Administrative Code (#125.12), New Jersey also precludes a residency requirement.

Municipal employees have sought the enactment of such laws to overcome municipal ordinances imposing residency requirements. There are two kinds of residency requirements imposed by municipal employment to residents of the community. For example, New York State's Nassau County (Administrative Code #13-1.0) imposes one year's residency within the county as a prerequisite to obtaining a county job. Other ordinances require municipal employees to maintain residence within the municipality (Ordinances of Buffalo, N.Y., Chapter 1, Sec. 5; Charter of Syracuse, N.Y., #8-12, subd. 2). Municipal ordinances requiring employees to live within a municipality or proximate to it are particularly frequent for police officers (Local Law No. 3 of 1970 of Kindston, N.Y.). In some instances, local laws imposing residency requirements are explicitly authorized by state law (New York Public Officers Law #30).

LEGAL DEFENSE OF EMPLOYEES

Several states have enacted laws by which they undertake the defense of their employees in the event of court action against them for actions performed during the course of the employee's official duties. California Government Code #995 provides for such defense when the employee is subjected to a civil claim. Similar laws have been enacted in New York State with respect to correction officers employed by the state (New York Corrections Law #24) and by the Correction department of any city (New York Gen. Mun. Law #50-j). Another New York State law (Public Officers Law #17) differs only in detail and provides similar protection to other state employees. New Jersey goes further. It indemnifies its teachers against both civil and, in some instances, criminal actions (New Jersey Ed. Law #18A:16-6 and 18A:16-61).

MISCELLANEOUS ITEMS

The following items are cited merely to illustrate the variety of state enactments subject to preemption in the absence of amendment to H.R. 9730. California (Govt. Code #18006) reimburses state employees for their moving expenses if, by reason of reassignment or promotion, they must relocate. A substantial number of states provide for 1-2 days of paid leave for educational conferences. By its statewide administrative standards, the New Hampshire State Department of Education has established a maximum teaching load for high school teachers. No high school teacher may be assigned a teaching schedule which requires more than five different class preparations for a given day or more than six periods of class instruction. An Arkansas statute (#80-1217) reflects a concern for the protection of an employer interest. It provides that the final month's pay of a teacher shall be withheld until the teacher submits to the county superintendent his daily register and other required statistical material. Florida statutes specify that teacher contracts shall be for a minimum of 196 work days and that faculty load in the state universities shall be 12 hours. Several state statutes authorize sabbatical leave, but place limits on its duration and support whereas Louisiana mandates sabbatical leave for all educational employees. These are only some of the bits and pieces from a substantial number of statutes dealing with mandatory subjects of bargaining. The principal investigator believes that the education codes alone may well include a thousand or more statutes subject to preemption under the NLRA.

EXCLUSIVITY AND ENFORCEMENT OF REMEDIES

Because of the nature of government, it seems obvious that some accommodation must be made for the right of people to petition their government for the redress of grievances (U.S. Constitution, First Amendment). This right may come into conflict with exclusivity where the grievances relate to employment by the government and where the grievant prefers someone other than his union to carry his petition.

A related issue is how the provisions of the NLRA can be enforced against a state. It should be noted that in *Maryland* v. *Wirtz*, 392 U.S. 183 (1968), the Supreme Court recognized that, because of states' sovereign immunity, some of the remedies ordinarily available under the Fair Labor Standards Act might not be available when a state is the employer-defendant. Recently the New York State Court of Claims (*PBA* v. *State of New York*, 70 Misc. 2d 335 (1974) dismissed a union claim that the state had violated a collective agreement because the alleged violation involved no money damages. The court reasoned that only the equitable relief of specific performance could satisfy the complaint and "the equitable powers of the Court of Claims are very limited and are restricted to enforcing a money judgment."

COMPULSORY ARBITRATION

Several states mandate arbitration to resolve negotiations disputes between their municipalities and their employees. Usually such laws are restricted to public safety occupations (e.g., New York

S.L. #209.4; Pennsylvania SB 1343, L. 1968; Oregon Statutes 243.730, #19), but New York City has enacted a local law covering all employees (N.Y.C. Administrative Code #1173-7. O.c). These laws benefit either governments or their employees, depending upon the particular circumstances of the situation. In general, however, they have been sought by police and firefighter organizations and resisted by many other unions, as well as by public employers.

SUPERVISORY EMPLOYEES

The National Labor Relations Act denies its protections to persons employed as supervisors (#2(d)). Supervisory employees in the public sector, however, now enjoy protected rights of organization and negotiations under many state laws (New York Civil Service Law #201.7(a); Florida Statutes #447.003(4); Minnesota Law #179.65(6); New Hampshire Chapter 98-c:1; New Jersey Employer-Employee Relations Act #34:13A-3(d)). In some instances school principals have been held to be entitled to protected status by interpretation of state law (New York-*Matter of Hempstead Board of Education*, 6 PERB 3002 (1973), affd. Board of Education, *Hempstead v. Helsby*, 42 AD 2nd 1056 (1973); affd. NY 2nd (1974)). In other instances, principals have been covered by explicit statutory language (Massachusetts, Minnesota #179.65(6) and New Jersey are examples). Were H.R. 9730 enacted without amendment relating to preemption, it is doubtful whether a state could enact tenure protections or bargaining rights for administrative personnel which Congress deliberately withheld (see *Ironworkers Local 207 v. Perko*, 373 U.S. 701 (1963)).

Summary and Conclusions

There are several perspectives from which to consider the state legislation potentially subject to preemption. One is the perspective of a particular type of law, e.g., retirement legislation. Another perspective is state oriented. Some states have a great deal more legislation than others on terms and conditions of public employment. The ability of some state and local public employers to adjust to federal legislation may be vitally dependent upon the nature and scope of the adjustment, a factor not necessarily apparent from analysis of separate items like retirement or tenure. Furthermore, the state perspectives are essential to understand the politics of preemption. A public employee union in a state with a poor tenure law may be willing to accept preemption of the tenure law for the right to bargain on job security. A public employee union in another state with a strong tenure law may be unwilling to accept preemption of tenure statutes for the right to bargain on job security. Public management may be faced with the same kind of tradeoffs, and its response is likely to be influenced by its state as well as its national situation. On the other hand, the formulation of national policy appears to require insight into the state by state impact of alternative preemption policies.

Actually, even summaries of state statutes would not provide the complete picture of preemption problems. The Minnesota education code alone includes 26 statutes which would appear to be preempted by NLRA coverage. This list does not include the retirement laws subject to preemption. The Florida education code appears to include 24 items subject to preemption. The Minnesota code includes legislation on mandatory subjects of bargaining not included in the Florida code, and vice versa. On the other hand, state agencies, such as state boards of education, often promulgate regulations on mandatory subjects of bargaining which have the force of law. Such regulations undoubtedly widen the legislative gap between some states and narrow it between others. The same conclusion undoubtedly holds for state civil service and state personnel codes.

It is also as essential to analyze the situation from the standpoint of "no preemption" as it is from the standpoint of preemption. This memorandum has been devoted largely to the situation that would result if state legislation were preempted. It should not be inferred from this that the problems of preemption are necessarily more difficult or more important than the problems resulting from a "no preemption" policy. For example, if there is no preemption, or only the kind of preemption suggested by 13(b) of H.R. 8677, the NLRB probably would have to interpret the statutes and constitutions of all 50 states at one time or another, but probably sooner than later. Every time one of the parties refused to bargain on an item on the basis that it was not preempted by the NLRA and hence not subject to bargaining, the issue would potentially be subject to appeal to the NLRB. Whether there is a feasible way to have the state courts decide such issues is open to question, to say the least.

As a matter of fact, a variety of alternatives will have to be considered in depth. Some of the more obvious ones are as follows:

1. Complete preemption of state legislation
2. Complete exemption of state legislation
3. Preemption (or exemption) of some state legislation

4. Preemption (or exemption) of some or all state legislation under certain conditions
5. Combinations of (3) and (4) above.

Actually, (3), (4), and (5) each encompass a wide range of alternatives which may have to be considered in depth. Again, however, it must be emphasized that all such legislative policy analysis will require comprehensive summaries of the state legislation potentially subject to preemption. The formulation of federal legislation which takes preemption problems into account adequately will be extremely difficult, but it appears to be absolutely essential to constructive national policy and to avoid a flood of litigation concerning preemption issues.

Discussion Questions

1. Would preemption of state laws by federal legislation tend to benefit employers or employees? How? Give examples.
2. Describe some of the long-range and short-term results of exempting state legislation—in whole or in part—under a new federal law.
3. If you were a member of Congress, how would you vote on a bill extending the NLRA to the public sector? Discuss your answer in terms of your constituencies and your own viewpoint of the national interest.

Reprinted from Journal of Collective Negotiations in the Public Sector Vol. 4(2), 1975

CHAPTER 18

The Need for Urgency in Federal Sector Bargaining

RONALD W. HAUGHTON

Drawing on my experience – not just as the chairman of the Federal Labor Relations Authority (FLRA), but also as a long-time mediator and arbitrator – I'll discuss the dynamics of the collective bargaining process and the major deficiencies of negotiation as it is practices in the federal sector.

The importance of contract administration cannot be overstated, with binding arbitration now mandated by the statute,[1] which is basic to every collective bargaining relationship. However, this relationship cannot begin until the parties have negotiated a contract to administer.

Collective bargaining negotiations, and the contract they produce, are not a one-time affair. They are inextricably tied to contract administration in a continuous process that makes the contract truly a "living document."

---

[1] The Federal Service Labor-Management Relations Statute, Title VII of the Civil Service Reform Act of 1978 (Public Law 95-454), effective January 11, 1979, replaced Executive Order 11491 as the framework for labor-management relations in the nonpostal federal service.

Contract negotiation is the incubation period for the collective bargaining relationship. It determines whether the relationship starts off on the right foot, and it sets the tone of the relationship for the long haul.

Like every other labor relations system in the federal program, the collective bargaining contract is our most important product. We are largely beyond the organizing stage in the federal sector. Sixty per cent of the work force is organized in exclusive bargaining units; and when supervisors and other excluded categories are taken out, the actual level of organization among eligible employees probably reaches or surpasses 70 per cent. President Carter said it best when he made the point in signing the statute into law that it "recognizes that the federal work force is largely a unionized work force."

The point I would like to make is that we are heavily into the contract negotiation (and contract administration) stage of collective bargaining relationships in the federal sector. Thus, the contract bargaining process warrants — but regrettably it is not getting — the highest level of attention by practitioners and students of our program.

In fact, we have to flash back several years to find a complete picture of the collective bargaining process as it was practiced in the federal sector. I am referring to the 1974 survey done by the then-Civil Service Commission and Office of Management and Budget at the instigation of the old Federal Labor Relations Council (FLRC) under Executive Order 11491 [1]. The survey produced a comprehensive "snapshot" of bargaining in virtually all of the 2300 units covered by negotiated contracts at that time.

It is the only survey of that magnitude even undertaken in our program, and provided a useful source of information on how the collective bargaining process was working. Overall, it was not a bleak picture.

The following profile was drawn after going through the survey to pinpoint what the typical bargaining experience looked like in the federal service back in 1974, based on the most common situations reported.

> The union was the moving party in requesting the negotiations, and the parties were at the table within a month. They wrapped up groundrules within a week, in a single bargaining session lasting a couple of hours. The parties were back at the table within a month for basic contract (as distinguished from groundrules) negotiations. They spent one to three months in negotiating the basic contract, in eleven to twenty weekly bargaining sessions lasting four hours each. All told, it took three to six months to deliver an effective contract from the date negotiations were requested [1, pp. 92-93].

That is not a bad profile . . . as far as it goes. But before the congratulations, let's take a closer look at some of the more disturbing aspects uncovered by the survey.

- From the request to negotiate, it usually took from a week to three months to get to the table — but it was not uncommon to take up to six months.
- Groundrules negotiations typically were wrapped up within the first week — but a number of them stretched on for as long as six months.
- The parties usually met daily, or at least weekly, on groundrules — but they were more apt to meet weekly or even only once a month or less often in basic contract negotiations.
- From the request to negotiate the effective date of the contract took several months, twelve to eighteen months in many instances and over two years in a number of instances [1, pp. 92-93].

The most discouraging finding from that 1974 survey, to me, was that in negotiations covering nearly 500 bargaining units, delays were reported in getting to the table following the request to negotiate. In assessing the reasons for these delays, the survey discovered enough to go around both sides of the bargaining table. Let me quote from that chapter of the survey. It is worth reading.

> The most commonly cited reasons were broken down as follows — in descending order:
>
> Delays on the union side: 1) lack of response or preparation, 2) studying the proposals, 3) preoccupation with representation challenges, 4) unavailability of union negotiators, 5) turnover among union officials.
>
> Delays on the management side: 1) studying the proposals, 2) unavailability of management negotiators, 3) reorganization of the unit, 4) turnover among management officials, 5) preoccupation with other negotiations.
>
> Delays on both sides: 1) mutually agreed-to time for preparation, 2) awaiting issuance of . . . amendments to Executive Order 11491, 3) impasse on groundrules, 4) mutual agreement to defer start of bargaining, 5) scheduling conflicts.
>
> Other reasons commonly given for delay in beginning negotiations — affecting both parties alike — included deaths and illnesses, holidays and vacations, workload requirements, and training of negotiators. Some delays were attributed to internal union activities — including election of officers. And both sides reportedly were involved in delays caused by their resort to national headquarters for assistance in preparing for the negotiations [1, p. 96].

If the same survey were repeated now, I wonder what the results would be. How many instances of intolerable, and avoidable, delays would crop up? Would they be attributable to many of the same, or to new or different, causes? These questions, and others, are as important as they are intriguing. Unfortunately, nobody knows the answers for sure — at least not on anything like the comprehensive scale surveyed seven years ago.

But there are some pointers the parties can take stock of, and apply, to help avoid repeating the kinds of delays referred to in current and future contract negotiations. Those pointers do bear repeating.

If there is but one point to emphasize in this regard, it is this: *There is a need and responsibility of both parties to inject a sense of urgency into the contract negotiation process.*

The traditional midnight bargaining deadline that confronts and motivates parties in the private sector is not a factor in the federal sector, where the strike spur simply does not exist. This does not mean that imaginative union and agency representatives cannot create a simulated deadline of their own. In government, we are expert at setting and meeting deadlines in other areas of operation — rigid budget deadlines, for example. There is no reason we cannot do the same, or that it cannot work, in our contract bargaining.

One of the groundrules for negotiation can be, and ought to be, a meaningful time-target. Thus, a sense of urgency, which all too frequently is absent from the federal bargaining table, can be established. When I say the time-target must be meaningful, it means that the negotiators must feel in their gut a sense of real failure if the date is not met. A fictional deadline can be worse than no deadline at all.

Groundrules agreement on a time-target, of course, is not enough to get an effective start on basic contract negotiations. The bulk underpart of the iceberg is hard, year-round work by both parties, so they can go into bargaining fully prepared.

Management from the first-line supervisor on up should be urged to make notes through the term of each contract in order to identify what it perceives as essential or desirable changes in the next round of negotiations.

By the same token, the word should go down through the union structure to be alert to problems from the employees' viewpoint so that their perceived needs and desires can be accurately reflected at the bargaining table.

This is how contract administration can be married to contract negotiation, to the maximum benefit of both. The time to begin preparing for the next negotiation runs from the day the current contract takes effect — not just a few days or weeks before it expires. If the parties follow this simple step then, well in advance of their initial meeting for the next negotiations, management and union representatives will have the data available to frame meaningful and realistic contract proposals based on actual experience. That can mean less time at the table and quicker settlement.

An element of gamesmanship comes in at this point. The experienced negotiator will prepare a complete contract proposal, including the items to be carried over from the current contract as well as new items to be added in the next contract. The strategy is to get the other party to work from your document. It is sometimes easier to defend your own language than to attack somebody else's. Sometimes, this can be half the effort.

Assuming both parties have done their homework and are ready for the first negotiation meeting, proposals can be exchanged and groundrules can be set for basic contract bargaining. The bargaining process should be given a high priority by both parties. They should make a mutual commitment to drive toward a settlement by a specific date, and they should make an earnest attempt to achieve a contract by that date, including meeting as often and for as long as necessary.

At first, when the parties have reached the table for basic contract bargaining, the discussions are apt to be on a pedestrian level while each party "feels out" the other. At this point, however, the noncontroversial items can be initialed with the understanding that "all bets are off" if a final settlement is not accomplished.

As the parties proceed to the more controversial issues, they may want to consider making subject-matter assignments to joint subcommittees. This approach offers important advantages that can significantly reduce the time it would otherwise require to reach final settlement. By referring the thorniest issues to joint subcommittees, the full bargaining committee can move on to those issues more amenable to quick resolution by it. The experience has been that the members of a joint subcommittee frequently can devote more time to the complexities of a problem than could the committee as a whole, and they acquire a sense of vested interested in "selling" what they develop as a jointly fashioned settlement proposal to the full committee.

This is not the only tactic that can be tried at this stage of negotiations, and it may not be feasible for a given situation. But it can be useful in many situations as a means of expediting the bargaining process.

There comes an electric point in any negotiation when the parties see a settlement within their grasp. A kind of natural momentum develops that should not be inhibited by artificially prescheduled negotiation times. Neither party, at this critical point, can afford to risk losing this momentum by an adjournment because it happens to be 5 p.m. on Friday. They have reached the time when settlement should be exalted over procedure, whatever schedule may have been agreed to in the groundrules, and to press on into the evening and even over the weekend if necessary. An extra few hours at the table at this point can avoid weeks or months of further bargaining after the momentum slows.

There also can come a point, of course, when honest differences of opinion require a break, a new procedure or perhaps even a new location. This is the time to use the services of the Federal Mediation and Conciliation Service (FMCS).

Skilled mediators are available from FMCS on almost a moment's notice, to come into the negotiations and help the parties narrow or resolve their differences. The very act of explaining the issues and positions to the mediator can, by itself, lead the parties to take a fresh and closer look at their differences and sometimes to settle them in very short order. If not, the mediator can be relied on to help establish a new, extended time-target where that becomes necessary.

IT IS ESSENTIAL THAT THE CONCEPT OF A DEADLINE, OR TIME-TARGET, BE MAINTAINED THROUGHOUT THE NEGOTIATIONS

The experience in both the public and private sectors has been that the process I have just described produces a signed contract in nearly every situation. According to the 1974 survey cited earlier, third-party assistance — primarily mediation involving FMCS — was used in negotiations affecting only 16 per cent of federal bargaining units.

In the private sector and all too often in the state/county/municipal sectors, the alternative to timely contract settlement is a decision to strike and a decision to take a strike. Congress has not only recognized that federal employees may not strike, under long-established law, but has provided a meaningful alternative — the Federal Service Impasse Panel, an entity within the authority.

The panel is one of the most high-powered and prestigious of all federal agencies. It comprises seven presidential appointees who know collective bargaining from A-to-Z, and a small but expert staff available to assist in resolving those final outstanding items that were not susceptible to mediation and that in other systems likely would result in a strike.

The Panel has an arsenal of methods available to it, including factfinding and recommendations for settlement, and ultimately the power to "take whatever action is necessary and not inconsistent with (the statute) to resolve the impasse." [2] A euphemism for final and binding arbitration authority, this brief provision for the Panel to "take whatever action is necessary . . . to resolve the impasse" [2], might well develop over the years into one of the most important ingredients in the whole federal collective bargaining system. They alone have across-the-board provision for peaceful finality.

The authority, of course, also can play a role in contract bargaining. While the determination of specific contract terms is left to the parties themselves, the authority can affect the process peripherally when there is a dispute over whether a contract proposal is negotiable. Currently, more than 200 cases of negotiability are coming into the authority at an annual rate.

The responsibility of FLRA to provide answers to these questions of negotiability, and the need to provide faster turnaround, are matters we take very seriously. We have assigned the highest priority to stepping up the processing of negotiability cases by the authority, and we have greatly streamlined our internal procedures and put staff in a crash project status to move these cases through at an accelerated rate.

I can visualize the situation when the parties reach that electric point in their negotiations, and management raises the issue of negotiability. If the union decides not to accept management's position in the matter, it is referred to the authority for resolution. It may take months to get an answer. Meantime, the parties have lost the precious momentum that made final contract settlement appear to be within their grasp when the issue of negotiability was raised.

It becomes doubly difficult to negotiate a contract to finality when critical issues are, in effect, tabled pending resolution by the authority. My fellow authority members and I realize we bear a heavy responsibility to provide answers in negotiability disputes as quickly as possible. But the parties must understand that they, too, bear a responsibility — to search for imaginative or innovative mutual solutions that will answer their purpose and avoid bucking negotiability problems over to the authority.

In the area of negotiability, FLRA must truly be regarded as the forum of last resort after all other attempts by the parties themselves to resolve the issue have failed.

In this paper, I have tried to give the benefit of my thinking on ways of making the contract negotiation process work more efficiently and produce quicker results. It is not my intent to give a short course on bargaining tactics, but to convey some of the ways a sense of urgency can be established and maintained in contract negotiations.

Congress itself injected a spirit of urgency into the process when it enacted the statute. For example, it pared from forty-five to thirty days the time for agency head approval of negotiated contracts.

Agencies and unions in the federal sector should be pursuing contract settlements with the same alacrity throughout the collective bargaining process.

REFERENCES

1. Committee Print Serial No. 93-51, House Committee on Post Office and Civil Service, pp. 92-116.
2. Section 7119(c)(5)(B)(3), Title VII of Public Law 95-454, at 92 STAT. 1209.

Discussion Questions

1. Why would the parties be apt to meet frequently in setting ground rules, but less often during basic contract negotiations? How much credence would you give such reasons?
2. The author exhorts the parties to find "imaginative and innovative mutual solutions" that might help "avoid bucking negotiability problems over to the authority." Give an example of a negotiability problem and some solutions that do not involve an outside authority making a decision on it.
3. Do you believe the concept suggested in the chapter, i.e., setting deadlines, is a workable solution? Why or why not?

Reprinted from Journal of Collective Negotiations in the Public Sector Vol. 10(3), 1981